REVIEWING MARIO PRATESI

A member of the Italian school of literary realism, Mario Pratesi (1842–1921) was a prolific author of poetry, fiction, and essays. He was widely read and much respected in his day, and while his works never became part of the Italian literary canon, he played an important role in chronicling and shaping the events and debates of the world he lived in.

This book uses the extensive holdings in the Mario Pratesi Archives at Victoria College in the University of Toronto as the basis for a unique study of the literary culture of post-unification Italy. Working with original manuscripts, extensive correspondence, biographical materials, and a vast collection of contemporary reviews, Anne Urbancic uses the methods of *critique génétique* not only to reconstruct the evolution of Pratesi's works through their successive drafts and published versions, but also to document the impact of book reviews and the press on Pratesi's literary style. An original and insightful history of book reviewing as a genre and a detailed study of its role in Italian history and culture, *Reviewing Mario Pratesi* opens up a new area for investigation within Italian literary studies.

(Toronto Italian Studies)

ANNE URBANCIC is a Senior Lecturer in the Department of Italian Studies and the Mary Rowell Jackman Professor and coordinator of VIC ONE (Northrop Frye and Lester Pearson Streams) at Victoria College, University of Toronto.

ANNE URBANCIC

Reviewing Mario Pratesi

The Critical Press and Its Influence

UNIVERSITY OF TORONTO PRESS
Toronto Buffalo London

© University of Toronto Press 2014
Toronto Buffalo London
utorontopress.com

Reprinted in paperback 2022

ISBN 978-1-4426-4871-5 (cloth)
ISBN 978-1-4875-4804-9 (paper)

Toronto Italian Studies

Publication cataloguing information is available from Library and Archives Canada.

This book has been published with the help of a grant from Victoria College, University of Toronto.

We wish to acknowledge the land on which the University of Toronto Press operates. This land is the traditional territory of the Wendat, the Anishnaabeg, the Haudenosaunee, the Métis, and the Mississaugas of the Credit First Nation.

University of Toronto Press acknowledges the financial support of the Government of Canada, the Canada Council for the Arts, and the Ontario Arts Council, an agency of the Government of Ontario, for its publishing activities.

   Canada Council   Conseil des Arts
for the Arts   du Canada

ONTARIO ARTS COUNCIL
CONSEIL DES ARTS DE L'ONTARIO
an Ontario government agency
un organisme du gouvernement de l'Ontario

Funded by the   Financé par le
Government   gouvernement
of Canada   du Canada

*This study is dedicated to Andrew and my daughters,
who have all graciously accepted that on my desk stands
a photo of Pratesi, not of them.*

Contents

Acknowledgments   ix

Introduction   3

1 Florence   21

2 Milan   44

3 Belluno   64

4 Florence Once More   83

Conclusion   109

Notes   113
Bibliography   147
Index   163

Acknowledgments

This book could not have been completed without the encouragement and help of many wonderful colleagues and friends. My sincere thanks to all of you. A sabbatical leave allowed me to take advantage of concentrated writing time, an occasion that Pratesi did not have, and lamented often and loudly. A generous research grant from Victoria University in the University of Toronto facilitated research time in Europe where some of the newspapers and journals that reviewed Pratesi are housed: the Biblioteca Nazionale Centrale di Firenze, the Gabinetto Vieusseux (Florence), the Biblioteca Comunale Sormani and the Biblioteca Braidense (Milan), the Biblioteca degli Intronati (Siena), and the National Library in London (Colindale Branch). These supplemented the information found in the extensive holdings of the Robarts Library in the University of Toronto. I also thank the heirs of Pratesi who provided important insights to Pratesi's life. Invaluable information came also from the Pratesi Archives housed in Victoria University Library Special Collections, and the *Pratesi Carteggio Inedito* site (http://pratesi.vicu.utoronto.ca/index.html). This site represents the work of undergraduate students from several faculties, graduate students, high school students through the University of Toronto mentorship program, senior alumni working as a team with Professor Carmela Colella of Brock University, Ontario, and myself. Over 1,600 letters and documents donated to the Special Collections section of E.J. Pratt Library at Victoria University in the University of Toronto were read, transcribed, and annotated; they are all available as an e-publication at the site above.

REVIEWING MARIO PRATESI

Introduction

It is a winter's day in Toronto, almost a cliché for Canada. How curious that Tuscan writer Mario Pratesi (1842–1921) should have his life ordered, recorded, and catalogued here in a city that probably never entered his thoughts, a city thousands of kilometres from his beloved Santa Fiora on Mont'Amiata where he was born, a city equally distant from his flat in the old stone house in via San Leonardo high above Florence, where he died. Praised for his precise and colourful observations and descriptions of the myriad villages, towns, and cities that attracted him or repulsed him, the closest Pratesi ever came even to hearing of Canada was in all likelihood a letter sent to him by Giuseppe Solimbergo (1846–1922), then consul of Italy in Montreal, who wrote to him in Florence asking for a favour, and in the most Canadian of ways, complained about the winter weather. How Pratesi's papers and letters arrived in Toronto constitutes part of a much longer, more complicated, and fascinating story which culminates with the generous donation of Pratesi materials to the Special Collections of the Victoria University E.J. Pratt Library on the campus of the University of Toronto.

Important and respected in his own time, Pratesi remained excluded from the Italian canon of major writers. One might well wonder, then, why he merits our attention today. It is because his rich correspondence justifies another look at him, not only for what it reveals about him and his works but also about his culture and about Culture. The letters written by Pratesi and those sent to him offer an entry into a world long gone, inscribed indelibly into History with upper case H. It is a History that casts its net widely, and fishes up from the Italian Ottocento only the most minute and partial answers to who, what, where, when, and why. The Pratesi letters make us stop and reflect on people whom few remember now. They allow us to reconsider their actions and events in a rather exciting and tumultuous world, and to consider the repercussions on our world today. The years of Pratesi's lifespan, taking in as they did the challenges to unify the Italian peninsula and the struggles of post-unification Italy, may even prove to confirm the famous words of Pratesi's English contemporary, Charles Dickens, to whom the Tuscan was compared by some of his peers: "the best of times and the worst of times."[1] The political upheavals (including the horrors of the Great War), the linguistic conundrums, the social changes, the literary tastes all reveal themselves in the rich corpus of missives to relatives, friends, colleagues, and acquaintances. The fertile exchange of ideas between Italian intellectuals and, in particular, their German and British counterparts, also comes to the fore. The letters offer seemingly tangential information that in reality serves to explain other events and ideas in Italy. Let two examples among many suffice. From the letters we learn that Pratesi's friend, the Englishwoman Jessie Taylor Laussot, later Hillebrand, was instrumental in introducing the music of Robert Wagner to the Italian peninsula. Through her letters with Pratesi we now also know that she was also the author of a fundamental book of music theory, heretofore always attributed to a man because she used a male pseudonym.[2] Another example can be found in the letters to and from his dear friend Giacomo Barzellotti who describes how the philosophy of Positivism made its influence felt on the Italian peninsula. Generally, the countries where positivist attitudes most took hold were highly developed industrially, particularly England.[3] That the philosophy, with its focus on science, should be adopted to the extent it was also in Catholic Italy points to the burgeoning confidence of the new country, to its more sophisticated new view of itself. Barzellotti's letters act as a harbinger of the social and political changes that would propel Italy, for better or worse, into the twentieth century. But more, Pratesi was no ordinary observer. A writer whose keen sense of descriptive precision garnered praise for him from his works as a youth to his last publications, Pratesi captured his world from various angles: the Manzonian emulation, the realist (he was referred to as the Tuscan *verista*), the decadent; he was serious, funny; he wrote as a poet, a master of prose narrative, and a pedagogue. He was the friend and correspondent of many similarly endowed observers, most actively engaged in a rapidly developing Italy as the country played out its roles on a larger stage beyond its own boundaries. Pratesi, too, involved himself in his world: not a politician or philosopher, he used his stories to trace the patterns of the common Italian, the men and women who participated every day in the D'Azeglian challenge of "making Italy and making Italians."[4] His characters reflect back to us the "real" Italy set in the world of Pratesi's imagination.

At the same time, Pratesi's letters play a fundamental metanarrative role: they reveal to us the writer at his work; we see him in his "studio," so to speak, as he creates, changes, debates, deletes. As we observe, it is not only the scratching of the pen we hear metaphorically. Outside his room resound the upheavals of a world undergoing immense change, and as Pratesi writes, he hints at, and often openly describes, the changes informing his social environment: major political changes with their concomitant effects on the History of Italy as the country struggled with her new roles in the geopolitical theatre of the world. But, we can also witness other evolutions and transformations, some openly discussed, some intimated: linguistic,[5] medical, and philosophical adjustments to new *mores* and attitudes; his letters reveal new technologies (especially in travel), new fashions, and new attitudes, all bringing with them his sensitivity to the human condition, as for example, he intuitively recounts in his letters of the period of the Great War, or as he evokes the memories of cherished friends upon their passing. Through his letters, we can almost relive the late Ottocento and early Novecento, appreciating the knowledges with which he enriches us. We can look back and see the epiphenomenal effects of Pratesi's world in his letters, interpreting retrospectively the events he describes or implies. We must remember, however, that Pratesi remained in his time, unable to see what we see. His diffidence towards an author such as Gabriele D'Annunzio, for example, was a reflection of his own personal taste, but also of his resentment that such an upstart should be preferred over himself in major publications.

With his every publication Pratesi invited his close friends into his metaphorical workshop to help him as he gave shape to his works, to criticize and to encourage him, the latter a role most important for an author beset by bouts of depression throughout his life. His friends were his informal critics. They acted as initial indicators of what the formal assessments of his works might say. Sometimes he took their advice; sometimes he chose to ignore it. Either way, when he saw his pages evaluated by formal critics writing in various journals and periodicals, he turned once again to his friends to grumble or rejoice.

In the absence of manuscripts, Pratesi's correspondence serves as the stuff of the *critique génétique* approach advocated by Louis Hay, Jean

Bellemin-Noël, and others (which, interestingly, initially often dealt with more or less the same time period in which Pratesi worked, but in France). This approach to textual examination or reflection allows multiple considerations of an author and his or her works, including theoretical, historical, and also comparative. It proposes that the critical scholar also enter into the writer's workshop, to assess all the elements that inform a piece of writing. Bellemin-Noël has referred to this as *avant-texte*, or what comes before the text. Such a study includes not only manuscripts but also incomplete sketches or drafts of a work, correspondence, and other similarly relevant aspects that together reveal the internal workings of the piece of writing, uncovering, as it were, the many juxtaposed threads woven through the text, even though these threads may seem external to the final authorially validated product. What interests practitioners of critique génétique has often been discarded by an author as extraneous or unnecessary or irrelevant to a finished text. However, considering such material in relation to the final written work deepens our knowledge and appreciation of how, rather than what, the author wrote. Furthermore, it gives us insight into the author and his time. Louis Hay, one of the first "geneticists," suggests that such a historical/critical perspective cannot be overlooked for "to say that the text is marked by social structures, ideologies, and cultural traditions is to say that it continues to speak of them, that in its warp and woof we can read at every moment, the truth of the time. Or rather a certain truth since the cultural imprint is inscribed in each text in a specific form."[6]

Bellemin-Noël, finding himself at a loss for a precise descriptor for the technique, which is methodologically unregimented and flexible, employed the term "textanalyse" (usually rendered as "textoanalysis" in English). Textoanalysis, according to Bellemin-Noël, also takes into consideration the unconsciously included, involuntarily revealing parts of a text; since his point of departure is the field of psychoanalysis, he uses the expression "l'inconscient du texte" (the unconscious of the text) to describe how he proceeds.[7] My present study has no intention of painting Pratesi's psychological portrait, and his hidden psyche is not the focus of my work. Yet, time and again, those very elements that critique génétique would deem worthy of consideration also offer glimpses into Pratesi's emotions, and suggest motives for his psychological deportment, which in turn substantially shaped his writing. These came to the fore even in the conspicuous absence of reviews, when he was an elderly man, irritable and irascible, working in what could be called his "late style" of writing.[8]

Adaptation of the lessons learned from the geneticists led to the discovery of what I will call an "inter-reader." Having accepted "the deep relation between writing and reading in all texts, the relation between the textualization of a writer's private representation and what one might call the verbal simulacrum, that is, the textual simulation that is later operative in the reader's representations," brought me to the intriguing issue of the book review.[9] Indubitably, the relationship that Pratesi intended as an author was the direct one between his work and his readers. But, in fact, the existence of a book review created an intermediary between author and readers, for the latter often became readers thanks to the recommendation of a book review. Indeed, to promote a book is one of the functions of a review. Nor does the inter-reader or reviewer have a simple typology. Pratesi's inter-readers existed on several not always distinct levels. First there were his friends, who, as such, had ready access and participated in the "avant-texte" of his work. Often, they even helped create aspects of the avant-texte by suggesting changes to the works as the writing process progressed. A second group of inter-readers was composed of objective reviewers, professional inter-readers who described his books in published periodicals but who did not personally know or work with Pratesi. Still another group comprised professional inter-readers who were biased. Among these, for example, we find Ernesto Masi, who had first expressed his opinion of *Le Perfidie del caso* (1898) in a private letter to Pratesi; later, urged by Pratesi, Masi adapted the letter so that it might be published as a formal book review in the journal *Nuova Antologia*. Another type of biased reviewer is the pseudonymic reviewer of Pratesi's first two narrative works, who likely reviewed the author at the request of the publisher, and who would have received some indication of the publisher's attitude towards the book to help him shape his review. Still another example is offered by Enrico Corradini, whose aim in writing a negative review was to criticize the periodical that had originally serialized Pratesi's work more than to denigrate the writer himself or his novel. The work of the inter-readers does not constitute an avant-texte for the book under review, of course, since their comments appeared after publication. But it ineluctably served as an a priori consideration for any work that followed. To make the situation of the inter-reader more challenging and fascinating is also the fact that these readers, and in particular the inter-readers who were Pratesi's personal friends, inevitably influenced one another, as they discussed his avant-textes among themselves. His correspondence often reports and compares their reactions to his works in progress, or works completed, and it indicates and comments on the formal reviews of his works that appeared in various contemporary journals and periodicals.

Gathering the reviews Pratesi received provided an opportunity to study the very genre of book reviewing. Each one of the formal reviews received by Pratesi helps us follow the history of book reviewing in Italy because Pratesi wrote during the years when reviewers and reviews finally and formally established themselves as a literary enterprise of their own in Italy. That not so many years before Pratesi, Alessandro Manzoni should have fretted more about his few readers rather than his formal reviewers suggests the relative newness of book reviewing in the first part of the nineteenth century. But, by the early 1880s when Ruggero Bonghi (1826–1895) began to publish his all-review journal *La Cultura*, the situation of books, of printing and promoting them, had changed irrevocably. Bonghi, whom a contemporary called a "major star" of the Italian literary scene, was acknowledged as the "intellectual president" of the important Florentine literary salon known as the Salotto Rosso, and he was "the political, literary and philosophical consultant "of its doyenne, Emilia Toscanelli Peruzzi.[10] In his preface to another publication, Bonghi himself marvelled at the unprecedented increase in publications that Italy had experienced from 1867 onward, so that by 1887 daily papers numbered 1,606.[11] An impressive number, indeed, if one considers the rather high rate of illiteracy on the peninsula at the time and the fact that most Italians did not even speak standard Italian, but communicated in their dialect.[12] In Pratesi's time, Italian book reviewing was still in the developmental stages when compared with contemporary England and France; nonetheless, Italian publishing houses had recognized the added economic value of having their publications receive a positive book review. Nor was the valuable publicity potential for the author's future works overlooked. In the years after Italian unification, as periodicals increased in number, many young and innovative Italian writers became household names. Among these is also Mario Pratesi, whose name may not stand out prominently in Italian literary history today, but whose prolific pen attracted the attention, mostly positive, of reviewers all along the Italian peninsula.

By the time that Pratesi read the first formal review of the novella *Da fanciullo: Memorie del mio amico Tristano* (Florence: Le Monnier, 1872), his first significant publication,[13] book reviewing in Italy had already made notable strides, as had related categories like journalism, periodical publication and their marketing, and also technical innovation.[14] The road, of course, was not always a smooth one. The history of book reviewing in Italy actually begins in France in the seventeenth century and then comes to the Italian peninsula by way of England. Ugo Foscolo, for example, learned how to write book reviews by imitating those of the *Edinburgh Review*.[15] Compendia of book titles and abstracts had existed before the 1600s, of course. Edward A. Bloom, in his groundbreaking study on book reviewing, reminds us of the *Bibliotheca* of Apollodorus of Athens in the first century BCE, of the *Bibliotheca Historica* of Diodorus of Sicily (whose work was undertaken under the rule of two Caesars, Julius and Augustus). Later, in the ninth century CE, Photius of Constantinople compiled the *Myrobiblion seu Bibliotheca*, which focused on ancient Greek literature.[16] But the invention of the printing press, with the resulting ever-widening availability of printed materials, also gave momentum to this genre. As books printed increased in number, and as readership also increased, the need for abstracting new works came to the fore. This was more than journalism (also going through growing pains in the seventeenth century), more than promotion; it was not quite literature per se, and it was certainly different from literary criticism, exegesis, or interpretation. Yet, all the elements above constitute a book review: Orteza y Miranda suggests that reviews act "as a change agent, creating a critical climate of opinion";[17] hers is an elaboration of Bloom's earlier description of reviews as "a valuable index to contemporary literary tastes and attitudes ... a genre in which journalism unites with literature and touches upon criticism."[18] Book reviews, therefore, are not to be understood as articles of literary criticism. Virginia Woolf explains that "towards the end of the eighteenth century ... the body of criticism then seems to split into two parts. The critic and the reviewer divided the country between them. The critic ... dealt with the past and with principles; the reviewer took the measure of new books as they fell from the press. As the nineteenth century drew on, these functions became more and more distinct."[19] Last, but not least, Roger Philip McCutcheon's study reminds us that book reviews, even in their primitive presentation as publication announcements found in various single sheet corantoes, serve also as promotional pieces for the book, its publisher, and its author, to a far more detailed degree than the title page of the publication, which previously normally served not only to identify the book's title and author but also for advertising or promotional purposes.[20] To go beyond the simple presentation of a title page as advertisement was especially imperative when dealing with translations of books from other languages where title page alone could not promote the work. Among the first and most notable "separations" between review and criticism to illustrate the emerging necessity for a book review is the following which appeared in the *Perfect Diurnall* in 1648: "There is now published the much expected work of that Famous, and Learned, and Iuditious Divine, Mr *Iohn Diodati* of Geneva, being his Annotations upon the Holy Bible, corrected and much enlarged, with a methodicall analysis before every book thereof: the first on the Subject ever yet in English. The book is very necessary for people of all Estates and conditions, and greatly beneficiall in private families for the better understanding of the sacred Scripture."[21] The embryo of future book reviews lies at the heart of this description, for it is simultaneously an ad for the book, an overview of the book's content, a brief assessment of its value, and an indicator of its intended audience, all elements that book reviews slowly began to incorporate in a more formalized manner.

Ruggero Bonghi's presentational essay in the first issue of *La Cultura* points to the *Journal des Sçavans*, published by Denis de Sallo, as the direct source of modern book reviews.[22] This is not only true for Italian reviewing, but for reviewing in Europe in general; histories of the genre confirm Bonghi's assertion. Started in 1665, the *Journal* (published both in Amsterdam and Paris) intended to "give readers (and scholars) an universal account of the state of learning."[23] Bonghi ascribes its birth to the need to let an ever-increasing readership "know what was happening in the Republic of letters," especially considering the great proliferation of new publications.[24] In that same year, 1665, the *Philosophical Transactions of the Royal Society* also undertook a similar activity in England; clearly, each publication gleaned and translated information and articles from the other. Three years later, in 1668, in Italy, Francesco Nazari, a Bergamasque abbot, modelled his similarly titled *Il Giornale de' letterati* after Sallo's *Journal*. The *Giornale*, published in Rome, appeared regularly until 1681 then, after 1683, more irregularly under the direction of Benedetto Bacchini of Parma.[25] Later, it was revitalized by Apostolo Zeno, Antonio Vallisnieri, and Scipione Maffei, according to Bonghi. Maffei's introduction to the new *Giornale* again cited a great need for such a publication because printed works were by now too numerous to be read all of them in their entirety, and therefore readers required a reliable source to let them know how to choose their reading material in order not to be misled by book titles about the contents therein.[26] Although the *Giornale* ceased regular publication in 1718, when Zeno moved to Vienna, it appeared intermittently until 1740, and then was reborn as the *Nuovo giornale dei Letterati*, which was active from 1774 until 1790.

Curiously, and for reasons which he does not explain, Bonghi's preface avoided any mention of the numerous other periodicals that proliferated in the eighteenth century, a regrettable omission that overlooks the important contributions to periodical publication of such noted pioneering papers such as the *Spectator* in England, but also the Italian *Il Caffè*. The latter existed under the direction of some of the most notable literary figures of their time: first under Pietro Verri (1728–1797), and later under his brother Alessandro (1741–1816), together with numerous other "caffetisti," including Cesare Beccaria (1738–1794) and Luigi Lambertenghi (1780–1860), who acted as editors over its seventy-four issues.[27] Perhaps more than other similar publications, *Il Caffè* marks the fundamental passage from news journal to a print forum for discussion of literature, politics, and other fields of knowledge.

Even less understandable is Bonghi's omission of the *Frusta letteraria (di Aristarco Scannabue)* [*The Literary Whip of Aristarco Scannabue*] important to the history of Italian book reviewing because the first prototypic Italian book review appeared here. Giuseppe Baretti, the founder, writer, and publisher of the *Frusta letteraria* was born in 1719 in Turin, but his peripatetic life, which offered him a solid formation in literary and journalistic publishing, evolved far beyond the city of his birth. He first published in Milan, but finding the environment there rather restricting, he left for London in 1751. London, for Baretti, was the city of intellectuals, of Enlightenment, of empiricism; it was anti-academic and anti-pedantic, innovative, receptive to new and open-minded enterprises, such as those offered by the continuing developments in the field of journalism. Baretti immersed himself as fully as possible in this exciting environment, where he was mentored by writer, critic, and lexicographer Samuel Johnson (1709–1784). Subsequent trips to Spain and France expanded Baretti's outlook on the world. He began to publish in English, including *The Italian library containing an account of the lives and works of the most valuable authors of Italy*, published in 1757 and likely the model for Mario Pratesi's friend Angelo De Gubernatis' similar compendia almost a century and a half later. Baretti was also the author of the *Dictionary of the English and Italian language* (1760). By 1763 he had returned to Venice, and at the beginning of October he released the first issue of the bi-monthly *Frusta letteraria*, using the pen name Aristarco Scannabue, and indicating Rovereto as the city of publication. In this premier issue he included a favourable review of the poet Giuseppe Parini's *Il mattino* (although the poet remained unnamed). Not all reviews were as positive as this one. Later Baretti even also "whipped" his own *Piacevoli poesie* (1751) in a sarcastically derogatory review. After the demise of the *Frusta letteraria*, in 1765, Baretti returned to England, continuing his literary career as critic there; his *Discours sur Shakespeare et sur monsieur de Voltaire* (1777) earned him the reputation as precursor of Romanticism.[28] Baretti died in London in 1789. After Baretti definitively left Italy for England, the *English Review*, one of the five contemporary reviewing journals, turned to Sir Robert Liston (1742–1836), who resided in Turin, for comments on foreign publications. Records also show that another in the list of five, the *Monthly Review*, was regularly sent to Florence. Thus, English and Italian reviewing as a genre continued to develop in tandem.[29]

Journals and periodicals flourished in Italy in the nineteenth century. New technologies for the production of paper came to Italy from England at the beginning of the century, and by 1812, also from England, arrived the possibility of continuous mechanized printing that did away with the need for hand-cranked presses and notably increased the quantity of publications.[30] Formats for publishing articles on ideologies, politics, literature, etc. established themselves more formally at this time and, similarly, so did book reviewing. As reviewing became more visible and prominent, reviews tended to enjoy more credibility than book advertisements because readers assumed that the book reviewer was an informed individual at the very least, or, at best, a recognized authoritative voice in the field.[31] Nevertheless, even with their growing acceptability, book reviews did not seem to be included on a consistent basis in the various publications available. Thus, the reviews first of Pratesi's *Memorie del mio amico Tristano*, and then later of his novel *Jacopo e Marianna*, both appearing in *Il Diritto*, were not part of a regular journalistic feature of that newspaper. Formal reviews of his later works, published as reviewing became more established and formalized, increase in number and are found in popular newspapers and journals throughout the peninsula. The Pratesi archives reflect this. Pratesi carefully clipped, or copied by hand, most of the formal reviews of his works. Still others were mentioned in his correspondence. For the most part, he accepted his reviewer as an "arbiter of taste and consumer adviser," as James Hoge has written.[32]

When Ruggero Bonghi first proposed the review journal *La Cultura*, he explained that the time was right for a publication focusing on reviewing: intellectual endeavours were increasing and gaining recognition in Italy, although the country still lagged behind England, France, and Germany, and even behind the United States and Russia. He described Italian intellectuals of the past as scholars locked within a windowless house of personal interests, without the possibility of seeing out to other intellectual "houses." Through his journal, he aspired to offer contemporary intellectuals a wider purview in their academic pursuits. Furthermore, Italy still had to cultivate a larger and more informed and appreciative reading public.[33] Such a public no longer excluded the middle class, as had happened previously when journals were intended primarily for the nobility or the clergy. Neither of the latter two groups could continue to promote contemporary letters, according to Bonghi. The first because it often preferred letters and research of no practical use, the second because it concentrated on, and limited itself to writings of an ecclesiastical nature, not attractive to the new bourgeois reader.[34] Bonghi also remained adamant that political bias had no place in his journal. He intended to use his reviews to attract a broad readership, but including the nobility and the clergy, in order to address a more extensive awareness of what Culture represented. Highly critical of what he deemed a closed understanding of the concept resulting in a narrow-mindedness that only harmed intellectual pursuits in Italy, and quoting from Hamlet ("There are more things in heaven and earth, Horatio, Than you think of in jour [sic] philosophy"),[35] he called for more tolerant attitudes towards new publications: "All books [sent to *La Cultura*] will be received and welcome as long as they demonstrate conscientious intellectual work and a committed desire to capture beauty in art and truth in science. To this committed desire of authors, the critics will respond with a committed presentation [of each work]."[36] Although he did not elaborate, he may have had reviewers such as Carlo Cattaneo (1801–1869) or Carlo Tenca (1816–1883) in mind. Both reviewers were notorious for their hostile appraisals of works; author, diplomat, and literary philosopher Niccolò Tommaseo (1802–1874) became a particular target for the first and poet Giovanni Prati (1815–1884) for the second. Critic Giovanni Bardazzi points out that Tenca was especially well known for the "recensione demolitrice" (the destructive review) in journals such as the *Rivista europea* and *Il Crepuscolo*.[37]

In order to achieve his desideratum for unbiased, authoritative reviews, Bonghi proposed a guiding framework, important because still accepted in the field of book reviewing today. First, reviews would openly identify the political, literary, or intellectual bias of the author; if the work required corrections (typographical, stylistic, factual), the critic would indicate these precisely. Furthermore, no critic would use the review as a forum for an attack against the author personally.

Reviews might be of various lengths, as appropriate; books from a variety of academic or literary areas would be reviewed. The journal invited a large number of collaborators of varied interests to participate. Reviewers could choose whether or not to identify themselves; reviews without an identified author (a practice that continued until the beginning of the twentieth century) would be the responsibility of the periodical.[38] Furthermore, works considered for review were not limited to those published only in Italy, and could focus on a number of thematic areas or fields of study (although he saw no need for books on mathematics or the natural sciences to be included). In addition, he hoped that academics and writers would find *La Cultura* a useful tool for information about forthcoming publications and for encouraging contact between authors and scholars interested in similar topics. *La Cultura* would also provide a space for obituaries. Bonghi wished his journal a long life. Indeed, after overcoming the typographers' strike that seriously delayed one of its early issues and jeopardized its acceptance by readers,[39] and later, after having been suppressed by the Fascist regime in 1936, the periodical continues today as a critical journal with articles on topics of interest to scholars of history, literature, and philosophy. To confirm the growing importance and value, and also increasing ubiquity, of book reviews for Italian writers as the twentieth century dawned, the clippings service Eco della Stampa, a seemingly natural offshoot of *La Cultura*, came into existence in Rome in 1901 with the sole purpose of monitoring print media for its subscribers. Among its earliest subscribers was Pratesi, who joined in the first year of the service, and through this resource, received citations and reviews of his works from publications he had no direct contact with. How greatly had the world of book reviews changed from the time he had written to Clemente Maraini asking the publisher as a personal favour to reveal the identity of his first reviewer, Diogene.[40]

Bonghi had hoped that his journal of reviews could open a windowless house of exclusive academics. Virginia Woolf, on the other hand, felt that in the world of reviewing, the windows revealed too much. Her work simply entitled *Reviewing* (1939) never mentions Italian letters, yet it describes succinctly all that Bonghi had aimed to accomplish in founding *La Cultura*, a confirmation that the genre had developed in parallel ways in both England and Italy as it became more sophisticated and more accepted as an independent genre. Woolf wrote her brief and informal pages from the dual perspective of reader and also occasional reviewer, commenting in her diary: "When I read reviews I crush the columns together to get at one or two sentences; is it a good book or a bad? And then I discount those 2 sentences according to what I know of the book and the reviewer. But when I write a review I write every sentence as if it was going to be tried before 3 Chief Justices."[41]

While Bonghi welcomed reviews and reviewers, Woolf did not. The field had changed enough in the almost fifty years that separate the two publications to have produced its own set of critics. Woolf, too, begins with the metaphor of the window, one where seamstresses sit as they mend old clothing, at the mercy of onlookers: "So our poets, playwrights and novelists sit in the shop window, doing their work under the curious eyes of reviewers. But the reviewers are not content … to gaze in silence; they comment aloud upon the size of the holes [in the metaphorical garment], upon the skill of the workers and advise the public which of the goods in the shop window is best worth buying."[42] She writes of the hefty and unavoidable power of the reviewers who deeply and personally affect the authors they appraise by ignoring authorial sensibilities and by compromising future sales through their negative reviews. She laments the popularity of the genre, saying that the increased number of reviews has no benefit for either the writer or the reader since reviewers often contradict each other, resulting in irrelevant considerations. She is concerned that reviewers, who generally write for daily or weekly or monthly publications, must produce reviews with increasing speed and frequency and decreasing reflection in order to meet editorial deadlines. In full agreement, she quotes Harold Nicolson who wrote in the *Daily Telegraph* (March 1939) that when a book review is truly honest, then it simply states in a public and published forum "why I either like or dislike their work; and I trust that from such a dialogue the ordinary reader will derive some information."[43] Woolf considers how to preserve the value of book reviews, suggesting facetiously that potential reviewers be required to show credentials similar to those of doctors, and outlining how a review might resemble a visit to the doctor, where reviewer and author engage in private and serious consultation. As Bonghi had written in *La Cultura*, Woolf, too, argues ultimately, despite her playful jibes, that reviewers play an essential role in the development of authors: "How many authors are there who would wish to have an expert opinion on their work? The answer to this is to be heard crying daily and crying loudly in any publisher's office or in any author's post bag. 'Give me advice,' they repeat, 'give me criticism.' The number of authors seeking criticism and advice genuinely, not for advertising purposes but because their need is acute, is an abundant proof of the demand."⁴⁴ However, she warns, contemporary reviewers do not help their own cause; if they disappeared, authors would probably write better, and readers would educate themselves in literary appreciation.

Curiously, in the pages following her brief treatise, its publisher Leonard Woolf (husband of Virginia) hastens to add his opinion to hers, contradicting her entirely. Insisting that the reviewer "has nothing to say to the author; he is talking to the reader," Leonard Woolf maintains firmly that

> the function of the reviewer remains fundamentally the same; it is to give to readers a description of the book and an estimate of its quality in order that he may know whether or not it is the kind of book which he may want to read ... It is not at all an easy thing to give a clear, intelligent and honest analysis of a novel or a book or poems ... The vast majority of reviews do give an accurate and often interesting account of the book reviewed ... The writer who wants to write works of art and make a living by doing so is in a difficult position. As an artist the critic and criticism may be of immense value or interest to him. But he has no right to complain that the reviewer does not perform the function of critic for him.⁴⁵

Mario Pratesi took the reviews of his works seriously, perhaps because he himself was often called upon to give his opinion on the writing of others, both formally and informally. He may have learned the art of constructive criticism through the conversations and discussions that animated the Salotto Rosso of Emilia Toscanelli Peruzzi, the genteel hostess of the much frequented literary salon in Florence. Mrs Peruzzi regularly sent copies of recently published books to the salon's participants, and solicited their own works from them, in order to offer constructive opinions and commentary. She was well known for her encouragement, promotion, and support (including financial) of young writers she considered worthy, among whom we find notable names like Edmondo De Amicis, Giannina Milli, Ada Negri, and Pratesi himself. Pratesi also recognized the value of discussing his works with trusted friends and especially with Cesare Abba, Giacomo Barzellotti, and Alessandro Gherardi. In the case of Abba, the discussions were almost exclusively epistolary since the two rarely met after the months spent in Pisa at the beginning of their long friendship in the 1860s. With Barzellotti and Gherardi there were more frequent encounters which indubitably became occasions for discussions of their respective projects and future publications. Pratesi's many postings to schools in various parts of Italy brought new friendships, and also opportunities for further informal critiques of his work. At the same time, formal reviews of his work brought him recognition from readers and critics, many of whom later also gave him informal opinions of his writing. All in all, the formal reviewers gave Pratesi their serious consideration throughout his life as a writer. Pratesi even merited a review for his first narrative work published, *Da fanciullo: Memorie del mio amico Tristano*; the critique may or may not have been commissioned by the publisher of *Il Diritto*, Clemente Maraini, but its overall positive introduction of Pratesi as an author worthy of note and full of promise set him on the life's path he had so long desired.

A comprehensive critical or historical overview of book reviewing in the Italian world of letters has yet to be written. The collection of Pratesi's reviews found in this study represents a view into a crucial developmental period of that history. His sampler is particularly rich because he saved many of his reviews, even copying in longhand those he could not clip out of journals. Concomitantly, public libraries and archives also came into their own during his lifetime, and the value of conservation in museums and other such repositories became ever more recognized and appreciated not only in Italy but in the Western world as a whole.[46] Thus, reviews not conserved in his personal archives are available through various libraries in Europe and North America. While Pratesi's personal collection of clippings, found by him or sent to him by friends and relatives or even those received from the clippings service Eco della Stampa, provide a unique direct contact with the author himself, and are especially valuable when they bear his scribbled comments, they nevertheless remain as single decontextualized cuttings. On the other hand, hunts through libraries and archives have revealed reviews of his works conserved in paper form or in microfilm. They allow researchers to see his reviews in their enriched original conditions, in relationship with other news pieces of the day, and including advertisements.

Pratesi wrote many works, principally poetry, that did not receive attention from reviewers. Furthermore, some of the informal reviews from acquaintances were often unhelpful, perfunctory laudatory nods expressing thanks for a complimentary copy of the work, sent out of courtesy. Overwhelmingly, those reviewers who paid him more consequential attention, informal or formal, found much to praise in Pratesi's prose, especially in terms of his linguistic richness, clarity, and precision.

In effect, over his long career, only two of the official reviews were dispiriting, both written by the same reviewer, Enrico Corradini, for his own periodical, *Il Marzocco*. Giacomo Barzellotti's negative opinion of the novel *Il Mondo di Dolcetta* (1895) (this novel was also one of Corradini's targets) was seen only by the circumspect Mrs Peruzzi to whom Barzellotti addressed it in a private letter. It is included here for the first time. Pratesi likely never knew of it. Although the number of formal reviews Pratesi received was not extraordinarily high, his works consistently attracted the attention of reviewers in major periodicals. But their number diminished as the years passed, as he grew older, more morose and cynical. Especially towards the end of his life did the silence surrounding his writing appear almost embarrassing; his late style of work only emphasized how out of date and deeply pessimistic he was in a new century, the twentieth, filled with innovative, but to him, unfamiliar attitudes towards writing and literature. It is inevitable, therefore, that a study of the book reviews he received, and the reactions to them, also provide what I will call a "shadow" biography of Pratesi; not the story of his life, not his psychological biography as Jean Bellemin-Noël might advocate, but the story of the book reviews of his life and how they ineluctably affected him and his writing. Pratesi emerges in this shadow biography as a man profoundly and earnestly dedicated to his writing, deeply engaged in the rapidly evolving world of Italian letters in the years of the unification of Italy, 1861–71 and afterwards (his first notable publications appeared in 1872), preoccupied with the positive promotion of Italian literature in Italy and beyond, and also a trusted and respected mentor to other writers, especially those younger. He acted as literary adviser to both men and women writers, suggesting, correcting, and encouraging until the pain of his debilitating final illness, a cancer, prevented him from working. The informal reviews of his works reveal an extraordinarily wide circle of loyal friends, many of whom exchanged letters with him over several decades.

Since this study took on the inadvertent responsibility of his shadow biography, it follows Mario Pratesi through the various cities in which he received the reviews of his works: from Florence through Terni, then Viterbo, Reggio Calabria, Milan, Belluno, and then finally returning to Florence where he lived the final years of his life. Pratesi wrote poetry, travel pieces, short stories, and novels; all genres garnered the attention of reviewers. While the focus here remains on his reviews, and not on a critical appraisal of his writing, the latter clearly informs the information provided here: the reviews are, after all, critiques of his work. The reviews cited and the letters quoted are all original and largely unpublished (in the case of the latter), or appear here for the first time since their original publication. The earliest review is from 1872, the latest from 1917.

To study an author and his works through the lens of book reviews has proved a truly unique but highly satisfying challenge. It has allowed me to examine primary sources previously unknown to contemporary studies. The reviews have unwittingly provided an initial sketch of the history of book reviewing in Italy, an unexpected consideration, also new to Italian literary history. The letters which gave birth to this project have served not only as a reintroduction to Mario Pratesi and his works, but have also described the world of the late Ottocento beyond the parameters of literature. They will undoubtedly continue to offer inspiration to critics in various fields.

The collection of materials upon which this study is based represents a rare and much appreciated view of late nineteenth-century/early twentieth-century Italy in myriad aspects, first and foremost literary but also political, social, philosophical, religious, pedagogical, etc. In these letters and documents, the world of Mario Pratesi springs to life in a unique, often surprising, always informative manner.

And what a world! Italy, finally unified geopolitically, inevitably began to feel the stresses and strains of taking up her new global identity. The world had grown: Italy could no longer consider her place only in Europe; North America and later (especially with the Ethiopian War) Africa made their presence felt in the Italian zeitgeist. New technological inventions, including in the printing industry, made time appear to speed up, shaking the traditional provincial or rural attitude that Italy had always embraced. The detailed debates about writing that only shortly before Pratesi's time afforded writers such as Alessandro Manzoni the luxury of long discussions with friends and colleagues about his works, about how they might or might not belong to Romanticism, for example, became curtailed conversations as movements fomented by Giosuè Carducci's new interpretation of poetry, by the *Veristi*, by the *Scapigliati*, by the Decadents and others overlapped each other, bringing new attitudes, and increasing numbers of readers as the middle class grew in numbers and strength. Nor could Italy ignore contemporary movements in other countries. As Bonghi had advocated in *La Cultura*, Italy was no longer a country where the nobility and clergy dominated; far more important was the middle class, now better educated, richer, and cognizant of its importance both in Italy and in the Western world as a whole. And Mario Pratesi, sensitive, dour at times, pessimistic, and articulate, tried with various degrees of success to make sense of it all through his writing.

Chapter One

Florence

Florence in the month of October insinuates a damp autumnal dreariness through its streets: those linearly aligned as parallel thoroughfares, as well as those tortuous twisty narrow lanes behind them. Somehow, walking home on a dark fall evening, Mario Pratesi lost his footing, stumbled, and fell. In his letter of 26 October 1872 to Giuseppe Cesare Abba, one of his closest friends, then living in Pisa, he laments the bruises and the pain; a medical historian might gather from his further description that he had suffered a concussion as well. In the same letter, Pratesi concerned himself to a far greater degree with another medical word: abortion. This he used metaphorically to describe his latest literary effort. "My little novel," he wrote self-deprecatingly, "or better, my abortion, has been printed since July, but not released. It will be released in November."[1] Not a month later, on 14 November, the first copies arrived in select bookstores in Rome and Florence, and on the 27th of the same month, Pratesi, now two days into his new teaching assignment in Pavia, reiterated morosely to Abba that he had had an abortion.[2] The word, used with Abba only in his early years of writing, indicates Pratesi's precarious state of mind as he tentatively begins a career his family never wanted him to have and initially did not support.[3] His father, in particular, had tried hard not to see it come to life, but once it did, grudgingly offered moral and financial support, as the correspondence between them shows. That the son should consider his writing here an abortive process speaks also to his lack of self-esteem as a writer, aware always that he is self-taught, unsupported, and always afraid of producing a useless mass out of his deep impulse to write. While he did not call later works "abortions," the fear of failure would never leave him.

This sense of depressed desperation characterizes much of the early correspondence between Abba and Pratesi. Both men were prone to prolonged periods of self-doubt, loneliness, and particularly on the part of Pratesi, a self-righteous anger over his suspicion that somehow he had been systemically overlooked as a writer and his talent ignored. These personality traits likely had their origin in his childhood and particularly in the death of his mother when he was only four years old; after her passing the subsequent difficult changes the household underwent as his father, Igino Pratesi, tried to raise the family continued to have negative influences on him. A well-meaning but strict patriarchal attitude, to which was added the arrival of a new step-mother,[4] ensured the psychological rebellion of this sensitive third son, who, unlike his older brothers, Tito and Dante, proved poorly suited for the military or police career his father had planned for him. Pratesi's depressive periods often accompanied moments during which his body was physically compromised as well, wracked by respiratory and pulmonary problems that at times culminated in intense coughing, lingering colds. Pratesi often coughed up blood. He had been in the throes of one of these respiratory onslaughts when he met Abba in April of 1865 at the trattoria run by Cencio Mastromei in Pisa.[5]

Giuseppe Cesare Abba (1838–1910) was already widely recognized for his heroic actions as a sympathizer of independence fighter Giuseppe Garibaldi when Pratesi came to know him. Their initial encounters and animated discussions lasting many hours in the little Pisan eating spot or in the Caffè dell'Ussaro were soon interrupted by the skirmishes of the third war of independence against Austria, in 1866, when Abba became actively involved, and Pratesi, due to his ill health, remained behind.[6] Their empathy towards one another became the glue that held their friendship together until Abba's death, and even later, in Pratesi's memories and recollections. In the almost fifty years of their friendship, they encouraged each other through life's vicissitudes. Each urged the other to continue writing and publishing. Pratesi was the more prolific of the two. Abba continuously held back; his published works revolved mostly around his military memories as a Garibaldino, and he felt that his descriptions of the exploits could not convey the exciting details of how the events had occurred. His best known work had begun as a project initiated by the leading poet of the day, Giosuè Carducci, who had solicited material from various military men for his intended biography of Giuseppe Garibaldi, the great hero of Italian unification. Impressed by the pages Abba had sent him, Carducci urged the latter to issue them independently. The work, titled *Noterelle di uno dei Mille edite dopo vent'anni* was published in 1880 and was his greatest literary success; it was later republished in 1891 as *Da Quarto al Volturno: Noterelle d'uno dei Mille*. But Abba had originally considered himself an author whose formation followed the school of Alessandro Manzoni, Italy's most celebrated narrative writer of the day. Inspired by Manzoni, Abba's first writing attempts produced *Arrigo*, a poem in five parts in the Romantic style. Abba wrote slowly and laboriously as he explained in the letters he exchanged with Pratesi, who urged him to finish the work and publish it as soon as possible. Abba's promises to do so remained largely unfulfilled, and publishers who knew them both even turned to Pratesi asking after the whereabouts of Abba's intended manuscript. When the poem finally appeared in print, Pratesi prepared a long review in the hopes of promoting it publicly; of his full review, the first sixteen manuscript pages remain, penned in his small tight handwriting.[7] Pratesi's intent was to promote his friend's literary talent, but his article on the merits of the poem would have not accomplished this end, wandering as it does from Byron to Goethe to Shakespeare. Pratesi writes here in a difficult and complicated erudite style, with copious quoting of Abba's verses, for which he provides an interpretation. The review is that of a neophyte writer attempting to establish his own writerly authority in his adjudication of another's work, quite unlike the reviewing guidelines that Bonghi would advocate later in *La Cultura*. A truly tedious review, fortunately, it remained unpublished, although Abba himself most certainly saw it since it was included in a letter to him from Pratesi dated 21 June 1866. On the other hand, Pratesi's overview of *Arrigo* should not be discarded; it offers us informative glimpses into the world of a developing young writer. First, the piece represents a sample of Pratesi's early expository style, the only manuscript remaining of his initial attempts to write prose. A nearly final draft, as is clear from the clean copy with astonishingly few revisions and considerations, the pages offer a compelling example of what Louis Hay and others would consider *critique génétique*. As he often laments in his early correspondence, Pratesi had no higher-level schooling; he sat in during university lectures in Pisa but was not a recognized student. Consequently, his style in the *Arrigo* review, unwieldy, almost unreadable, offers a mishmash of strategies appropriated from writers familiar to him, and is presented through his personal lens of quasi-hagiography, given that he was writing about and for his close friend. But his lexical choices here are already noteworthy for their variety and precision;

similarly, we see good evidence of his skill for keen observation and analysis, literary characteristics that hint at his future success as a writer. Second, because his work imitates articles he considered samples of good critical writing, it provides us with a relatively reliable exemplar of contemporary book reviewing, which at the time still remained more literary criticism than review, still intended almost exclusively for an erudite reader. Pratesi's essay on *Arrigo* served yet another purpose. The exercise of critiquing the works of a close and much admired friend helped Pratesi shape his own work. Abba's *Arrigo*, like most of Abba's work, took its inspiration from his personal experiences and observations as a soldier and his memorialization of those military events. Pratesi, on the other hand, began to understand writing as more than simply recollecting and reproposing his own life experiences. Such a task proved rather daunting; in a letter of June 1867, not long after having written the *Arrigo* review, he confessed to Abba: "Art is such a sublime thing which one does not reach without Herculean effort or without a calm and serene mind. For some time now I have given up hope of reaching it: bereft of everything and defeated by my destiny. Nonetheless, although Art has brought me only tears, I don't stop loving her with all my heart."[8]

For Pratesi, then, Art had become a severe mistress, and moreover, one that did not readily help him hold body and soul together. His father, resigned to the fact that this third son had definitively closed the door to a paid military career, watched and fretted as Pratesi courted his elusive Muse. His financial situation a disaster, Pratesi borrowed money from his father, who was already taxed by the demands that five children (the youngest, Corinna, subject to chronic illness) made on his meagre pension. Pratesi found various poorly paid positions in order to support himself so that he could write, a luxury which then could be done only in spare moments. He explained to Abba in 1870 that his primary Muse was Hunger, and his other Muse the Truth, but curiously, somehow, the positions he accepted, in reality, became nourishment for both.[9] In the summer of 1867 he found employment as a secretary to Niccolò Tommaseo (1802–1874). The "Grande Dalmata," whom Italy recognized and revered for his patriotism, his philosophical, poetical, and literary writing, and whose work as lexicographer remains valid to this day, was blind and despite his renown, despite his literary activity and output, he lived a life of desperate poverty. His fifth floor lodgings in the Lungarno delle Grazie on the banks of the Arno river became Pratesi's temporary refuge: "The work is hard, and the fruits of my labour miserly. But Tommaseo is a man of integrity, and I find comfort in his words, often affectionate and cordial," Pratesi confessed to Abba.[10] Thirty francs per month had to suffice. But, disastrously, Pratesi fell in love with Tommaseo's sixteen-year-old daughter, Caterina. Perhaps in seeing the love and respect Tommaseo demonstrated towards his wife Diamante, Pratesi envisaged a similar future empathy between himself and the daughter.[11] Tommaseo terminated the employment.

The departure from the great author's house cast heavy emotional and physical repercussions on the young Pratesi, as his response to Tommaseo and also his letters to Abba indicate. In the former, Pratesi hints that he is considering suicide.[12]

Pratesi's psychological demons, released in all fury by his dismissal, hounded him all through 1868 and, in fact, actually culminated in an attempt to end his life.[13] The event affected his whole family, and his father agreed to have him hospitalized in the Ospedale Psichiatrico San Niccolò near the Porta Romana in Siena. Again, Pratesi's devotion to Art allowed him a modicum of fortune in his misery. He came under the care of Dr Carlo Livi, the director of the hospital. Livi, a leading expert in psychiatry, believed that psychological cures were hastened by allowing patients to practise activities of their own choosing in order to encourage the healing process. Pratesi wanted to read in order to expand his self-education; even more, he wanted to write poetry and prose. Thanks to his father's anxious care for his son, the young patient had access to books. For the elderly father, carrying these to the hospital could not have been an easy feat for it meant that he had to cross the hilly terrain of the medieval city, from Porta San Marco to Porta Romana, only to be told that he could not see or speak to his son when he arrived at the hospital gate.[14] After seven months, Mario Pratesi was discharged from the sanatorium. During his stay, he had written some poetry, including *Per una morta fanciulla, La chiesuola di Ponte alle Grazie*, and *L'Angelo custode*,[15] all published soon after his homecoming in 1869. In effect, this period of profound difficulty and inner turmoil became a writing school of sorts for him, allowing him to initiate in a concrete manner his career as a poet. Unfortunately, the publication of his poems also gave rise to his self-doubts, and his sense that his work as a writer was not valued as it deserved, an attitude that in some of his correspondence comes across as a pathetic search for self-esteem.[16]

Nor did he overlook his love for narrative prose while hospitalized.[17] Mario Guidotti, eminent Pratesi scholar, indicates that Pratesi wrote his first novella, *Le Memorie del mio amico Tristano*, around 1869. Carlo

Madrignani and Giancarlo Bertoncini concur in their seminal study of the work. Existing letters do not indicate more precisely when or where Pratesi planned and revised this work, a gem that Guidotti rightly refers to as "a little masterpiece."[18] But, despite the bitterness of Pratesi's announcement to Abba in mid-May 1869 that he had finally been released from "the crazy hospital with its 350 crazy people where his brain had turned to liquid," we can understand that his artistic Muse had not abandoned him at all during his stay at San Niccolò. His letter accuses the hospital of killing his Muse; had she not been destroyed Pratesi asserts that

> I could have drawn her from the depths of my feelings, in my own way and not following others, I would have called her to me. I wanted to find inspiration in the minute and simple facts of life, to find the ideal in the reality of the common, to bring to light what is most hidden, least valued and esteemed in the world, to show the aesthetic sense of those things that happen naturally every day, to see the tears in certain social situations and certain outward appearances both in nature and in human existence; a homespun art, simple, passionate, lyrical and satirical at the same time in order to reflect all the colours of the social prism, all the harmonies of life and nature.[19]

His words are rather reminiscent of the lament and regrets we hear echoed in the words of the protagonist of the novella and suggests that, in this youthful work, Pratesi has achieved precisely the goals he described to Abba above. How different this "homespun," "simple" approach is from his review of Abba's *Arrigo*. It is not inconceivable, therefore, that writing the novella fundamentally informed the psychiatric therapy proposed by Dr Livi.[20] Certainly, *Le Memorie* constitutes a rare example of Pratesi's literary corpus because there is no epistolary evidence of the work as it progresses, nor even mention that he has even undertaken such a project. It is highly unusual for him not to ask his friends for comments or reactions as he wrote. His correspondence with Abba indicates explicitly that he received scarce letters while hospitalized, and his few letters from family members confirm this. The booklet was already written in 1869, as Guidotti indicates; the 1883 edition of the novella (published together with the poem *La Tarantella sul Lido*) also retains the original 1869 dating on its closing page.[21] That the novella should have sprung to life as a fully formed work in the scant months following Pratesi's release from San Niccolò is unlikely, especially because Pratesi soon found full-time employment as a teacher. Of greater likelihood, therefore, is its birth in the sanatorium and subsequent reworking following Pratesi's release from the hospital. Not long afterwards, the story appeared in instalments and with revisions in the Roman daily *Il Diritto* on 19, 20, and 21 March 1870.[22]

While no literary critic has yet explored in depth the idea that *Le memorie* contained pages linked to Pratesi's psychological healing, Carlo Madrignani suggests in his preface to his study on the various editions of the book, that the piece represents a "secret" work that does not readily adhere to the thematics that will interest Pratesi's later writing.[23] By describing it as "spontaneous microhistory" of literary exceptionalities because of its emphasis on orality, on the marriage of character, landscape, and memory, and on the simple ordinariness of everyday life,[24] Madrignani intuits how important the work must have been to the dysfunctional Weltanschauung Pratesi experienced at the time of writing. Furthermore, the pages effectively illustrate Pratesi's attempt to focus on an intimate and vital part of himself;[25] the work born of this desire reveals the deep relationship between the narrative and the author,[26] not autobiography but pseudoautobiography, an observation that is supported by one of his earliest pieces of prose, which he significantly signed with the pen name "Tristano," not uncoincidentally the name of his protagonist in *Le Memorie*.[27]

Although, most unusually for this author, there are no glimpses into Pratesi's writing workshop as the novella progressed, and therefore no informal critiques; the work received at least two formal reviews, both unreported in previously published bibliographies. The first, appearing on 7 February 1872 in *Il Diritto* (where the story had appeared in serial form), was part of an "appendice," an appendix, as it were, to the daily paper, a section reserved for instalments of serialized novels, and only occasionally, for book reviews. The anonymous reviewer signed his column Diogene, claiming that in the manner of his Greek counterpart who sought honest men, he searched for good writing. And in *Le Memorie* (now retitled *Da Fanciullo: Memorie del mio amico Tristano*), one of three books reviewed together, he claimed to have made a delightful discovery.[28] He lauded the realistic universal appeal of its melancholy, and he praised its affectionate portrayal of simple but inexpressible human desires. The details of Pratesi's verbal portraits, including the cat, nobly, calmly, sitting on its haunches, tail neatly wrapped around himself, struck the critic as particularly effectively done. "What a beautiful jewel this novella," he wrote towards his conclusion: "I had to put it away, dear reader, so as not to be tempted to quote several pages. Bravo, signor Pratesi, publish, publish more such novellas, and we shall read them all ... ladies will find their own gentleness reflected in them, the idle will find them a pleasant way to kill time, the worker will see in them noble sentiments, and finally even we, poor pariahs of literature, will be allowed to forget the many troubles of life, and we will learn to write better Italian."[29] Nor did the review end there; the author continued for another column to extol the beauty of Pratesi's poem *La Tarantella sul Lido* included in the same volume. Beautiful indeed, he exclaimed, but not as beautiful as the story in prose. Similarly, an anonymous review in *La Perseveranza* of 28 December 1872 found the style of *Le Memorie* particularly notable. The review examines Pratesi's second long prose narrative, *Jacopo e Marianna*, and works by two other writers, and while this critic was not as effusive with his praise for *Le Memorie*, he nonetheless expressed the hope that Pratesi would continue to write. Far more important is this reviewer's assertion that Pratesi, together with the two other authors considered, were proponents of a new school of literature, the school of realism.

And so, Pratesi's Muse had not died at the hospital of San Niccolò after all. A most demanding mistress for him, ultimately she proved a most loyal companion for the rest of his life. In the angry tirade to Abba quoted above, his insistence that he would have achieved far more as an author had he not been unjustly thwarted by circumstances and depression, initiated a refrain that changed little through the years as he matured. Nonetheless, his Muse continued faithfully at his side as he wrote, reworked, and rewrote each of his works.

By the time he read the first reviews of his work, Pratesi had become a teacher. He moved to his first, infelicitous position in the Collegio Cicognini in Prato near Florence, an assignment he announced to Abba in his letter of 13 May 1869. His work at the prestigious school included daily supervision of his students, and he hoped to take advantage of such an opportunity to instil in his young charges positive and inspirational attitudes. But disappointment awaited him, as the position took up the greater part of his time, imposing upon him numerous mundane duties. Furthermore, the boys he taught took him by surprise with what he interpreted as their maliciousness.[30] He soon left Prato, and by November he had returned to Florence, now employed as a copyist in the Archivio di Stato di Firenze where he made lifelong friendships with the director Cesare Guasti, and one of the other copyists, Alessandro Gherardi. The work, though tedious, at least allowed him some time to write. He began another serialized story, "Le viole di Marianna." It recounts the life of the romantic and idealistic youth, Jacopo, and his love for Marianna, a young orphaned girl forced to live with cruel relatives. Their feelings for each other find obstacles at every twist and turn especially in the degenerate suitor Signor Pierino, in whom, as Guidotti says, love becomes a "desperate sentiment."[31] The couple is supported by the honest and caring Nevio, Jacopo's friend and, according to Guidotti, a character based on Pratesi himself.[32]

By mid-September 1870 he informed Abba of its completion: "I have finished my story. Twenty-eight chapters have burst from my heart. I have put my soul into it, my tears, my anger, and my Sienese language; nevertheless, I don't really believe I have produced anything good."[33] He persisted in self-doubt as he corrected and changed the drafts. He fell ill once again and stopped writing, confessing to Abba that "I have too great a respect for Art, whom I adore, to work when I feel incapable of drawing inspiration from my imagination. Oh God, how unhappy I am! What suffering, what torture this is! I cannot even cry any more!"[34]

While he would have liked Abba to view the draft of his manuscript and comment on it, the deadline demanded by *Il Diritto* approached; the paper required the story by January 1871, although it did not appear in print until September. In March, Pratesi finally sent Abba a copy of the opening chapter to review, despite the ill health that had continued to trouble him since December. To add to his preoccupations was also the fact that his work as copyist at the Archivio di Stato was to end by the fall of 1871.

Abba read "Le viole di Marianna" attentively, and offered the first of several "friendly" reviews that in the coming years Pratesi would solicit for all his works. For the most part, no manuscript copies of Pratesi's work remain to give us an opportunity for *critique génétique* as Bellemin-Noël theorized. Nevertheless, in these prepublication assessments and also in post-publication comments, we do have an insight into the author at his work, accepting of the critiques at times, dismayed at others, but overall attentive and responsive to the efforts of his friends to provide an honest appraisal of his pages. Abba overall offers a positive review of "Le viole di Marianna," but his words clearly indicate his belief that Pratesi has strayed from "traditional" Italian literary forms to more unpalatable foreign trends:

> I have received your instalments and I'd like to give my sincere opinion of your work; ... what doesn't go well to date or may not go well later, I will

not say yet, not until the whole is published ... Of what I like I will say a little now that the work is mostly published. The language is beautiful, even too much so; I mean you can really feel the elements of literary Tuscan, and if you used some slightly more common expressions it would be more appreciated. The style is all yours, and anyone who doesn't know you would intuit your character and your physiognomy from it, because one can't write like you do unless one has suffered, suffered a lot, enough to be able to ignore the suffering. The characters are well written, but not all of them as well as the artist, with whom I swear I've conversed, so alive does he seem. If you could do the same for other characters of yours, if we could see them as completely as we see your Nevio, your work would garner more applause ... Continue Mario, you have found your path. But let me warn you about one thing. Pay attention to how the plot develops, make it seem Italian. Don't give the reader any surprises.[35]

Abba explains himself by advising Pratesi to follow a chronologically linear plot development, to avoid jumping from the coffin to the birth. Perhaps in this suggestion he reflected his own penchant for a diaristic format in writing, linear par excellence. As far as Abba was concerned, the work should flow like a river, "so that once you've gone upstream you don't have to repeat the work of going upstream once again later in the book." The comment is clearly his criticism of the influence of foreign authors, and Abba decries the Italian penchant for imitating them: "This is one of the defects of our times, one that we've adopted from foreigners. You've fallen into the trap a bit too much, and I found in this story of yours that the fabric is beautiful and ours, although there are threads that don't belong to us ... however, your sin in this is not so great as to be unpardonable."[36]

Abba does not name the authors he refers to. But, paradoxically, as we can read above, he also advises Pratesi to use less of the Tuscan idiom. Why this critical tension? His reiteration of it indicates that the issue was of some interest, and of some concern. Certainly, the French Gustave Flaubert was known in Italy by this time for his novel *Madame Bovary* (1857) as were the poems of *Les fleurs du mal* by Charles Baudelaire, published in the same year. Émile Zola also had an established presence in Italy, and in particular with his recent novel *Thérèse Raquin* (1867).[37] The same could be said for other foreign authors: French, German, and English. Abba does not elucidate in any detail what he means by foreign elements except to say that the traditional Italian plot follows a strict chronologically progressive order. It does not indulge in flashbacks or flash-forwards. Italian plot development, according to Abba, should be as heard in the stories told by grandmothers, who recount in linear fashion.[38] Had Abba overlooked the fact that even Alessandro Manzoni's *I promessi sposi*, the seminal Italian novel, eschewed the rigid chronological structure he now advised Pratesi to adopt? How could he have done so when emulation of Manzoni's writing style was one of his own goals? While we shall never know the reasons for the contradictory critique, we can attempt some conjecture. By now Pratesi had been welcomed into the Salotto Rosso of Emilia Peruzzi, where authors, Italian but also foreign, eagerly participated and were discussed. Pratesi had also begun to frequent the home of German historian Karl Hillebrand and his English wife Jessie Taylor Laussot. Nor would Abba have forgotten that his friend's principal promoter and publisher was Swiss. Far removed from this active literary environment, Abba may have anticipated that Pratesi would inevitably be influenced by the myriad foreign authors in his new circle of friends, acquaintances, and mentors. In contrast, Pratesi's friend Giacomo Barzellotti, who had travelled and studied in Germany and England, saw no problem with foreign influence, even speaking publicly on the desirability of such exchange.[39]

The next informal review makes up the larger part of Abba's letter of 22 October 1871. Having read more carefully, Abba still remains unconvinced by his friend's literary style. He continues to consider it un-Italian:

> Too often one can sense the literary artifice, and the hand of the writer, which previously wrote so well in *Vita dell'infanzia* and in poems, seems foreign to our beautiful sun. Yes, my dear Mario, the plot of your novel is not Italian although the concept is Italian ... you come and go up and down, trying hard to rein in your characters, who balk at your intentions for them. If, after the first chapter ... you had allowed the reader to take the reins of your story, handling them together with the reader, describing the events and introducing him to the characters as they appear and as the events required, you would have been more successful; but your jumping here, overlooking there, hurrying and then slowing down is probably not appreciated by your readers in Italy, who remember our old traditional stories clearly, as you yourself have often told me.

Abba offers his friend details on where the plot and, more importantly, the characters, undermine the text. On the other hand, he particularly appreciates the protagonist Jacopo, who, although he might have been treated with a lighter hand, assumes admirable verisimilitude:

> The passage where you describe him seems to me among the most beautiful ... Poor Jacopo! How he makes me feel your own presence. I have re-read that passage, and each time I like it more, proof that this is work well done. And Marianna, such a sweet creature, who is she? Did you know her? Or did you imagine her? In any case you can't read of her without loving her, and in loving her, experience a feeling of gentleness in your heart. Bravo, Mario, this is how a woman should be portrayed, this is how she should feel love, unhappy or otherwise, her character should be such if she is to be considered an angel, if she is to be a good wife and mother.

Mostly, however, Abba is impressed by the language that Pratesi uses, but with a reservation. He still senses too much of a literary Tuscan register, and advises Pratesi to make it more pure, closer to the spoken tongue of everyday people. There remained one further criticism, Pratesi's penchant for ellipses: "That use of ellipses I did not like. You have to specify things; you must not allow others to add their own ideas. Ellipses seem like an excuse [for not being clear] and detract from the simplicity of the whole. If you publish the story as a book, take that stuff away."[40]

Nor was Abba the only informal reviewer for "Le viole di Marianna." Niccolò Tommaseo had also gladly received the work of his former secretary. Despite their difficult parting in 1868, the two had remained in contact, Pratesi always at a respectful and admiring distance, the elderly Tommaseo always willing to give advice when requested. That the letters to Pratesi from Tommaseo were dictated to his daughter Caterina (now acting as her father's secretary) seemed no longer a source of regret or rancour.[41] In a letter Pratesi received more or less at the same time as Abba's detailed observations, Tommaseo had made similar comments: "You should write ... prose; keep to current language as you do it with ease and nonchalance; keep this in mind even for minor details, avoiding certain forms that one does not find in spoken language."[42] A year later, once the story had been published as a book, no longer "Le viole di Marianna" but *Jacopo e Marianna*, Tommaseo reread the work. His critique this time was more ideological in nature: he took issue with the negative portrayal of the clergy in the novel, wondering rhetorically if Pratesi had only met corrupt priests, as the novel might suggest, and never corrupt laypersons.[43] Despite the latter's sincere respect for

Tommaseo, it was inevitable that Pratesi's shabby treatment of the clergy should irritate his former employer, an apologist for Christianity perhaps to the same degree that Pratesi insisted on his anticlericalism. Tommaseo had already made clear his displeasure at Pratesi's depictions of priests when he had read *Le Memorie*: "Why do you insist on portraying priests as persons to be ridiculed, as if there were no laypersons who are even more ridiculous? Scorn does not perfect, disdain does not inspire valour; a ray of goodness illuminates long miles of darkness." Nonetheless, the tone of Tommaseo's letter was encouraging as the closing lines show: "But continue to write as you do, in your frank manner; however, avoid using some of those phrases that you would not have heard spoken by people [who are not highly educated]."[44]

Another of his close friends, philosopher Giacomo Barzellotti, whose preoccupations with his thesis and the beginning of his academic career had taken him far from Pratesi in the years of this first novel, had enquired about the progress on this current work in 1871, while Pratesi was still writing. Pratesi sent him a copy in the summer of the following year, and Barzellotti, having read the novel in a rather short space of time, wrote to express his delight and also to give his opinion, which he knew would be valued. First, and foremost, he admired the use of language, a pure vivid Tuscan; he commented positively on the plot development, and unlike, Abba, he found that *Jacopo e Marianna* did not follow the disarrangements in plot so popular in the works of foreign authors. The elegant simplicity of the story was also a positive aspect, especially since not one of the characters was out of place or superfluous. Barzellotti continues: "In [your portrayal of the characters] there is evidence of the feeling you have for harmony and proportion in art; and given our era of detailed descriptions with overly detailed minute particulars, which tire us out [as we read], I compliment you for what you have done."[45] Aware that he may be exaggerating the praise, Barzellotti explains that despite the faults in the novel, his first impressions are positive. More importantly, he promises a published review, and in December he announces to Pratesi that he has almost finished "an article, and not short, on your novel, an article I would like to publish if possible in the [*Nuova*] *Antologia* so that the announcement of your novel can be read by men of letters; if not, I shall publish it in the *Gazzetta d'Italia* or in some other paper."[46] The article appeared in January 1873, as promised, in the *Nuova Antologia*.[47] It, too, helps us see the emerging development of book reviewing, for in effect, despite its length, and despite the author's acceptance that it was an "article" not just a review,

Barzellotti nevertheless intended that it be used for promotional purposes rather than be considered a piece of literary criticism.

Other readers also offered informal critiques of *Jacopo e Marianna*. Inadvertently revealing that he was rather behind in his reading, Carlo Corsi (1826?–1905), writer and military strategist whom Pratesi likely came to know through his older brothers in the service, applauded "Le viole di Marianna" for its Tuscan language and delightful pages.[48] *Jacopo e Marianna* also became the catalyst for Pratesi's long friendship with statesman Sidney Sonnino (1847–1922), who had written to Emilia Peruzzi about it. Signora Emilia (1826–1900), the gregarious and intelligent doyenne of the Salotto Rosso, a literary and political salon in via Borgo de' Greci in Florence, hosted many prominent men (and women) in the years immediately following the unification of Italy. She promoted young authors of the day, personally choosing them, inviting them to the salon, lending out their latest publications to others in order to solicit comments and critiques. Soon after the publication of the *Jacopo e Marianna*, Sonnino expressed his delight in reading it, noting in his letter of early December 1872 to Peruzzi that in particular he appreciated the straightforward and graceful language.[49] Even years later, in 1905, another of Pratesi's friends, Sofia Bertolini Guerrieri-Gonzaga (1873–1961), who was given a copy of the novel by the author himself, wrote of her admiration for his exquisite use of language, the vivid descriptions of landscape, and for his ability to capture and hold her interest.[50]

By early 1873, three rather long reviews of the novel had been published: in *Il Diritto* almost immediately upon its release (19 November 1872) where the reviewer again was Diogene, in *La Perseveranza* (28 December 1872) where the reviewer remained anonymous, and in the *Nuova Antologia* by Barzellotti. All of them praised Pratesi's work highly; in two he was compared to Dumas, fils. Attilio Brunialti (1849–1920), who, as Pratesi discovered when he queried *Il Diritto* editor Clemente Maraini, was the reviewer behind the pseudonym Diogene, reiterated his opinions in a personal letter to Pratesi. The latter had clearly written to the reviewer, miffed at the comment that there was little real patriotism in the protagonist, Jacopo, who according to the review, thinks not of Italy, but only of his own village bell-tower. Brunialti replied by return post, as the correspondence dates show, with additional private praise for the work:

> It's true that I may have insisted too much on something that seemed an inherent aspect of your Jacopo. But what can we expect? You know what animals readers are, we can't just say their eating troughs are filled with

select feed; we have to find some bits of straw. As for me, in order to tell the full truth about your book, I would have said even better things, but in order not to raise suspicion, I had to have my lantern seek out some faults, even a little one, in order to mitigate my praise, so that the review would suit the sceptics too.[51]

Brunialti had ended his review with the comment that Pratesi's work augured well for the future of Italian prose. His private opinion of reviews and reviewing, derogatory as it may seem, is also valuable for it highlights the growing public expectation in having a balanced overview of a book; reviews could not just praise or censure, but had the obligation of pointing to both the strengths and weaknesses of a work.

A month or so later, *La Perseveranza* offered a similar opinion as that of *Il Diritto*. Counting Pratesi as one of three promising young novelists, the reviewer considered both *Le Memorie* and *Jacopo e Marianna*, with emphasis on the latter.[52] Acknowledging that melancholy informed the works to a great degree, the reviewer justified this attitude by calling attention to Pratesi's personal experience with severe melancholia. He does not shy away from pointing out that the plot requires better construction and development and that it often touches upon banality. But, he goes on to say, Pratesi's greatest skill is in language, "the language and style produced by his pen have and demonstrate all the flexibility, the vividness, and the precision of the Tuscan tongue." Having referred to the three authors under scrutiny as young members of a new school of literary realism, he ends the review by focusing on Pratesi: "In these his first works there is more than promise, there is a guarantee of a future. All he has to do is continue along this path."

Barzellotti, too, writes in a similar vein. He begins his article with a detailed overview of the plot; he finds some weaknesses with its development, as did the reviewer from *La Perseveranza*. Nonetheless, he points out Pratesi's fresh approach, his narrative lyricism; he notes that the author's poetic soul imprints itself in the pages of the novel, affirming that in this, Pratesi is closer to the style of the Italian master Alessandro Manzoni (1785–1873) than that of Sir Walter Scott. He touches on some inexpert character descriptions, particularly in the fact that the characters do not evolve personally or morally in the work; he notes that in their intimate selves there appears at times a certain psychological rigidity. He ends the review by reconfirming Pratesi's linguistic and stylistic mastery in the novel, remarking that Pratesi "captures the spontaneity of the heart and knows how to translate it into words." He foresees a long literary life for his friend.

The letters remaining between the two do not reveal Pratesi's reaction to Barzellotti's review. It is possible that Barzellotti consulted with Pratesi in preparing the review although in this period the two seemed not to have frequented each other. Pratesi had departed to teach in Pavia by the end of November, and Barzellotti spent those weeks in Germany, England, and France. Barzellotti's letters indicate his intention to see his friend in Florence in December, and their discussions may have taken place at that time, just prior to the publication of the piece in January 1873.

Unfortunately, the prognostications of Barzellotti, Brunialti, and the anonymous reviewer in *La Perseveranza* that Pratesi would enjoy a long life as author were disregarded completely by another newspaper column that almost thoroughly derailed Pratesi's career as writer and teacher.

A scathing ad hominem attack written by an unnamed student from the Istituto Tecnico where Pratesi had been assigned as teacher of Italian literature was published in *La Canaglia* of Pavia at the end of January 1873.[53] The paper, issued weekly, claimed a republican bias. The student, who did not mention Pratesi's literary works at all, presented him highly sarcastically as a saint:

> Mr Pratesi is a saintly man, more holy than Professor Santa Maria, more immaculate than Rozzi, *virgin and martyr*, whom the gentlemen of the Deputation [of the Ministry of Education], guided by the patriarch [Pasquale] Villari and by the Holy Spirit, as the link between two [warring] factions in Pavia, exemplified by Don Lucido and Bargoni, have chosen to teach Italian literature at the Technical Institute.
>
> And in [Pratesi], literature has a valiant champion and the students of the Institute an excellent teacher. Suffice it to say that he spends the whole hour explaining either the virginity of Mary, or papal infallibility, or the miracle of St Anthony and his pig.
>
> In the midst of all the corruption and atheism …, surely Mr Pratesi will be able to lead our youth along the straight path and teach them true morals, and eventually lead them to paradise.

Don Lucido Maria Parocchi (1833–1903), the new bishop of Pavia, was clearly a fierce conservative. Although Pavia had had no bishop for the previous thirteen years, his appointment in 1871 was not accepted by the secular government, who denied him l'exequatur or official authorization to act as bishop. Nonetheless, he continued in his appointment.

In 1873 he founded the paper *La Scuola cattolica* and became its director. Angelo Bargoni (1829–1901) was the member of parliament and prefect for Pavia at the time. Having been the minister of education in 1869, in 1870 he proposed a bill for obligatory schooling in Italy. It was he to whom Clemente Maraini directed Pratesi with a personal letter of introduction when the latter arrived in Pavia. Bargoni had been among the early editors of *Il Diritto*, now under the leadership of Clemente Maraini.

Perhaps Pratesi found himself between two contrasting ways of teaching in a city where a pre-existing conflict made life difficult for him, especially in a school that, according to an article in *La Perseveranza* of 20 December 1872 did not yet have a full complement of faculty required after the curricular changes that had been put in place by the Ministry of Education (Ministero della Pubblica Istruzione) in 1871. Pratesi was one of the newly hired teachers. He admits to having contact with Bargoni, through Maraini and also through another mutual friend, Atto Vannucci (1810–1883), historian and Italian patriot then residing in Pavia. Vannucci was well known for his criticism of the Church's secular power, and Pratesi observes the irony of being called a saint in the *Canaglia* article given whom he frequents.

The article thoroughly shook Pratesi's confidence, always fragile in nature. Completely taken aback by its vehemence, he complained about the column and the effect it had on him to many of his friends including Gherardi, Maraini, Tommaseo, Abba, and also to his family. Their sympathetic responses went largely unheeded because Pratesi felt cut to the quick. He began the process of transferring schools, a request soon granted to him. Assigned to Viterbo, he fervently desired to leave Pavia as soon as possible: "Here I am then, all alone, in a town where even the comfort of Art is lacking, as is the comfort of Nature (because this plain, in my eyes, is sad indeed); I am among people who do not like me and I don't like them; rather, I am among enemies against whom I have done nothing. This is my bread! ... I have no other refuge but my lacerated soul."[54]

The greatest pain then, whether imagined or not, was that Art had abandoned him as he felt she had while he was in the sanatorium. Certainly, he sincerely regretted that he saw in his students "a great deal of indolence, and meanness,"[55] and he protested that he did "everything possible to impress in their minds the idea of Truth, of commitment to duty,"[56] that his teaching strayed far from the bigoted religious approach the article implied. But it was his faithful Muse who suffered most as a result of the satirical column. Pratesi fell once more into a depressive state, and along with it, he confided to Abba, came physical debility. He could no longer write, and he now regretted having written at all especially that saccharine, useless and stupid, terrible novel which people have wanted to "spread around like a bad joke. The thought of having to leave behind that useless imprint, that abortion, that baby, that fruit-fly wing which, in the three months it will outlast its author's life, will achieve nothing if not the confirmation of my weak, miserly, dried-up talent torments me more than my illnesses."[57] Some weeks later he announced that he had put aside the new short story he had started because his "hair had turned white, [his] heart and brain were worn out" by his depression.[58]

As he struggled psychologically, his friends came to his rescue to ensure that he might continue to follow his Muse. They provided him with copies of other reviews of *Jacopo e Marianna*, fortunately all positive. On 15 March 1873, *L'Opinione* of Turin hailed him as a young writer worthy of a place among the best Italian authors and, in particular, signalled his fresh and vivid use of language.[59] On 11 April, in Florence, Giuseppe Solimbergo (1846–1922) writing in the *Gazzetta d'Italia* concurred that *Jacopo e Marianna* stood among the best of recent publications because the author engaged in "true art, the most difficult to achieve." The reviewer bestowed particular praise on Pratesi's language and style, although he found the use of chapter quotes not to his liking. The review ends by advising Pratesi to "reflect within himself, continue and grow in his adoration for his art, to observe, meditate, and have faith in himself, in his strengths and to proceed in this direction. Over and above the honour that will come to him, he can rest assured that art will give him comfort most pure and great, such as is rarely bestowed in the bitter world in which we live."[60] Even several months later, in July, *Gazzetta del Popolo* wrote in a similar vein. The reviewer, Gian Leopoldo Piccardi, like Pratesi's friends in their informal reviews, noted that some of the language seemed too local, but "his style is simple and clear, and it flows like the waves in a river." Most importantly, Piccardi, as had others before him, also attributed to Pratesi a new mode of writing, calling him a writer of the realist school, "true and always natural."[61]

The compliments received for the novel were also enhanced by a personal letter sent to Clemente Maraini, editor of *Il Diritto*, by author, translator, and playwright Giulio Carcano (1812–1884), which Maraini published in his paper and which was also reproduced in the *Vita Nuova* of Siena and in *L'Istitutore di Torino*. Essentially, the letter reiterates the praises of the official reviews. Carcano is optimistic that in Pratesi

> a new talent reveals itself, bringing honour to him and to Italian letters. His is a difficult genre, as I've known for a long time. In what I call the harmony of truth, one must join the ideal to the real. What must always be felt is a sense of poetry ... And this secret Pratesi knows; his art is refined and he has the ability to create and depict, to make the reader feel and also cry. Something in his work reminds me of Dickens, although at times he is more profound than the Englishman. And there is more. That magic of writing how people think and speak, without being annoying, nor erudite, nor trite gives the story frankness and truth that should be envied. How fortunate Tuscany to have him ... And tell your valiant young friend that he should not tire himself out on the road he has chosen with such great promise.[62]

Maraini, of course, showed the letter to Pratesi, who passed it on for his family to read, as the correspondence with his father indicates. Since the letter is dated 11 November 1872, it is clear that Carcano received an advance copy of the novel from Maraini. How curious then that the editor should wait until April to make the laudatory letter public. We can understand that in publishing the private letter Maraini intended to boost sales of the book but the number of months between the publication of the novel and the insertion of the letter brings other considerations into play. In other words, there seems to be more to this situation.

Undoubtedly, Clemente Maraini was also the influence and promoter behind some of the positive reviews Pratesi's work had received, and in particular for the two separate laudatory reviews that appeared in *Il Diritto*, first for *Le Memorie* and then for *Jacopo e Marianna*. Furthermore, Giuseppe Solimbergo, who reviewed the book for the *Gazzetta d'Italia*, was a friend on whom Maraini could easily call for a positive review. In fact, Solimbergo later wrote for *Il Diritto* before a diplomatic career took him to other countries, including Canada. In what other ways, and, more importantly, why, did Maraini focus on the promotion of *Jacopo e Marianna*? Why such attention to the early works of a still relatively unknown author?

Clemente Maraini (1838–1905) was born in Switzerland and had studied engineering in Rome before finding employment in Constantinople and then on the Suez Canal. Upon his return to Italy, he worked for the railway in the Abruzzo region of Italy. He became editor of *Il Diritto* in

1867. The position took a heavy toll on him personally and financially; to his credit, the daily enjoyed its highest popularity under his direction, which continued until 1879. The newspaper was not his only interest. In 1873 he helped co-found the Banca della Svizzera italiana, and later, in 1885, the Banca popolare ticinese.[63] *Il Diritto* under Maraini's direction was a daily newspaper of political orientation; it depended also on articles culled or summarized from other periodicals. But Maraini was also supportive of new authors, and he introduced their works in *Il Diritto* in serialized form. He had likely come to know Pratesi through the publication of *Le Memorie*, which not only appeared in *Il Diritto* but also was published in book form by the typographer (and later owner) of *Il Diritto*, Giuseppe Civelli. A friendship and personal sympathy grew between Maraini and Pratesi. Maraini's family in Rome showed its incredible largesse and compassion towards the young Tuscan author. Welcomed into their home, he became a lifelong friend, and continued his correspondence not only with Clemente, but also with his sculptress wife Adelaide Pandiani (1843–1917), and their two children, in particular their daughter Mimi (b. 1868), who continued corresponding with him throughout his life. Pratesi, on the other hand, often acted most irritably and unkindly towards them; his prickly nature came to the fore in an especially rude and ill-tempered manner in the early months of 1874, when he mistook a letter from Clemente's younger sister Giulia as a demonstration of her romantic interest with a view to an eventual marriage. The family, although perturbed by his behaviour, did not take offence, and fortunately, the misunderstanding was eventually ignored. Pratesi borrowed money from Maraini just after the publication of *Le Memorie*; Maraini felt no need to have the sum returned to him, inviting Pratesi instead to ask for more financial support in order to allow him time to write without interruption.[64] Their correspondence shows that Maraini was instrumental in securing for Pratesi the teaching position in Pavia. Together with Luigi Luzzatti (1841–1927), then secretary to the Ministry of Agriculture, Industry and Commerce, the ministry under whose aegis fell the staffing of technical institutes in Italy, Maraini ensured that Pratesi could establish himself well in that city. When his attempts were not successful, Maraini again encouraged the young Tuscan to move elsewhere, announcing soon after the debacle of the *Canaglia* that he was personally engaged in efforts to find another teaching position for Pratesi.[65] To his great surprise, Pratesi also eventually discovered that Maraini had covered all the costs of publishing *Jacopo e Marianna*.[66] In part, then, Maraini's effort in promoting this book could be interpreted as self-serving because it would help him recover funds personally invested. On the other hand, the two reviews which he may have influenced or commissioned concurred with other reviews in their excellent opinion of the novel. Furthermore, a close examination of the issues of *Il Diritto* for 1873 reveals that beginning on 5 February and continuing until the issue of 26–7 December of that year, there appeared daily, and in some issues twice each day but on separate pages, advertisements for *Jacopo e Marianna*. The starting date of this free publicity, which reached 4,000 readers every day, is significant, for it immediately follows the vitriolic sarcasm printed in the *Canaglia* at the end of January.[67] A comparison with other authors promoted by Maraini in *Il Diritto* shows that the attention given to Pratesi's work was generously anomalous to say the least. Almost certainly, Maraini took on the financial responsibility for the inclusion of the advertisements. Pratesi himself was unable to commit to such a prolonged expenditure; nor were his family or friends able to pay for such publicity. Why Maraini should do this presents an intriguing conundrum. Known for his kindness towards his own extended family, to Pratesi he had no obligations beyond those required between publisher and author. Pratesi's friend Alessandro Gherardi gives us a clue to Maraini's character in calling him "a true pearl of a gentleman."[68] The answer may also lie in Maraini's firm conviction that Pratesi had noteworthy literary talent, and that the personal attack in the *Canaglia* had undermined him gratuitously. But perhaps more relevant was Maraini's recognition that in Pratesi he found a younger version of himself. In one of his earlier letters to Pratesi, Maraini revealed not only a fraternal concern and sympathy, but also admitted to a similarity in both physical constitution and psychological disposition:

> I hope that with the better weather your cough will disappear, and together with the cough you will chase away that bad companion that is Melancholy. You are young, you have talent, and if this is of value to you, you have a friend who wants to see you content, happy, and tranquil and busy. This may seem a contradiction of terms but it is not. I, too, have a melancholic temperament and am introverted; to win in the battle of life, I had to overcome myself first. You have such intelligence and character that you will also overcome yourself if you want to. And for this your sincere and loyal friend would be happy.[69]

Similar words echoed in a later letter in which Maraini again described how closely his own character corresponded to that of Pratesi.[70] Maraini may have felt responsible, in part, for Pratesi's difficulties in

Pavia since he had been instrumental in finding that unhappy position for Pratesi, and thus his support of Pratesi's writing may also have assuaged some of the guilt. Like Pratesi's Muse, he never abandoned the young author.

Maraini had an accomplice in Luigi Luzzatti. Only a year older than Pratesi, Luzzatti entered politics very early, and by 1869 had been appointed as undersecretary in the Ministry of Agriculture, Industry and Commerce. Later he would become prime minister of Italy (1910–1911). He, too, had felt the sting of Pratesi's prickliness, and like Maraini, had hoped the position in Pavia would be a satisfactory one for the author. Like Maraini, he saw in Pratesi a promising writer profoundly hurt by the anonymous venom of the *Canaglia*.[71] He agreed to allow a transfer of schools, a position that would come into effect some months later. But since Pratesi was loathe to accept the stipend still owing from his Pavia assignment without fulfilling his required duties, Luzzatti devised an alternate project for him as his speech writer. Pratesi told Abba:

> I hadn't been in Florence a fortnight, when I was told to go to Venice, commanded (the term they used) into service with Commendatore Luzzatti … I've been dying to visit Venice for ages, and once I received the letter assigning me there, I could only think of the Oriental City, the city of serenades and lagoons, over which the immortal tears of Byron flowed; and I left immediately … I felt fortunate to leave Florence for a new city. But now I can't tell you how desperate are the hours here in this irresistible city that fills my heart with energy and song, which disappear as soon as they appear. I'm dying here … I keep dying here. I don't know how my life continues. I feel like a slave … Mr Luzzatti is always kind to me while I am not [so kind to him] because I can hardly hold back my discontent.[72]

Pratesi did not die in Venice; quite to the contrary. The tedious secretarial work that Luzzatti had given him bore fruit. If the letter of 30 May indicated to Abba that Pratesi no longer felt the calling of his Muse, by the end of July she had returned and vigorously claimed him for her own again: "As long as you find yourself in the presence of a beloved woman, you don't feel what she instils in your heart: only once you leave her, the accumulated passion explodes. This is what Venice makes me feel now that she is no longer before my eyes. She seduces with the sadness of her power in the past, her misery in the present in the great splendour of her monuments, her poetry of traditions, nature, and memory."[73] His Muse, now embodied as Venice, led to a new piece of writing. Maraini and Luzzatti were there to welcome her as she returned to Pratesi, Luzzatti with a teaching position for the young author in Viterbo while Maraini greeted her enthusiastically by publishing Pratesi's report about Venice which appeared in ten instalments in *Il Diritto* between 17 and 29 November 1873. These "Noterelle Prese a Venezia di M.P." opened for Pratesi a new genre, hodoeporics or travel literature, that would bring delight to readers and critics alike, and that would garner continuing critical praise for him in the years following.

Chapter Two

Milan

Viterbo. Five hundred kilometres separated the acute bitterness Pratesi had experienced in Pavia from his new teaching assignment further south along the peninsula. Ninety kilometres away was his birthplace, Santa Fiora, and in the opposite direction, more or less the same distance from Rome were Maraini and Luzzatti, who continued to promote him, support him, welcome him. About 175 kilometres away was Siena, home of his father and younger siblings, whom he wished to avoid. And a little further away was Florence, where many of his friends could be found and where Emilia Peruzzi determined to admit him to the prestigious circle of the pear in the Salotto Rosso.[1] Despite protestations and some peevish reactions on his part, Pratesi remained close to Signora Emilia and to her attempts in gathering the intelligentsia of the time long after the heyday of the Salotto in via Borgo de' Greci in Florence, and he faithfully continued his correspondence with her at her residence in Antella until she died in 1900. Viterbo was a provincial town living at a provincial pace. Relatively close yet a most necessary psychological distance from the torture of teaching his forty-seven charges at the Istituto Tecnico of Pavia. In Viterbo, a small group of twelve students awaited him. Pratesi's initial reaction to the official news of the new assignment (he had known of the transfer informally since April)[2] revealed his negative attitude towards teaching at the Istituto Tecnico there.[3] As the days passed into weeks, however, he established a routine and found he had time to write again. Karl Hillebrand (1829–1884), the eminent German historian, and his English wife Jessie Taylor Laussot (1829–1905), promoter of Wagner and founder of the choral circle Società Cherubini, had opened their doors to Pratesi in Florence and by now had become close friends. Hillebrand sent word to Pratesi in Viterbo through Giacomo Barzellotti that he hoped for some articles or stories from Pratesi to include in his new German periodical; since money remained a pressing consideration for Pratesi, Hillebrand indicated that his friend would be well paid for his work.[4] He hinted that he would immediately republish *Jacopo e Marianna* in his own paper if it were translated into German.[5] Furthermore, the Christmas season of 1873 brought the opportunity to visit the Maraini family in Rome, and they undoubtedly encouraged him to continue writing.[6] By the spring of 1874, Pratesi, who had succumbed to another bout of depression, had nevertheless written a new novella, which he decided to offer first to *Il Diritto*. He informed Clemente Maraini:

> In these past few days I have written another rather humble little story that I have reflected upon a great deal, but which is finished now, and is complete as far as the characters, the plot, and the development are concerned; now I just have to revise the draft. I hope it will be ready by the end of the month and I shall send it to you to publish in *Il Diritto*. It's called "A Brawl or Love and Corruption." The title is somewhat patriarchal and slapdash, but it reflects the concept of the story. I'm really pleased to be able to give you something.[7]

The letter continued on an unusually confidential tone as Pratesi shared with his publisher and mentor what he had learned about himself as a writer:

> This piece came to me rather easily[?] and instilled in me the confidence that I don't lack for talent in writing popular short stories. To nourish this talent, which has faced the obstacles of my perverse fortune, it's useful to have the great desire, as I do, that ordinary people may have good literature among all this flippancy and indifference and materialism, literature in which there is a commendable faith, mover of miracles as Guicciardini and Goethe say, not the kind the Vatican promotes but the kind felt by Manzoni and Mazzini, the greatest spirits of our peninsula in this century.[8]

He ended the letter with a description of his writerly process, a glimpse into his workshop: "When I start writing, I can tolerate nothing else; my preparation for classes becomes insufferable, I lose sleep, and I am irritable to the point that I can't even stand a fly buzzing around me. A great torture indeed. I need patience, and onward!"[9] Finally, buoyed by optimism and a sense of purpose as a writer, pleased with the success of his work to date, he responded in late August 1874 to a letter from a deeply depressed Abba, encouraging his friend to persevere in his own poems and manuscripts, urging him to overcome the feelings of personal insufficiency and worthlessness. In this letter, for the first time to Abba, indeed one of only two occasions in his vast correspondence, Pratesi admitted that his stay at the psychiatric hospital in Siena six years previously had been occasioned by a suicide attempt.[10] At that time already, he had felt the profound need and desire to write, to express his passion for truth and beauty through literature. But he had found himself so thwarted in his attempts to concentrate on writing that he felt suicide to be the only solution for him. However, he added, he had now abandoned such an idea forever.[11] A Pratesi of similar optimism rarely comes to the fore, especially because his letter to Abba ignored totally his personal circumstances at that time: although on holidays, he was physically unwell; furthermore he was still grieving over the loss of his mentor Tommaseo who had died in May. In addition, he was assailed by continued self-doubt over his failed courtship of Tommaseo's daughter Caterina while employed as the secretary to the Dalmatian writer.[12]

He found time and energy to write, despite his health and his pedagogical duties to his students. The short story he had mentioned to Clemente Maraini, now retitled "Belisario," was done, and his friend Giacomo Barzellotti urged its publication.

A prolific writer himself, a professor who was not wont to procrastinate with publication like Abba, Barzellotti had forged a friendship with Pratesi that would last a lifetime. If Abba responded to the melancholia to which Pratesi was prone, Barzellotti reflected the same intellectual curiosity and the same sententious character as Pratesi. Kindred spirits in so many other aspects, Barzellotti's optimism challenged Pratesi's despondency. But, unlike Pratesi, Barzellotti, a man highly ambitious in all his aspirations, committed far more energy to political endeavours.

Giacomo Barzellotti (1844–1917) came from Piancastagnaio, near Pratesi's birthplace. In all likelihood their friendship began in Pisa in 1865 when both of them studied there.[13] As Fatini notes, Barzellotti's impressive background of studies and excellent preparation almost immediately opened opportunities for him in the academic world, beginning with the publication of his thesis in 1869 by the Barbèra publishing house.[14] Familial wealth allowed him to travel extensively through Europe for research. He soon became well known and also respected for his position as a positivist philosopher, courted by various universities throughout his life, and offered tenured academic positions, including at Pavia, Naples, and later Rome. His numerous writings give ample proof of his reasoned, humanistic thinking, his finely honed skills as critic, and also a certain ease of expression. It mattered little if he wrote academic treatises, literary articles, critiques of books, or poetry. While Abba's letters served as a source of mutual compassion for Pratesi, Barzellotti instead offered him objective empathy, firm self-conviction, and moral strength. Only at the end of his life, when family problems began to weigh on him in a particularly onerous manner, did Barzellotti succumb to an emotional outpouring of his travails. And Pratesi, always an ally, never refused to listen. In announcing the death of his friend in 1917, Pratesi wrote to the Marquise Lina Trigona that he had been overtaken by the mute sobs of a soul that remembers but that will never again experience those memories: "59 years of friendship. A similar passion for studies that united us, a passion that animated our conversations as youths and old men, now over forever … He appeared insensitive because he suffered his personal problems in silence, strongly as will a philosopher and as a good man."[15] Barzellotti's intellectual and reasoned attitude to their friendship presented itself from their earliest letters; just prior to Pratesi's hospitalization in the psychiatric clinic in Siena, Barzellotti appealed to a sense of future potential, urging his friend not to remain in the emotionally embittered present: "You have found so much strength in the unhappiness that has oppressed you; you have continued your studies, focusing on Italian and Latin; the latter has opened for you a window onto a new literature, a new history, a new order of studies. Look within yourself, and you will not find yourself lacking."[16] The same reasoned humanistic approach revealed itself in Barzellotti's review of *Jacopo e Marianna* in the *Nuova Antologia* (January 1873). His opinion was not new to Pratesi, who had read a substantially reduced version in Barzellotti's letter of 2 August 1872. His conclusion that, with more experience, Pratesi would demonstrate he was indeed born to produce memorable literary works reiterated in tenor and content his personal advice to Pratesi in the early years of their friendship.

Pratesi relied on and appreciated his friend's frank and keen observations. Nor did Barzellotti disappoint. His critique of "Belisario," Pratesi's tragic story of a Sienese shoemaker thwarted in his love for the young Barbara, demonstrated his attentive reading of the piece.[17] Barzellotti had received the manuscript from another mutual friend, the linguist Isidoro del Lungo (1841–1927), who had made some minor annotations in pencil on the manuscript itself. Barzellotti, however, engaged with the text on a much more detailed level. He sent Pratesi his first observations after having read only the initial thirteen pages. His overall impression was positive and encouraging:

> I found your usual simple, natural, sparse writing; your style of observing and describing. The first two or three pages seemed this time, too, as I told you before, a bit studied and belaboured, you can feel in them the strident grating of classical levers as your story proceeds, but then the style takes on a gentler flow, as you intended. As I read, I made a note (in the margins ...) of details that I didn't like or that I'd like changed, and that you can change in the page proofs, but they are really little things. Let me point out a few.[18]

The list, while not lengthy, highlighted his acute sense of observation. A second similar letter followed once Barzellotti had read the whole story. He must have anticipated Pratesi's displeasure for he assured him in the letter that his comments are those of a reader of sound common sense.[19] His letter praised the work as a whole, but noted the dark tone, typical of Pratesi's works. While he agreed that every author has the right to present his own view of life in his works, he expressed his concern that in "Belisario" Pratesi had been rather heavy-handed in negativity, and that consequently, his work took on too much of a similarity with *Jacopo e Marianna*. He criticized the plot development, the only aspect where he felt Pratesi had not succeeded in his writing, He noted a lack of clarity in information, a need for more efficacious description, and he pointed to specific pages and examples where in his opinion the story fell short. His conclusion that the novel was a good one nonetheless, worthy of publication, came with the advice that Pratesi make changes to the work before sending it to a publisher.[20] Some days later, at more or less the time that he returned the manuscript to his friend, Barzellotti repeated his suggestions. His tone again was objective, almost impersonal, straightforward, as was characteristic of his writing:

> Let me tell you again what I wrote in my last letter, and what Del Lungo also has asked me to tell you: your story, despite the fact that we can't say it has an engaging plot (because the plot development does not seem to have succeeded well), remains nonetheless a work with many truly beautiful pages, and even as is, with minor changes, by removing some

sections rather than adding new ones, you can still send it to the [*Nuova*] *Antologia* where it will be appreciated by readers.[21]

Once more he anticipated Pratesi's reaction: "I beg you to send [the manuscript] soon. Protonotari [editor of the *Nuova Antologia*] will review it and then it will appear in the *Antologia*. He has already committed space to it so you cannot withdraw it now. Send it to me so that I can take it to the offices of the journal."[22] But Pratesi reacted just as Barzellotti had feared: he withdrew the manuscript from consideration by the *Nuova Antologia*. He offered it instead to Clemente Maraini, who invited him to send the manuscript to *Il Diritto*.[23] And then, he changed his mind once more, and locked the unpublished story away.

By the end of May 1875, Pratesi, again discouraged in his writing, had also lost confidence in his teaching; he found his position in Viterbo increasingly difficult. Barzellotti chided him:

> Why have you abandoned your story? Why, since you've revised it over the past few months, as you said, don't you send it to the *Antologia* instead of keeping it in a drawer? It could even have been published just as it was, and to your credit, and now, I'm sure it will make a completely different impression in its weaker sections because what I know of your way of correcting and refining your writing assures me that you have most certainly changed the story. So decide to send it, and don't get discouraged now that you've arrived [as an author].[24]

Almost a year later, the story was finally published in the *Nuova Antologia*. Pratesi, still lacking in self-confidence, begged Abba for a candid evaluation of the published work, insisting on sincerity because it was "the sacred duty of friendship."[25] He himself was not particularly well disposed towards his own work, and his dissatisfaction with the situation he found himself in had been exacerbated by his growing antagonism towards the school where he taught and by his displeasure for the penalty imposed on him for wounding his adversary in an ill-advised duel. Besides a fine, he was also banned from staying in Viterbo and sent to Acquapendente, some fifty kilometres away, for a period of time. He lamented to Abba: "To give you an idea of my frame of mind in writing that little story, imagine a sailor whose ship has been smashed by a continuously raging storm and who nonetheless carries on obstinately, alone, without a crew, against the wind, and against the current. And what have I accomplished? ... an abortion. Except that it is really more a meditation on life than a story."[26] The word "abortion" to describe his work sums up once again Pratesi's continuing lack of confidence, even self-pity, and personal dissatisfaction. Abba, beset by his own diminished self-esteem let Pratesi wait more than three months for a response.

At long last, a letter came from Abba with commentary on the story. Praising the high degree of verisimilitude in the descriptions of the Tuscan landscape, and some of the scenes between characters, Abba commented, again without providing explanation, that the structure of the whole was not Italian, as had also been the case with *Jacopo e Marianna*, and the work suffered for this: "But beauty is always beauty, even if it adopts northern or tropical forms."[27] Most of the comments, however, took as their point of departure not literary dexterity or competence, but a decidedly psychological outlook; Abba reflected none of Barzellotti's straightforward discourse about which literary techniques and motifs worked and which did not convince: "I read your 'Belisario.' I read it twice, and found in it your soul, greatly afflicted yet strengthened by the battle. I found in it that disdain that does not suddenly appear but that is etched on the face of those who suffer, deep and ineradicable. It's not an arrogant disdain but one tempered by sadness and by the constructive desire that one day, no matter how distant, this human race will become better."[28] In the meantime, Pratesi had received a post-publication review of "Belisario" from Barzellotti. Its positive and complimentary tone, always expressed in Barzellotti's reflective and carefully measured words, indubitably brought Pratesi great pleasure:

> You want me to tell you my frank opinion, and here it is. I liked [the story] because in it I found truth in its plot and descriptions, without exaggerations, much feeling, characters on the whole excellently described and many events keenly analysed: your style, as usual, is very good and artistically delicate (such that, as Hillebrand and I agreed, stories like yours have not been published in the *Antologia* until now, and it seems we won't have other similar ones except from you). The plot and its development, as I said, are a little thin and tenuous ... perhaps because of lack of action and the slow pace. Keep in mind, however, that I may be wrong; consider this opinion as a completely personal impression.[29]

As was his wont, Barzellotti could not refrain from some detailed observations on possible improvements, but he concluded in a most congratulatory manner: "[Future improvements] will be aided by the exhausting studies you have undertaken, and which I approve and I admire in you, because despite so much sorrow and so many difficulties you have had the energy and the courage to shoulder them."[30]

A similarly complimentary letter arrived also from Adelaide Maraini, wife of publisher Clemente Maraini. In her hurried handwriting with its overly large looping letters, perhaps unsuspectingly, she told Pratesi all he needed to know to bolster his morale as a writer. She informed him that despite his withdrawal of the story after having offered it to her husband for *Il Diritto*, Maraini nonetheless continued to hold him in high esteem, and was working actively, despite his own ill health, to have Pratesi moved to a more suitable position away from Viterbo. She tried to minimize Pratesi's self-deprecation towards "Belisario," assuring him that both her husband and also Protonotari, who had published the work, had discussed it together praising it. She added: "I have read it and found unparalleled beauty in its sentiment, its knowledge of the workings of the human heart, and refined nuances. What I found there is perhaps similar to *Jacopo e Marianna* because the topic and the plot are not new. This is the sincere truth."[31] Mrs Maraini was not a literary critic or even a critical reader as were Pratesi's friends, for most of whom literature and writing and publishing were vocations. On the other hand, she became a more likely spokesperson for all those educated readers, likely members of the bourgeoisie, who perused the *Nuova Antologia* and stopped to read "Belisario." Far more than the others with whom Pratesi corresponded, Mrs Maraini reflected the tastes of his reading public, and in the absence of contemporary formal reviews of the story, it would not be incorrect to surmise that her opinion took on a readerly authority, belying Pratesi's claim to Abba that he had produced another abortion. Quite to the contrary, with "Belisario" began Pratesi's most prolific period as author.

Having found in the novella a genre particularly well suited to his disposition, Pratesi began to work on a new one, "Un vagabondo," the story of Redento (also called "Carestia"), the young homeless wanderer.[32] Pratesi's ill-humour, continual dissatisfaction, and moodiness, often accompanied by various physical ailments, again created difficulties for him as he penned this work. By now he also desired keenly to leave his post at Viterbo, and sooner rather than later; he remained deeply offended by his demotion in seniority and status there, a consequence of the duel.[33] Finally, in a letter to Abba of 6 December 1876, he announced his forthcoming move to nearby Terni, and less than a month later he informed Abba that he had indeed already left Viterbo for his new assignment.[34] Clemente Maraini had again intervened to facilitate the move. But Pratesi felt ill served; he complained to Barzellotti at the beginning of March that his salary for both January and February had yet to be paid; for him Terni was the worst hole in Italy.[35] He lamented that he had just experienced the most terrible ten days of his life, challenged again to another duel, which he resisted. He admitted as well that the anger he had felt at the insults of the *Canaglia* in the city of Pavia had resurfaced in Terni. Later that year, his assignment as acting principal of the school for a brief period forced him to put "Un vagabondo" away without completing it.[36] Alessandro Gherardi asked about it in his Christmas letter of 1877,[37] but not until mid-September of 1878 did Pratesi mention it again, this time to Adelaide Maraini, saying that he had begun to work on it again. To Abba he wrote that he had finished it quickly between late October and early November of that year; later that year he claimed to be displeased with the work, sorry that he had not burned the manuscript.[38] Nevertheless, he sent it to the *Nuova Antologia*, which accepted it for publication in its November and December issues. The response of readers must have brought him great comfort. Almost as soon as the third and final installment appeared, his father, Igino, never generous with positive reinforcement, informed him of the praises he had heard.[39] Atto Vannucci (1810–1883), well-known and well-respected patriot and man of letters, who had remained a staunch support from their first encounters in Pavia, sent him two pages of compliments, thanking him for the pleasure he had provided by writing the story; Vannucci lauded the style, the inspiring plot with its conclusion "that brings comfort to all those honest souls who still believe in virtue."[40] He urged Pratesi to continue producing similar works. Alessandro Gherardi, although burdened by his heavy work obligations at the Archivio di Stato and also by family problems, took the time to give him a long, and rather detailed, post-publication review of "Un vagabondo." Gherardi echoed the words of Vannucci. He could not put the story down until its end; the characters, with the notable exception of Giuditta, were realistically depicted and, on the whole, admirable. The descriptive passages were noteworthy, although somewhat undermined by the expository prose, which did not impress him equally. He lauded Pratesi's dexterity with language, although pointing out examples where it became too erudite. Overall, he concluded, "I could say many other things, more in praise than in censure, of course, because of today's novelists and short story writers, I don't know if any can surpass you nor even reach you as far as dignity of concepts, of true and profound awareness of art and elegant form are concerned."[41] The next day, Sidney Sonnino, who would in the future have a profound effect on Italian politics, wrote to Pratesi. After Sonnino had been introduced to the Tuscan's work through the Salotto Rosso of Emilia Toscanelli Peruzzi, the two had struck up a friendship. Now that he had recently started his own periodical, *La Rassegna settimanale*, he wrote to invite Pratesi to contribute. Despite the fact that we have found no official reviews of "Un vagabondo," Sonnino's invitation confirms that Pratesi's literary pieces had brought him acclaim.

Firmly established now as an author of novellas, he responded to Sonnino's invitation with "Dal Monteamiata a Sovana," a travel piece, the other genre at which he would excel.[42] The article brought admiring praise from Leopoldo Franchetti (1847–1917), co-director of the *Rassegna* with Sonnino.[43]

Pratesi spent the summer heartened by the welcome received from the *Rassegna settimanale*; he finished another novella, "Un corvo fra i selvaggi" which the *Rassegna* happily accepted and published in its issue dated 14 December 1879, but actually available some days earlier.[44] In sending Pratesi extracts, Franchetti urged him: "If you have other themes in mind, write them, write them, write them. It's likely that these will ensure a career for you. The sketch you sent us proves that you find the right characters even in Terni and environs. When you've written a few of these, you can publish them together in a volume."[45]

"Un corvo fra i selvaggi" found a most receptive public, struck likely by Pratesi's profound and sensitive treatment of the theme of nature against grace. In it he challenges the reader to determine which of the two main characters represents the unaffected uncaring offspring of nature, and which the soul: the raven or the man. The Hillebrands wrote immediately to applaud their friend. Karl Hillebrand gently pointed out what he considered one or two weak sections, but his enthusiasm for the work as a whole was unmistakable: "I have read and reread your sketch with immense pleasure and would like to congratulate you. Here is the genre, the form, and the framework that most suits your talent. You'll remember that I have I always told you this, and the great success that this little piece has found confirms my first impression. Why long novels with complicated plots when this more natural and more simple genre is in you? ... I hope that this victory will encourage you and that soon we shall see another example in this genre."[46]

Jessie Taylor Laussot's exuberance exceeded her husband's:

> For several days I've chastised myself for not having answered your letter which brought me more pleasure than you can imagine. Yesterday, however, I was so moved by your "Corvo" that I don't want to delay any longer in telling you how much the piece enchanted me ... I found Sunday's *Rassegna* among my papers and began to read the "Corvo" and was so surprised and enchanted that I read it through twice ... [Karl] will give you his own opinion, rather more important than mine, but I just need to say to Messer Mario that it's not only when I see a beautiful landscape that I want to write about it, but also when I read something beautiful, and so I felt the need to tell you that the "Corvo" is the most artistic and beautiful thing I have read in a long time. Excuse the compliments. I don't often give them, and my enthusiasm doesn't grow like potatoes; you can take both [compliments and enthusiasm] as being sincere and not without value.[47]

She immediately thought to share the story with her wide circle of well-heeled and polyglot friends living in various countries of the continent: "Twenty or so copies of this issue of the *Rassegna* will travel throughout Europe to introduce Messer Mario and to make his work esteemed in its true value."[48]

Barzellotti also commented enthusiastically; the letter has been lost but a subsequent letter reiterated his delight at the novella.[49] The following September Barzellotti reread the story and again found it "one of the most beautiful and ingenious pieces that have been written in Italy for many years, and perhaps unique in its genre." "Do give us another one," he exhorted his friend.[50]

At around this time, Pratesi had also come to the attention of Angelo De Gubernatis (1840–1913), an eminent scholar of Oriental mythology who had undertaken the compilation of biographical dictionaries of contemporary writers. He asked to include Pratesi in his book, and Pratesi, not completely happily, supplied some information.[51] Around the same time, Atto Vannucci, in another act of acknowledgment of Pratesi as author, dedicated his book *I Martiri dell'Indipendenza italiana* to him in a similar act of peer recognition.[52]

Pratesi's popularity as writer had increased, and his circle of peers widened. Friends and readers, it seemed, waited expectantly for more from him. Pratesi obliged. The story "Quaresima e carnevale" appeared in the *Rassegna settimanale* in late February 1880.[53] Later called "Il dottor Febo," it recounts the story of a blind miner who must disguise himself as a begging priest in order to feed his family. The focus of the *Galgenhumor* is the hypocritical society in which Febo and his family must fight in order to survive. Abba, always the procrastinator and beleaguered by family commitments, provided his usual positive but very general appraisal. The letter, dated more than a year after publication, 16 April 1881, is noteworthy for two reasons. First, because his emotional diatribe set up a false rivalry between Pratesi and his contemporary Edmondo De Amicis (whom Pratesi admired and had read since 1874), a rivalry that might ascribe Abba's warning about outside influences on Pratesi to a jealous fear of losing a friend. Second, in the letter, Abba tempted Pratesi with the idea of leaving aside the highly successful novella format that had brought his friend so much acclaim to return to full-length novels.[54] Because Pratesi was already thinking of anthologizing his published stories in a full-length book, Abba's idea to start a new novel would not have been unwelcome to him, especially since he trusted Abba's opinions.

For the time being, however, Pratesi continued with the shorter novella format rather than longer novels. Once the school year ended in the spring of 1880, he contributed a fine critical essay of subtle reflection on the *Canticle of Canticles* to the *Rassegna settimanale* in May.[55] Freed from teaching responsibilities, he also reworked "Un ballo nel monastero," a story he had begun at least some months earlier, and which Karl Hillebrand wondered about in his letter of 8 December 1879.[56] It recounts the struggles of the impecunious schoolteacher, Maestro Vincenzo, wise, good natured, and reasonable, and of the last friar remaining in the convent, who undertakes a macabre joke that leads to tragic results. Again, the *Rassegna settimanale* published the story happily, and since it, too, met with a felicitous reception from readers, Sonnino asked for further contributions.[57]

In October, Sonnino reiterated his invitation, although it had become clear to Pratesi that the journal was suffering some financial setbacks.[58] Sonnino remained optimistic, however; furthermore, his letter also announced that the *Revue Britannique* had translated and published "Un ballo" in French.[59] But Pratesi had other more pressing concerns at this time. Unhappy also with his teaching position in Terni, he asked for yet another transfer, and to his great disgust and immense disappointment, received an assignment to Reggio Calabria, far from anyone he knew or who knew him. He arrived in Reggio on or around 10 November 1880.[60] His immediate disdain for what he considered a filthy city, its repugnant people, and its antipathetic schools formed the content of several vitriolic letters to various correspondents.⁶¹ Pratesi felt forgotten, a resentful relegate to Reggio.

Quite to the contrary, friends worked on his behalf to ensure that his writing circulated. Jessie Hillebrand had proved more than good as her word; not only had she promoted Pratesi's "Corvo" among her friends, but she herself translated it into English, and had it published in the *Cornhill Magazine*.⁶² The translation, it appears, was to be a surprise for Pratesi.⁶³ He must have derived great delight from a formal review of the translated story, published in the *St James Gazette* (10 February 1881); his archives contain manuscripts of three separate translations into Italian of the article. In it, the anonymous critic assures readers that the story is one of those few pieces of writing that increase in merit upon rereading for "it is a remarkable story, worthy of being known to a far greater degree by English readers because the style in which it is written makes it appear that it really happened. It is original not only in its content but also in its style, and in the way it is developed. The author does not remind us of any other writer, he is freshly risen from nature and, in an age of old themes and conventional situations, it is not strange that this story has been translated into English and German."⁶⁴

To have an English readership meant prestige and financial remuneration for Pratesi. Fully cognizant of this, even long after he had stopped writing new stories, he attempted to have other publications translated into English, unfortunately to no avail.⁶⁵

The aphorism that "nothing breeds success like success" may certainly be applied to these years of literary fecundity in Pratesi's life. Although he himself remained in Reggio, physically and resentfully far removed from them, his friends in Florence actively worked on his behalf. Vernon Lee (pseudonym of Violet Paget, 1856–1939), whom he may have met as early as 1875, and who, thanks to her friendship with the Hillebrands, frequented the same social and literary circles as Pratesi, made exceptional efforts to ensure that his works remained readily available. With her powerful voice in both British and Italian literary activities, she introduced Pratesi to the publishing house of Piero Barbèra. Not having published with Barbèra had always torn ungraciously at Pratesi, especially since the publishing house had accepted his friend Barzellotti into its fold years before, when he completed his doctoral thesis.⁶⁶ A note in 1872 from writer and academic Augusto Conti (1822–1905) suggesting that Pratesi's works would be welcomed by the publisher for consideration either went unheeded or resulted in a rejection from Barbèra for, in a subsequent letter, in which Pratesi complained about his assignment to a small town like Pavia, he blamed it on not being among the writers promoted by that publisher.[67] But Vernon Lee took up the challenge of a Barbèra publication. Pratesi by now had several successful stories; some he had allowed friends to see, although the pages remained unpublished.[68] Sonnino continued to request new contributions.[69] An anthology of these would represent a natural next step. Thanks to both the "Corvo" and "Un ballo," Pratesi could claim an international audience and could count on continued readership; the financial risk of Barbèra's undertaking of such a project would not have been a great one. These were precisely the aspects that Lee emphasized in her letter introducing Pratesi to Barbèra:

> I take advantage of my literary relationship with your Publishing House to introduce to you my friend Mario Pratesi, a young Tuscan writer of most beautiful and distinctive talents, whose sketches "Un Corvo fra i Selvaggi" and "Un ballo nel monastero" made a great impression last year in the *Rassegna Settimanale*. Mr Pratesi is looking for a Publisher for a collection of short stories and "sketches," which, if one may judge by his other works, should please your reading public. I believe this letter will prove beneficial not only to Mr Pratesi but to you as well, and to your Publishing House.[70]

Her letter proved auspicious. Barbèra personally contacted Pratesi to invite him to publish with them.[71] By early December the project was well underway. From his desk at the Archivio di Stato, Alessandro Gherardi encouraged a speedy publication but warned his friend not to overcorrect the original stories at the risk of losing the freshness of their first impression.[72] Here again we have a glimpse of Pratesi at work: a writer who corrects and then overcorrects.

Pratesi did not concentrate solely on this new endeavour. He had other preoccupations. Increasingly miserable at Reggio, he turned yet again to his friends for help in finding other teaching placements. Sonnino was now also among those who regularly took up the cause on Pratesi's behalf, as the latter became ever more determined to leave Calabria. Through his despondency, Pratesi continued to write. When "Il Signor Diego" appeared in the *Rassegna settimanale* in the 20 November 1881 issue, it garnered an exceptionally strong review from fellow author and poet Giuseppe Martinozzi (b. 1850). Addressing Pratesi as a "miraculous painter" and "only great poet that our Siena has had in nine centuries of existence in history," Martinozzi could scarcely contain his exuberance for the work: "I feel that your portraits have the strength of being alive, a carnality so firm and true, a depiction so naturally animated that the great number of other Italian artists seem like watercolourists compared to you. For a long time I have avoided literature known as pleasurable but I don't recall ever seeing anything so tremendously and originally (I'm trying my best to explain myself) vivid and penetrating as your unforgettable characters."[73] Barzellotti also noted that his friend had achieved literary excellence in the short stories written at this time despite the continuing difficulties and setbacks in Reggio; Barzellotti deemed them the best of Pratesi's works, praised by all who read them.[74]

In the months following, Pratesi returned to the *Nuova Antologia*, offering the journal a new story, "Padre Anacleto da Caprarola," reinitiating a publishing relationship that would last until the end of his life. It tells of an elderly Dominican friar who cannot accept the societal changes taking place all around him. His uncompromising attitude condemns Padre Anacleto to the same derogatory observations that he often made about others. Almost as soon as it appeared, in October 1882, Pratesi also presented the story to Barbèra for inclusion in the new anthology, which was nearing completion.[75] Barbèra agreed.

That previous summer Pratesi had finally been granted a transfer from Calabria to northern Italy beginning with the new academic year. His new assignment was in Milan, a marked change for him since previously he had always been posted to sleepy small towns. His workload in a larger urban centre now increased conspicuously; his students numbered over ninety. Furthermore, he had undertaken time-consuming research for Vernon Lee who had begun her studies for the volume eventually published in 1884 as *The Countess of Albany*. In this work she thanked Pratesi profusely for his invaluable collaboration, which included "the examination by myself and my friend Signor Mario Pratesi, of several hundreds of MS. letters of the Countess of Albany existing in public and private archives at Siena and Milan."[76] Despite his myriad distractions, the publication of his anthology remained of primary importance for Pratesi during this period. He fretted about the corrections; he fussed about the title he had chosen, *Miseria*, and sensing it would not prove attractive or interesting, proposed other titles. He worried about its presentation, as he wrote to Barbèra: "I have put much thought into all those stories; let the volume not appear superficial to readers; and I have not written for frivolous women nor for common dandies who look only for curiosities and for something they call the *interest* of the story. Please do the very best you can."[77] Finally available in the late spring of 1883, the volume, definitively titled *In Provincia*, was an extraordinary success.

Friends complimented him: Cesare Guasti (1822–1889), now director of the Archivio di Stato where Pratesi had worked in Florence, assured him that the book contained many laudable aspects of which Pratesi could be proud;[78] other friends, among whom Cesira Siciliani, Enrico Panzacchi, and Adelaide Maraini sent similar notes.[79] But it was the official critical reaction to the volume that ensured what Gherardi called Pratesi's fortune, metaphorical and fiscal.[80] The review of the *Gazzetta Letteraria* feigned trepidation upon seeing such a hefty volume, but, the critic wrote, he soon was convinced that the pages were so well composed, that the five hundred pages seemed even too few. "This is a beautiful book," he elaborated, "worthy of a prominent place in the libraries of people with good taste." He continued with positive comments on the verisimilitude of the situations, the lively dialogue, and the clearly depicted characterizations. Fresh and elegant on the whole, he noted that the volume concluded with a particularly noteworthy jewel, the *Memorie del mio amico Tristano*.[81] Vernon Lee extolled the attractive attributes of the volume with a laudatory review written in English, a review that, ironically, few Italians would have read, just as, on the other hand, only few English readers could read the Italian *In Provincia*. Writing in the *Academy*, she lamented that Italy had yet to have a true contemporary novel of an "original, modern and truly national mould." She elaborated:

> This moment has not yet arrived, and the Italian novel is still a hypothetical matter; but even now the humble molecules of Italian fiction can sometimes unite into a work which is remarkable, and beautiful, and valuable, and which must last. Such work is that of Sig. Mario Pratesi, whose volume, *In Provincia*, appeared a few weeks ago. It is the first flower of that seed of realism and fancy which, for the last ten years, has been scattered unnoticed throughout Italy; it is the real reality of humbler Italian life, seen with marvellous accuracy of vision, but selected with admirable instinct for the beautiful and the important; it is the work of a fastidious and wayward fancy, but executed by an eye which has seen everything, and by a hand which can portray anything; it is essentially what the art of the future must be, if it is to be anything at all: impressionism directed by idealistic selection.[82]

Her words hinted that Pratesi had moved beyond a style dependent on realism, and into what she called "impressionism"; clearly, Vernon Lee had discerned his development as an author. Her contagious enthusiasm reached English Italophiles, among them a young writer, Alice Werner (1859–1935). Werner, who would later become well known as a professor of Bantu and Swahili at Cambridge University, wrote to Pratesi three weeks after the *Academy* review to ask permission to translate *In Provincia* into English.[83] The project proved fruitless as such but in her volume *The Humour of Italy*, published in 1892, Werner remembered Pratesi's work and included three of his pieces: a short selection from "Il signor Diego" and *Da Fanciullo* and the complete story "Doctor Phoebus" ("Il Dottor Febo"). In her comments on the authors represented in her book, she noted that Pratesi

> is at his best when describing the scenery of his native mountains … [He] is intensely sympathetic in his manner of depicting life. He does not aim at an "objectivity" which seems to glory in appearing cold and heartless; but he does not dwell unnecessarily on his pathetic scenes. He relates them with grim brevity, and leaves them to produce their own effect. He has an eye for the ludicrous, but it does not predominate in his view of life; he never laughs, but he often smiles quietly, and sometimes grimly.[84]

In Italy, reviewers of *In Provincia* appeared somewhat more cautious, but nonetheless considered the work positively. Aristodemo B**** lauded the art of the short story or novella, pointing out the difficulty of writing well in this genre, and the expertise of Pratesi in producing such notable examples. He noted the author's tendency to melancholic themes and character representations. Openly disagreeing with Ruggiero Bonghi's review in *La Cultura* that the stories often resembled pedagogical exercises to teach morals, he maintained that Pratesi was "so conscientious as an artist, that he easily overcame the bonds of such [scholastic] servitude."[85] Bonghi had focused on the constraints that the stories of the collection suffered as a result of Pratesi's insistence on didacticism and morality, aspects that brought the reader to the quick conclusion that the author was indeed an academic. He felt confident, however, that with time Pratesi would prove to be a very fine writer.[86] The *Illustrazione italiana* noted that the exquisite language used by Pratesi came at the expense of captivating plots; Pratesi's stories were unable to "grab the reader by the hair and drag him to the last page." On the other hand, the review called Pratesi a "serious writer, a writer who has set for himself the model of linguistic purity and richness."[87] The reviews offered by Bonghi and in the *Illustrazione italiana* appeared in articles that evaluated multiple works, an observation that must not be overlooked; while Vernon Lee and Aristodemo B**** focused only on *In Provincia* in their critical pieces, Bonghi and the *Illustrazione* reviewer had considerably less columnar space in their respective publications for their opinions. That they should divide their space so that more or less equal attention was given to Pratesi and the two literary notables and champions of the school of *verismo* literature, Giovanni Verga (1840–1922) and Luigi Capuana (1839–1915), is significant. To admit Pratesi so favourably as part of a masterful and popular trio working in the same literary genre certainly increased his exposure and worth as an author. It meant that, with the two other great *veristi*, Pratesi's works, too, were appreciated for their realistic portrayal of the poor and disenfranchised, for their photographic fidelity in setting the scene, for their use of language, for their unembellished view of life. Barbèra clearly concurred, for a second edition of the anthology was published a year later, in 1884. In 1892, the volume had already found its place in a listing of the most recommended books published in Italy.[88]

Having found success at last, and now finally established in a teaching position more to his liking,[89] Pratesi drafted new works. Once more, he enjoyed the critical attention of Vernon Lee, whose own renown in Italy had also grown in the meantime. She reviewed the second edition of the anthology, this time in a long, full-page article published in Italian in the *Fanfulla della domenica*. Not merely a rewriting of her English review in the *Academy*, in this new piece, her support and enthusiasm for the short stories of *In Provincia* remained constant and undiminished. She pointed out that those who came to Italy from beyond her northern borders, from Switzerland and England, in particular, by far preferred Pratesi over writers like Verga, Matilde Serao (1856–1927), and the young Gabriele D'Annunzio (1863–1938). While these others may present an objective and impersonal view of Italy, she claimed, Pratesi had the talent to make northern visitors feel the essence of Italy through his writings:

> He is a realist, but not a realist of *pochades* who suggestively throws down four brush strokes of colour; he is a patient, searching realist, clear in his design, precise in his shades, as at times is Manzoni, as is Flaubert. In his stories he portrays things you will never forget ... But this is not all ... despite his realism, Pratesi is an idealist ... [in the sense that] instinctively,

and looking to please the silent desires of his own soul, he works according to the *"besoins actuels de l'âme de son auditoire"* [the real and deeply felt needs of his readers] as Stendhal wrote referring to the great singers of the late 18th century.[90]

The review continued with specific references to *In Provincia*, and concluded with Lee's observation that she truly felt she had met and known the characters Pratesi depicted, as if they had really lived. She wrote that, in essence, he had been able to see the "stupendous and strange land that is this Italy," through fresh, as if foreign eyes, when first impressions are most memorable.[91] Her words echoed those of Barzellotti, who wrote to his friend some weeks previously that his newest novella, "Catuzza," was among his best work especially for his depiction of the characters.[92] "The style is truly beautiful," commented Barzellotti, "and I believe that you did well not to overcorrect. So, continue on like this, because you are not only the usual Mario but you have progressed [in your art], and Carducci ... speaking a little while back about contemporary writers put you at the front of the line, pointing you out as the one on whom the [*Nuova*] *Antologia* could most depend." But, he continued in his well-tempered and objective fashion, "you should try to put references to current situations, to things being discussed today, etc. into your stories."[93] Gherardi made similar observations, pointing out that the sad moral fall of the lead character Catuzza, was perhaps even too realistically portrayed, and might have the opposite effect intended by Pratesi; that is, instead of condemning the sin, the reality of the depiction might even exonerate it. Gherardi, like so many of Pratesi's friends wondered:

> But, my dear friend, why don't you detach yourself sometimes from these disconsolate images of a sick or perverse society? You, who so highly admire virtue and integrity of character, who warm to every generous thought, and who feel the affection of friends and family so intensely, why don't you ever seek some theme that will move that part of your heart and soul, and not always depict themes of the sadness, horror, overwhelming disdain that you feel towards the evil and the squalour of mankind? You have a true talent for writing; try to make it the best and greatest.[94]

His Muse had brought him to success, it seemed. He was praised, recognized, read. And yet, there remained hints of tension. Friends and critics reminded him in various ways that his pessimistic view of the world was too real, too off-putting. He depicted his characters as might a gifted painter, but the plots were weak. Furthermore, while he excelled at the short story and the travel piece, he wanted to do another novel. His choice of title for *Miseria* in contrast with what the publisher chose, *In Provincia*, clues us into his unhappiness, an interior pessimism extended to his characters, as opposed to how he was accepted in the literary world, an appreciated realist. Personally, he felt alone: estranged by distance from his family; his friends, including confirmed bachelor Barzellotti, had married and had families. Pratesi now was middle-aged and looked for a new project of writerly self-affirmation. He was only five hundred kilometres to the north of Viterbo and his first real literary successes. But in his soul, he felt much much farther away.

Chapter Three

Belluno

The years in Milan, at the Istituto Tecnico Carlo Cattaneo, slipped into a recognizable and even welcome routine. Pratesi continued to complain about the cold weather and pine for the milder temperatures of Tuscany. But, as his correspondence reveals, although alone initially, Pratesi found a warm welcome in the houses of many new friends and acquaintances, several of them writers, like the playwright and novelist Gerolamo Rovetta (1851–1910), or highly interested, informed, and fascinating readers like Donna Laura Visconti Venosta, Count Angelo Villa Pernice and his wife Rachele, and others. He enjoyed the invitation of the *Illustrazione italiana* to contribute. He published some new poetry.[1] He wrote detailed review articles, in particular of Barzellotti's study *Santi, solitari, filosofi: Saggi psicologici* (Zanichelli, 1886)[2] and of Adelaide Maraini's statue *Saffo*,[3] which earned him much praise from Alessandro Gherardi who considered the review "a true jewel of a powerfully evident expression of the truest and most noble feeling for Art."[4] And, he fell madly and deeply in love with Clotilde, daughter of the Marchese Matteo Ricci, granddaughter of one of the most notable figures of the Risorgimento, Massimo D'Azeglio, and great granddaughter of Alessandro Manzoni. Last, but certainly not least, she was also the wife of Milanese composer Gaetano Coronaro (1852–1908). Despite diplomatically coded warnings from several friends, the affair continued until it became clear that Pratesi was no longer welcome in Milan, and that it was imperative for him to leave. Archival evidence suggests that he may have fathered a daughter with Clotilde.

The relationship, for all its ups and downs, imbued in him a fresh energy for his writing. Years before, Abba had hinted that Pratesi should once again pen novels, not just shorter novellas. Vernon Lee had also nudged him in that direction with her praise, as had Barzellotti. And so, despite his numerous teaching commitments at the Istituto Tecnico, Pratesi decided to turn once more to the longer story format. He was even encouraged by the publisher Barbèra, who had initially envisaged another anthology of novellas but then changed his mind for financial reasons, as Pratesi confirmed in letters to his father and to Giacomo Barzellotti. Pratesi repeated to both of them that Barbèra had favourably compared Pratesi's literary mastery of descriptive prose to that of Émile Zola in *La Terre* (1887).[5] Pratesi had a complete manuscript, originally entitled *Accanto al cimitero* at the ready, and he sent it to the publishing house, which accepted it and contracted for an initial run of 1,000 copies. Barbèra changed the title to *L'Eredità* before releasing the book in 1889. Again, the original title, refused by the publisher, reveals Pratesi's inner disposition: always pessimistic, always wary of happiness. And it also reveals his essential reluctance to go beyond the thematic formula he found comfortable. On the other hand, this novel captured the zeitgeist brilliantly.

L'Eredità, it seemed to critics, was his masterwork. Guidotti suggests that the work showcases the best aspects of Pratesi's literary talents including a full grasp and control of expression to match the contemporary psyche.[6] In other words, like Verga with *Mastro don Gesualdo*, published in the same year, Pratesi appeared to have recognized the deepest anxieties of contemporary Italy and was able to translate the confusion, the disquiet, and the agitation of his sociopolitical environment into a contemporary literary setting. The 1880s were years of much sociopolitical upheaval all across Europe, and with the expanded use of trains, the telegraph, the telephone (the latter two invented only decades earlier), as well as the linotype machine (invented around 1884), news spread more quickly, demanding equally quick reactions. Nor could Italy remain unaffected. The 1880s in Italy witnessed many changes of government due to crises both national and international; these were also years of Italian colonialist expansion into Africa, of widespread Italian emigration especially towards the Americas, of incidents of increased death through natural causes (particularly the earthquake of 1882 and the cholera outbreak in 1887), of unprecedented growth in industry, and in the demands of the ever stronger middle class. The invention of the Kodak camera in 1881, seemingly innocuous, also played a role as tragic events were no longer relegated to nebulous countermemory status, but could be confirmed in tangible form through photographs. Verga's grainy pictures, for example, certainly confirm how dependent he was on photos in shaping the characters of his books.⁷ Consequently, it comes as no surprise that two major icons of unsettled and unsettling times also belong to the same period: Nietzsche's *Also sprach Zarathustra: Ein Buch für Alle und Keinen* (with its admonitions that God is dead and that all events recur eternally) and Edvard Munch's angst-filled painting *The Scream* with its beleaguered protagonist representing Everyman both appeared in 1887. In this uneasy environment of contemporary Milan, Pratesi wrote *L'Eredità*.

Set in Siena in the early nineteenth century, it recounts the vicissitudes of an elderly farmer, Stefano, who wants to better his lot, become rich, and in the most Machiavellian of ways, rejects his land. He sets himself up as gravedigger, a post he then plans to pass on to his son Domenico, called Filusella (to whom he tries to teach the subtleties of the trade with humorous results). The other son, Amerigo, is sent to the city to learn about viniculture. Stefano intends calculatedly that Amerigo will eventually take over the lands inherited by his childless brother, Nando. But the dishonesty, blind ambition, and corruption exact their tragic toll on the family and have repercussions beyond, including on Amerigo's mistress Zaira. The graveyard where Stefano works and schemes offers moments of particularly well-described realism rendered through effective and lyrical prose.

Vernon Lee was among the first of Pratesi's friends to comment on *L'Eredità*, praising it for its elegant style, but lamenting the unrelenting focus on "the dirt of this life" that undermined Pratesi's talent as humorist, in the sense of recorder of contemporary mores. She wondered rhetorically if it were possible that all life was so luridly sad as he represented it in the novel.⁸ Barzellotti voiced similar concerns, but concluded philosophically that the pessimistic tone was in keeping with the characters who "reflect the fatality of a natural determination that permeates them all"; he took the occasion to warn Pratesi that the theme, continuous throughout his writings, restricted variety in them, adding however, that Pratesi had succeeded admirably in producing a novel depicting the realities of the Tuscan countryside with its villages and small towns. The book would bring Pratesi added success, Barzellotti concluded, and readers would recognize in it a mature writer of great merit who ably reflected the zeitgeist of Italy: "Those who appreciate art and our traditions, and want to see them in harmony with new forms of literary style to express beauty and truth will not be able to avoid recognizing in your book one of the most notable works written in Italy in the last several years."⁹

Jessie Hillebrand considered the book a masterpiece but faulted it for being too "Zolaesque" in its description of brutal characters.[10] Years later, Antonio Fogazzaro also wrote to express his admiration for the Italian nature of the novel, and the moral stance described there. If his enthusiasm wavered, it did so because he personally did not like brothels or prostitutes and clients described in books and he worried that Pratesi, in focusing on such negative and distasteful themes, might appeal to a reduced number of readers as a result.[11] The novel continued to receive praise long after Pratesi's death. Mario Guidotti, for example, called it "without doubt the strongest, most cohesive of Pratesi's works, and it will be able to remain in the history of Italian literature. It is his 'non plus ultra' ... [It is] one of the best narratives of the second half of the Ottocento to be placed beside the masterpieces of Verga and Fogazzaro ... And finally, it is a modern novel, in the most authentic sense of the word. A novel of aesthetic, social, and human values; Pratesi disappears and ... [what appears is] Poetry: free, clear, definite."[12] *L'Eredità* is the only one of Pratesi's works to be made into a film (*La viaccia*).[13]

The official critiques appearing in various journals following publication reflected the observations made by Pratesi's friends. In *Lettere e Arti*, reviewer A.A., wrote similarly: "All in all, we must conclude with a rather favourable judgment, when, in a story like this one by Pratesi, one finds such variety and beauty of characters, all acting through passion. Only one defect do we find in Pratesi's art, that of overnarration and lack of action, which makes the reader turn away. But when he does describe actions, he does so marvellously."[14]

The *Rassegna nazionale* began with a confirmation that a book by Pratesi was always a welcome read, even with its minor defects, which, although small, should not escape criticism. Pratesi's style most attracted this critic's attention: "unique, clear, strong: his precise Tuscan language, his natural naturalness (as opposed to a studied, forced naturalness)." But the critic found fault with the general plot, suggesting that pages would have to be expunged before youths might read the novel. Some things, he continued, were better left as a suggestion so that they not lead into moral degradation; to describe them leads to indifference and from indifference of evil to desire for evil, the path may prove short indeed.[15]

The novel with its accolades and ensuing literary renown, and for someone as impecunious as Pratesi, brought welcome respite from financial worries. However, he remained as irascible and pessimistic as always. His negative attitude generally derived from his obligations at school that diminished his writing time. He informed Abba in the spring of 1887: "Nothing is new here: I live *alone: people continue to assassinate me with all possible tricks of human treachery*; the workload is overwhelming ... [I am tired of teaching] and perhaps I shall think about leaving. How terrible are certain young people that you have to see and put up with in schools."[16]

Similarly, he complained to Barzellotti: "Here I lead my usual life: I know many people, for the most part disagreeable: no man and *no woman*, which is worse, who might give some nourishment to a starving soul, or with whom I might feel in harmony. Around me nothing but horrible and ungrateful dissonance; I could never have believed I might arrive at such a level of disgust, where human treachery has brought me."[17]

But, in fact, the emphasized phrases of his letters pointed to more than rhetorical emphasis. This was the period in which his affair with Clotilde Coronaro was most intense although nearing its end. Pratesi's closest friends, foreseeing the inevitable outcome of a liaison with a married woman of the noble class, urged him to terminate the affair. Instead, Pratesi continued the relationship, volatile and ardent on both sides, until he was eventually persuaded by Coronaro's cronies and colleagues that for his own safety he should quit Milan.

Nevertheless, these brief years of impassioned emotional upheaval proved fruitful for him from a literary perspective. In addition to *L'Eredità*, he published "Ricordi veneziani," a much read series of impressionistic essays on Venice in the *Illustrazione italiana*, proving once again his mastery with travel articles.[18] Similar to the "Noterelle" he had published in *Il Diritto* sixteen years previously, these latest articles brought the suggestion from Barzellotti that they be published as a single volume, and eventually Pratesi gathered them, along with several other essays into the volume *Di paese in paese*, published by Galli in 1892. Another of the essays included in the book, "La Villa di Massimo D'Azeglio," which the *Nuova Antologia* featured in its issue of 1 November 1890, brought applause, and requests to anthologize it in a collection intended for schools compiled by pedagogue Luigi Morandi (1844–1922).[19] Once again, the critics voiced their unanimous enthusiasm for the volume. Significantly, the reviews of this book reveal Pratesi's increased popularity and literary recognition. Periodicals in Rome and Milan reviewed the book, but of equal significance is that much smaller papers and papers beyond Italy also wrote about it. The ever supportive *Il Diritto*, even without the nudging of Clemente Maraini who was no longer involved with the periodical, called Pratesi a "gentle writer" whose hodoeporic observations dominated the book, at the expense of the poetry and "Una iettatura," a novella (originally called "Catuzza") he had also included. According to the anonymous critic, Pratesi wrote in the language of the heart, in love and passionately, revealing a soul "trained in Beauty": "Pratesi the prose writer is lifted beyond the everyday, while Pratesi the poet is not."[20] Domenico Oliva (1860–1917), editor of the mighty *Corriere della Sera*, read the volume with "great interest and true intellectual delight" and promised to write of it in the paper.[21] The *Vita moderna* of Milan dedicated a long article to the work.[22] The critic, playwright Gerolamo Rovetta, was ostensibly a friend of Pratesi's, and his views can be considered biased. On the other hand, in his praise of the volume, Rovetta may actually have brought disservice to Pratesi by pointing out that the work was not meant for everyone, just the select reader who would appreciate the delicate artistic impressions, gentle and aristocratic, that to many would appear as word games, exercises of style, academic dilettantism, and even unimportant chatter. Rovetta, too, felt that the novella and the poetry should have found another more appropriate venue. He concluded by confessing that he had learned much from Pratesi's work, and consequently, could appreciate art, and the description of art, to a far greater and more informed degree.

The *Corriere di Palermo* also felt that the inclusion of the novella and the poetry undermined the volume. The critic, Aramis, considered Pratesi a fresh, original, and vivid writer, whose book was most beautiful in content and presentation and whose travel pieces seduce the reader: "they contain something of Stendhal and more of Taine, but if their approach overlaps somewhat, this does not diminish [Pratesi's] original style in any way." Claiming in his conclusion that, with Pratesi, Italy has no reason to envy the writers of France, he maintained that he felt Pratesi's excitement in writing, and also his own enthusiasm for the descriptive passages of the volume, especially of Venice, for Pratesi had imbued them with a most uncommon evocative power, had given them a soul, and had made his readers imagine them in the best of lights, heightened by the fascination of the richest of palettes.[23]

In smaller periodicals, the reaction was similar. *L'Avvisatore alessandrino*, contrary to Rovetta, felt the book was accessible to all, and commended in particular the simplicity of style complemented by an "admirable purity of language." Of the five titles the paper had received for review, Pratesi's was the only one to receive particular attention in this column.[24] *La Sentinella bresciana*, applauding the volume as a whole, nonetheless opined that the inclusion of the short story "Una iettatura" seemed forced; the book should have ended after the essay on the Villa of Massimo d'Azeglio, according to the unnamed critic. Rather than publish his weak poetry, the writer concluded, "Pratesi should give us another book which takes us to other places, other cities, other countrysides: this is the specialty of Pratesi; let the rest go and give us other impressionistic travel pieces that will most certainly be as beautiful as those of this volume."[25] A. Ricchetti, critic for *L'Adriatico Gazzetta di Pesaro* did not mention the poetry or the novella; he wrote instead that Pratesi's worked distanced itself from the usual banal travel literature available; he called it a splendid work "for its pure forms and original thought ... not one page of this thick volume will be read without sincere intellectual pleasure."[26] In a complete reversal of the other perspectives, Nevio in *La Fortuna* (Fano) ignored the travel pieces, and commented instead on the poetry, which he claims recalls that of Carducci: "Pratesi calls these *verses*: he should call them profound and true *poetry*, and he will not be wrong. Considered as a whole, his poetic writing does not reveal a complete harmony with his thoughts and feelings perhaps because he has not found his voice yet. So much the better for the future of our slandered and neglected state of contemporary literature."[27]

The focus on the poetry is unusual, and Pratesi must have been pleased that his Muse continued to reward him for his attempts in all the genres. He carefully preserved these reviews, which likely brought him some comfort during a period of illness and exhaustion so intense that he returned home to Siena leaving Milan behind, and applied for a leave from teaching. In all probability he remained unaware that his work had also gained a positive reputation outside Italy; his silence on the matter confirms this. Suffering dark moments of low self-esteem, Pratesi would have found great satisfaction in knowing that both a Swiss critic, Jämes-Ed. Colin, and a German reviewer, Dr Franz Söhns, bestowed high praise for the work in their respective journals. Both admired, in particular, the descriptive and attractive travel pieces. Colin perceptively envisaged the work as a cohesive whole, a meta-voyage culminating in a rest after long and satisfying travels, a respite allowing time in the final chapters to enjoy the poetry and the novella. He urged his readers to pick up the volume and experience a most pleasant surprise. Söhns turned to Horace to end his laudatory review: "'In Summa:

Omne tulit punctum, qui miscuit utile dulci,' 'he who combines the useful with the delightful wins the prize.'"[28] The words would surely have comforted Pratesi in his despondence had he read them.

The two articles provide an interesting perspective on book reviewing as well. Written one in French and the other in German, they offer a glimpse and a confirmation into the development of book reviewing as a genre in other parts of Europe. Ruggero Bonghi had correctly envisaged a template for book reviews in his introduction to the first issue of *La Cultura* more than a decade previously. Here was evidence, years later and in other countries, that his model for an effective, informative review was a viable one.[29]

Pratesi's leave of absence was granted to him by late September 1892.[30] Early October found him recovering in Florence but beset by insomnia and unspecified pain; his letters point to continuing depression. He insisted on keeping to himself, inciting a concerned Emilia Peruzzi to admonish him, warning him that it was not good for him to isolate himself from friends and acquaintances.[31] But by December he had returned to Milan, knowing that the love affair between himself and Clotilde Coronaro was definitively over and with it any possibility of his remaining in Milan. So, once more he asked his friends to help in finding another teaching assignment. His departure from Milan did not take place in the most amicable of circumstances, but his new position, facilitated as usual by the intervention of Clemente Maraini, as superintendent of schools in the small alpine city of Belluno, offered him increasing financial security. His beginnings there were inauspicious, full of tedious forms and boring bureaucratic practice. His writing continued and began to include annual pedagogical essays intended as sources of professional development and reflection for the teachers under his jurisdiction. However, he could not leave his stories aside, and as he became more accustomed to his new position, he turned to a fictional world again, choosing on this occasion a setting in pre-unification Italy. The story developed with difficulty, as Pratesi admitted to Barzellotti in August of 1893, and although he himself remained dissatisfied with it, it was the novel he personally held most dear: "I have written a long novel notwithstanding my many troubles; that is, its body has all the bones, all its joints, its veins, and its limbs, but you know what that means. I now have to breathe life into that body, which is the style. Which means starting all over again and rewriting all thirty chapters."[32]

Il Mondo di Dolcetta made its debut in serialized form in the *Nuova Antologia* through the fall of 1894 and then early spring of the following year.³³ Choosing once more the environs of Siena as his setting, Pratesi recounts the story of the young Dolcetta who has abandoned her familial home because of various difficulties and has found employment in the house of a corrupt and arrogant aristocrat. Her fall from grace and eventual death from tuberculosis is told in pages of painstaking detail, where every one of the many characters is described, every event elaborated. The political and social agenda Pratesi set for himself in depicting accurately the Grand Duchy of Tuscany as it was in 1859, just before Italian unification, adds a heavy rhythm to Pratesi's prose.

Once the first instalment appeared in the *Nuova Antologia*, Barzellotti noted this cumbersome quality to Pratesi, who replied by describing the difficulties suffered during the writing process. He emphasized that, in the story, he had wanted to portray the Italian character and life in Granducal Florence in a historically correct manner; he worried, however, that his attempt would come to naught. He blamed his own physical condition, compromised by the fatigue caused by his unappealing superintendency in Belluno: "You don't know under what difficulty and travail of mind and body it was written ... I'm not happy with the work. You'll see its intent and concept: I wanted to portray life in Italy and the Italian character, but perhaps I've only created a hole in the water."³⁴

This is a revealing moment; his admission of his own dissatisfaction with the work anticipates negative impressions to come. Pratesi had also forgotten Barzellotti's boastful confidence of a few years earlier that his own works were popular with readers because he kept up with topics readers demanded.³⁵ Pratesi, in his painstaking attempt to perfect the historical verisimilitude of the novel, had disregarded the fact that readers must also derive pleasure from their reading. He soon discovered that the Grand Duchy of Tuscany was not a theme that would resonate pleasurably with his public.

Barzellotti read the novel in moments stolen from his own project on Taine, and promised a more thorough commentary once he had read the entire novel. For the time being, he complimented Pratesi for having produced a mature work, worthy of his talents.³⁶ Adelaide Maraini, too, found some of the chapters overly long and detailed and in this way detrimental to the story development.³⁷ Jessie Hillebrand also felt that the novel's verbosity weighed heavily; the details overwhelmed the novel as a whole. Nor did the emphasis on overt moralizing attract her. Kindly, she attributed her opinion to her English upbringing, writing that, as a result, the novel lacked verisimilitude for her.³⁸ Giuseppe Cesare Abba, too, expressed similar reservations:

When I found myself in the midst of that repugnant world of the young woman from the moment she was taken by that other woman, I liked the story less ... Everything the people among whom Dolcetta lives was laboured, long, and tiring to read ... I did not enjoy your novel to the same degree [in all its chapters]. But it seems to me that you are always fresher in your imagination, and of a braver spirit when you can sustain such a complicated story and make it appear as a simple concept.[39]

Pratesi himself must have anticipated similar reactions. As he sent complimentary copies to colleagues and friends, he added long missives explaining what the novel was about, and why he had written it, and how difficult the environment and circumstances in which he wrote. Giuseppe Chiarini, Ferdinando Martini, Giuseppe Martinozzi, Ernesto Masi, Luigi Luzzatti, and probably other notable names in politics and/or literary criticism received similar letters in early February 1896. It seems that, by this point, Pratesi had changed his mind about his own initial dissatisfaction with the novel, challenging the recipients of his complimentary copies to find its positive aspects by adding the flattering remark that only few would truly understand and appreciate the novel, and that the recipient was in the select group of such attentive and discerning readers. The letters, all written at the same time, stand out for their similarity of content, their unusual length, and also their tone of almost pathetic resentment at not having his literary efforts appreciated.

Nor had Pratesi's intuition missed the mark. Among all his novels, *Il Mondo di Dolcetta*, which he sincerely considered his masterpiece, was found to be least worthy of the honour. Yet, *Dolcetta*, of all Pratesi's novels, attracted the greatest number of book reviews. Critics, as always, generously praised the precise use and clarity of language. Ernesto Masi, who had received one of the missives suggesting that he was particularly well suited to critique the novel, noted its similarity to Antonio Fogazzaro's *Piccolo mondo antico*, also published in 1895 (but started a good decade earlier). His ambiguous final sentence to the brief revue likely did not serve to encourage its promotion or sales. "Overall," he wrote in *L'Arte*, "the novel was good, precise, profound, lively, and (at this point it is necessary to add), *old fashioned.*"[40] Masi probably intended his observation as a compliment, but in the fast-changing world of Italian letters and literary styles, in the world of innovative and daring new authors like those of the *Scapigliatura*, which openly challenged contemporary mores, like D'Annunzio, even like the gutsy Anglo-Italian

Annie Vivanti, Masi's words crippled the work. *Dolcetta* clearly harked back to a time that Italy considered past. The Grand Duchy of Tuscany, for all Pratesi's insistence on its verisimilitude because he had witnessed it, was over. If there remained a collective memory of it, the release of the novel just at the time Italy saw her new dreams of imperialism soundly thwarted in Ethiopia would also not have endeared the novel to readers.

Like Masi, the critic Silvius in *Il Pallano* (Lanciano) also described the novel in ambiguous terms. But those who read between the lines, rapidly grasped the subtle hints at the novel's weaknesses: while the book may be interesting, he pointed out, it consists of three hundred densely printed pages, rather localized Tuscan language and *ribobolo* (meaning idiomatic expressions); Silvius' ironic use of the strictly Tuscan literary term *ribobolo* emphasized the criticism vis-à-vis a wider Italian reading public. There is no need for reading between the lines in Silvius' observation that "this is not a novel such as can be imagined novels might be, or such as one would hope they might be, as are written and have been written ... If Pratesi who is most certainly already preparing some new work, puts some effort into condensing it, into knowing how to give it a unified centre from which his fantasy might depart, we shall, in the near future and without doubt, have a novel that will be an honour for him and for this country."[41]

Towards the end of March, the *Stella di Mondovì* gave the novel its full editorial approval, calling it natural, verisimilar, and spontaneous.[42] At the same time, another small periodical, *La Provincia* (Teramo), found fault with the fact that the work had originally appeared in serial form; consequently, as a novel, the piece was too drawn out and comprised too many episodes, even though the author's talent was excellent and vigorous, and accustomed to producing the best literary fruit.[43] Similar sentiments were voiced also by the critic of *"Il Capitan cortese,"* by the *Rivista bibliografica di scienze e lettere* (Naples) and by Dottor Pangloss, reviewer of the *Cacciatore delle Alpi*. In sum, the novel, in their opinion, merited praise for its many positive aspects, and its weaker elements did not detract from its general excellence.

These reviews published in relatively small periodicals are an excellent indication that Pratesi's publishers promoted his works throughout the peninsula, including in smaller towns and cities. These were papers with a relatively small number of subscribers. What of reviews in journals and papers with much larger, and much more cosmopolitan and sophisticated, readerships ?

Domenico Oliva, in his brief review in the *Corriere della Sera*, uses almost the same words as the critic of *Il Pallano*; he notes that the novel, "the result, no doubt of a long and lovingly undertaken study, [is] filled with good, or rather, excellent aspects but which lack a unifying concept and cohesion." He ends his review with the affirmation: "We have the right to expect better from Pratesi."[44] In light of his previous high praise of Pratesi, whom he lauded as an author whose works provide "true intellectual delight … [such that] his estimation of Pratesi was not only confirmed but increased," how the words must have rankled.[45]

Worse followed. The *Marzocco* of Florence proved almost cruel in its assessment of the novel. The review by Enrico Corradini, found it boring, dry, both in feeling and intellect, a jalopy of a literary vehicle with far too many details, with language too locally Tuscan.[46] Years later, when Pratesi prepared to republish the novel, in 1916, the deep hurt of this unexpected cut still affected him. His archives contain two typescripts of the review with his handwritten defensive comments (the same on both, although placed differently on the pages).[47] Pratesi had clearly been taken aback by the vehemence of the review, so much so that perhaps he had missed the mitigating factor that Corradini's anger was actually directed at the journal the *Nuova Antologia* more than at Pratesi. Corradini confesses unabashedly at the beginning of his article to using Pratesi as a "scapegoat" in order to illustrate the low standards of the periodical.

Unfortunately for Pratesi, the *Fanfulla della domenica* also openly ridiculed *Il Mondo di Dolcetta*. Addressing Charles Dickens in an apostrophe, the anonymous critic pleaded with the English author to teach Pratesi what true *humour* might mean;[48] it certainly did not mean "the madness of wanting to add humorism at all costs and without spontaneity, nor [did it mean] psychological vivisection without a firm and precise hand. So intent was Pratesi on intellectual acrobatics that the reader became irritated." The critic provides an example: Pratesi uses the metaphor of giving birth "giocondamente" (gaily): "Here we have a nice little heresy," the critic points out, "even if it is a metaphor … because no woman, as far as I know, at this supreme moment has ever abandoned herself to hilarity."[49] According to Pratesi, nor did the French journal *L'Italie* spare him for it focused on the tiresome work in reading the novel, and its resulting soporific effect.[50]

Even Barzellotti, who did not comment publicly on the work after his initial compliment of a year earlier, was taken aback by the comments of the *Fanfulla* although he privately agreed with the gist of the review.

In a letter Pratesi almost certainly never saw, Barzellotti wrote to Emilia Peruzzi asking if she had read the work:

> Have you seen our friend Pratesi's *Mondo di Dolcetta*? I, his very close friend who respects him highly, am sad to have to say that it is not his best work because of the usual terrifying pessimism with which he has depicted our society; according to him it is evil and so, described as such by him, it leaves the impression of distressing aridity and disgust. I am particularly unhappy that just today the *Fanfulla della domenica* printed a very negative review of Mario's book. I'm upset because I know how touchy he is. But, and I have to say this, he insists stubbornly on presenting only the negativity of the world, which is not the only nor the most true perspective. I'm persuaded every day that pessimistic *realism* (which is now beginning to be less in vogue), besides being boring, is also a great mistake, and while Art must be *realistic* it should not just reproduce the dry reality of positivistic point of view, otherwise it is not art.[51]

Letters indicate that the paths of Pratesi and Barzellotti did not cross at this time, and so Pratesi's complaint that his friends had reacted by refraining from making comments indicates that he understood the reasons for their reticence. Even the kind Emilia Peruzzi tactfully avoided the whole matter when she wrote to him to thank him for the novel by claiming preoccupation with her sister-in-law's illness and her worries about the political difficulties occasioned by the war between Italy and Ethiopia.[52] Pratesi did not press the issue with her in his response to her.[53]

Pratesi's heavy-handed historicizing certainly contributed to the negative reception of the novel, especially at a time when, as Barzellotti hinted above, realism had already given way to other movements, particularly in the Decadent style. But perhaps two other seemingly extraneous elements came into play to increase the lack of enthusiasm in Pratesi's readers and critics. First, Antonio Fogazzaro's *Piccolo mondo antico*, set in the same period as *Dolcetta* and with its similar plot, had enjoyed much success after its publication in 1895, and this served to make *Dolcetta* appear derivative, unoriginal. And from the world of opera came Giacomo Puccini's *La Bohème*, with its own consumptive penniless protagonist; that the opera should insert itself so successfully into the world of bourgeois leisure activities just as Pratesi published his novel may also have had an impact on how the latter was welcomed.[54] Too similar in theme, with similar characters, Fogazzaro's book and Puccini's opera overshadowed Pratesi's work.

The number of reviews Pratesi received for *Il Mondo di Dolcetta* points to the development of the genre itself. Ruggero Bonghi would have been proud of these reviews for how closely they followed his guidelines set out in *La Cultura* some fifteen years earlier. Barring the few anomalies like Corradini's tirade, the genre had matured as an instrument of critical appraisal: informative, fair, thorough, but not overly long. The review as promotional vehicle for publications is also seen here. More and more periodicals now habitually included a review column; nor were reviews limited to the popular daily papers with numerous subscribers. By this time, the smaller papers, many with runs of well under 1,000 copies, commonly incorporated book reviews into their issues. Undeniably, however, the larger papers, including the *Corriere della Sera* (about 50,000 subscribers at the time) most influenced the taste of the reading public. How adverse for Pratesi that those were the very titles to evaluate his novel negatively.

Years later, when American literary critic Joseph Spencer Kennard (1859–1944) wrote a milder more tempered review of the novel in his study *Romanzi e romanzieri italiani*, Pratesi could not see beyond the negative reaction his book had aroused in 1896. This review, too, was sent to Luisa Anzoletti in 1916 along with his angry comments. While Pratesi acknowledged that Spencer Kennard treated him more kindly than the Italian critics, he accused the American of considering him only superficially and dismissively, ignoring the psychological consequences of the actions of the characters: "Mr. Spencer sees none of this … Yet it is in this, and in the description of Tuscan life in the time of the last Grand Duchy that one finds the essence of the novel, its reality, and its truth which critics and readers overlooked because they were hostile or blind or superficial. And without mentioning unworthy articles like the one by Mr Corradini, even the brief and incomplete observations of someone like Mr Spencer do harm to the novel because they present a minimal picture, without [considering] the most characteristic and essential aspects."[55]

Spencer Kennard had recognized in the novel its elegance of language and what he called its "delicate bonhomie," but as did many of Pratesi's friends, the critic found the negativity of the work to be problematic, noting that it saw life as discouragement and meanness despite its "accurate, finite, harmonious and even writing."[56] Pratesi copied out the review in two manuscripts; Spencer Kennard's comments of above are graced in both copies with a marginal note by Pratesi: "This is absolutely false."[57] Perhaps in his resentful anger he had forgotten that he himself had fretted about the frightening view of the world he had portrayed in the novel.[58]

Always the loyal and supportive friend, it was Giuseppe Cesare Abba who mitigated the discouraging opinions of Pratesi's critics. In his Christmas 1896 letter he consoled his friend by pointing out that *Il Mondo di Dolcetta* owed its poor reception to one major aspect: it instilled a sense of discomfort in the majority of readers and critics who recognized themselves as actors in the corrupt world the novel depicts. Hence, the critical asperity.[59] More recently, a contemporary review of unabashed praise for the book has come to light, written by an unsigned critic for *Minerva: Rassegna internazionale e rivista delle riviste*, at the time directed by Federico Garlanda (1857–1913). It is not inconceivable that Garlanda, who held the Chair of English Language and Literature at the Università di Sapienza in Rome, himself wrote the review. The critic's positive comments on the novel focus on the well-developed plot line (enhanced immeasurably by the publication of the story in novel form rather than left in serialized sections), and extol the language and style of the work. He concludes with the invitation to all to read the story of Dolcetta and feel their hearts beat more quickly as they appreciate how the author has worked his rich and highly nuanced palette even in the most difficult moments of the plot: "You will forgive the author certain prolixities, which he could have avoided in places, and a few rough images that weigh down an otherwise most excellent work."[60] Pratesi almost certainly did not know of the review; had he read it he would undoubtedly have alluded to it, used it to justify his own attitude towards the novel. In the very least he would have mentioned Garlanda or *Minerva*. He likely would have appreciated deeply how the review mirrored in many ways his own reflections on the novel and the changes it required once he began to prepare it for a re-edition in 1916.

As Renato Bertacchini points out in his 1963 edition of *Il Mondo di Dolcetta*, the versions overseen by Pratesi were three: the serialized story published in the *Nuova Antologia* (1894–1895), the Galli edition of 1895 based on the *Nuova Antologia*, and the corrected *Rassegna nazionale* re-edition of 1916, which Pratesi considered his preferred version, and which he had changed and reworked (despite its many typographical errors still remaining).[61] Guidotti, working from published texts in the absence of manuscripts, points out that the differences between the two versions were not of a fundamental nature: various vocabulary changes, some long sentences shortened, some apostrophizing phrases deleted, thereby attenuating the rhetorical narratorial questions posed to the reader; Pratesi also removed some references to time and place.[62] Following Guidotti, Bertacchini also confirms that the corrections are numerous but in a sense not overtly substantive: no chapters or characters purged or added, no diminishment of the deeply pessimistic view informing the novel as a whole. Pratesi, in his continuing conviction, as he says in his testament, that he paints a faithful picture of pre-Risorgimento Siena as no other author has ever done, opts for minor revisions. Bertacchini observes that Pratesi changed the novel by attenuating the heavy-handed prose, especially in the many rhetorical questions addressed to the reader; he also inverted some of the sentences to make them more effective, and some of the exaggerated metaphors and similes were replaced with more precise and efficient expressions, especially in his use of adjectives. Bertacchini provides numerous examples.

In comparing the editions, although not in manuscript as *critique génétique* might prefer, we can nevertheless catch a glimpse Pratesi in his writer's workshop and admire the effects of his personal disappointment and resentment at how readers received *Dolcetta*. He remained angry, but he learned from his failure. Years later, still full of rancour, Pratesi may not have himself appreciated how nuanced his rewriting was; in his reworked edition, further to Bertacchini's examples, we can also observe a diminished authorial presence, which allows the characters to speak more independently and with a new sense of agency. Furthermore, Pratesi's notable expertise as a travel writer, a reporter of landscape, proved detrimental in a novel focused on the tension between characters and their mores and motivations. Thus, with subtle omissions or repositioning, Pratesi gives his protagonists more prominence, literally more space, in the 1916 edition.

Let us look as a case study at the third chapter of the novel, entitled "Seduzione" (Seduction), where the young Dolcetta meets Giulio Marchionetti for the first time. In the *Nuova Antologia* serialized version, for example, the protagonist sews near a window that opens onto a street. She is observed by the local riff-raff hanging about the apothecary shop. Sometimes she laughs to herself. In the later version, the window at which she sits gives onto a relatively larger space described as a small square, and she allows her work to fall aimlessly into her lap as she turns towards the apothecary shop of the wealthy Sor Telemaco and laughs at her observers. The act of looking back at those watching her establishes her as being less naive, less ingenuous than in the original version where she seemed unaware of being scrutinized. And this is certainly emphasized in Pratesi's changed observation from how (in the first version), at times, she appeared as if she wanted to see someone pass by her window to how (in the 1916 edition), at times, she took on the demeanour of wanting to have someone she desired pass by the window. By adding the element of desire, Pratesi prepares us more effectively for her reaction when Giulio Marchionetti deliberately absents himself from her; as readers, we can appreciate Pratesi's change from describing the young seducer's absence as an element that "entered acutely into her heart," to his absence, "like some ethereal element, penetrated her heart." Her desire for him is not evident at all in the first edition. The space of her seduction is also enlarged, from a nearby meadow ("prato") it becomes in the later edition more edenic, the place "laggiù sull'erba molle del praticello celato dalle mura castellane e dal bosco" ("over there on the soft grass of the little meadow obscured by the castle wall and the woods"). Furthermore, Dolcetta is given more dialogue in the second version, and particularly significantly, the revised chapter ends no longer with seducer Giulio Marchionetti's words, but with her escape from him "tutta stordita, palpitante, affannosa" ("stunned, trembling, panting"). Clearly, despite her desire, she perceives the danger he poses for her, and while in the first edition she does not defend herself, in the second she hides behind the fact that in the social order of her station in life she is not deemed worthy of loving him, and tells him so. Pratesi permits this new sense of agency to recur throughout the chapter also by offering more reflexive verbs, thus pointing to how the subject was implicated in the action (e.g., above he corrects Dolcetta "lasciava cadere di mano [il suo lavoro]" to "si lasciava cadere di mano [il suo lavoro]," from Dolcetta allowed her work to fall from her hands to Dolcetta allowed herself to let her work fall from her hands), subtle nuances that enrich Dolcetta's character by taking her beyond the strict binary of innocent girl seduced/immoral seducer to a young woman aware of what is happening but unable to stop the events. Pratesi also makes implicit phrases into explicit clauses with a named subject/agent and verb rendering the chapter less academic, more reminiscent of how an ordinary person might tell the story.

These changes helped in re-establishing the attraction and relevance of the work, as Bertacchini suggests in his introduction to the 1916 edition. Without naming them, Barzellotti too evidently felt the effects of these as he discussed the impending revised addition, and he commented to Pratesi that he was confident that the new edition would be more appreciated by readers than the first.[63]

Nonetheless, that Pratesi was completely surprised by the general negative reaction to the first edition of his novel is clear in his letters at the time and even many years later. He overlooked, perhaps, that his friends had warned him about the weaknesses of the novel even in its earlier serialized form. In his attempt to repeat the success of *L'Eredità*, perhaps he also ignored the similarity of theme and plot development not only between these two works, but among several of his novellas as well. In the rapidly changing world of Italian literature, innovative and even audacious works attracted readers and positive critical attention far more readily than his conservative, heavily descriptive and decidedly Tuscan pages. Whether he liked it or not, by the end of the nineteenth century there existed in Italy a consumer market in literature. The reading public clamoured for works that reflected new tastes and new attitudes, new energies. Ernesto Masi's remark that the work was old fashioned reflected the reaction of Pratesi's contemporary readers. In hindsight, Guidotti claims in his critical overviews, the novel is a work of the most modern intentions, anticipatory of attitudes that only decades later would be appreciated.[64] He echoes the words of Pratesi's friend and colleague, Renato Fucini: "When I think that at times I have compared myself to you in the way you observe, feel, and write, I become ashamed. I won't say more. Work my dear friend because your cocoon is not yet finished, and you have much much more silk inside of you."[65] Fucini's letter reached Pratesi in the late summer of 1896. By that time critics had forgotten about *Il Mondo di Dolcetta*. Pratesi had not forgotten, he would never forget, and twenty years later, in 1916, he republished the novel with corrections, finally also repudiating the previous version of 1896 in his will.[66] But he stubbornly held onto the negative attitudes, the pessimistic outlook.

What had gone so irrevocably wrong in the planning, writing, and publishing of *Il Mondo di Dolcetta*? The letters of the period and later that allow us to see Pratesi at work show us a man beset by interruptions that took time away from his manuscript: illnesses, the bureaucratic minutiae of his job as superintendent, even the weather in Belluno impeded him. We can see the tension between his realization that he was a successful author yet still plagued by hesitations over the work as it was serialized and then published. We can also surmise the disappointments to its critical reaction, disappointments that stubbornly instilled in him the growing conviction that the work was not faulty, but that, instead, critics and friends had not understood it, that they somehow had set out to undermine him. In her engaging biography of American author Louisa May Alcott, who wrote some three decades before Pratesi's *Dolcetta*, Susan Cheever points to a similar process suffered by Alcott as she penned her first serious novel *Moods*. Alcott, according to Cheever, only found her voice again (with the successful *Little Women*) when "she stopped Writing and began to write."[67] In other words, the process had overtaken the creativity of the story and its characters. Cheever's observation rings equally true for Pratesi.

So, like Alcott with her book, Pratesi moved on with his life, forced to accept the lukewarm, even hostile, welcome given to *Dolcetta*. As another school year opened, he also began to work on another novel, even with the disappointment of the previous one. The young author who doubted himself, and felt unable to write because of his doubts, had matured, still followed his Muse, still remained faithful to her.

Chapter Four

Florence Once More

Belluno lies about a hundred kilometres north of Pratesi's much beloved Venice. A small city, it is surrounded by the splendid mountains that give it its name but also render it oppressive at times. If nothing else, Belluno offered Pratesi a decided measure of reliability; for the first time in many years, he did not worry to any great degree about keeping body and soul together, thanks to a regular salary. But, Belluno was isolated and cold: meteorologically and metaphorically, with long lonely winters and few opportunities for friends. Friendships initiated years, even decades, before his posting there continued but were often fraught with laments of aging, illness, family setbacks and regrets, and death. Many of his friends, including Barzellotti, Abba, and Sonnino, had accepted onerous political appointments in Rome, and contacts became more and more irregular. In Belluno, by all accounts, Pratesi was an excellent superintendant of schools, a well-respected man. At the same time, the vicissitudes of his daily life rarely brought welcome challenges; most were petty disturbances that took up enormous amounts of his time and energy. Bureaucracy had never appealed to him, even when as a youth he had rebelled against working in the police office in Florence; time and maturity did not make bureaucracy any more palatable.[1]

Around this time, the correspondence in his archives tapers off somewhat. The factors are numerous, including those listed above. It is not unfeasible that other societal changes also played a role: the railroad and tram made visits an easier undertaking. The telephone, although not by any means ubiquitous, became an effortless substitute for letter writing.[2] In keeping with his administrative position, Pratesi's writing in Belluno now included annual columns to the teachers or students in his charge. The pedagogically oriented themes nevertheless brought compliments even if somewhat perfunctory.

In late July of 1897, Pratesi announced in a postscript to Barzellotti that he had sent a new story to the *Nuova Antologia* for consideration.[3] This despite the fact that Barzellotti had alerted him in June of ongoing internal problems at the journal resulting in its eventual sale to another publisher. Barzellotti warned Pratesi that no new articles were being accepted by the new publisher, Maggiorino Ferraris (1856–1929).[4] When, by the end of July, Pratesi still had not had a response from Ferraris about his manuscript, he apparently decided to forgo his usual custom of serializing his story and then publishing it as a book. He sent the full manuscript directly to another publisher, Emilio Treves; it was published as *Le Perfidie del caso* in the summer of the following year.[5]

How the title evolved does not remain recorded in any of Pratesi's documents. It represents, however, a small change in his customary Weltanschauung: less concrete than the titles of his other novels, it assigns the vicissitudes of human endeavours to chance. He recounts the story of an artist, Carlo Ghiberti, and Palmira, the woman he chooses as a model for his Mary Magdalene. She possesses ineffable beauty, which in the end becomes a suffocating burden for both of them and, as the object of perverse desire, leads to her death. The novel seems almost a reaction to the bittersweet reception of *Il Mondo di Dolcetta*, a work he had sincerely felt solid enough to take its place as his magnum opus. Critics have observed that, in *Perfidie del caso*, Pratesi appears to have changed his attitude towards writing. In its tone, clearly shaped by the current trend to decadence, ennui, and refusal of established social conventions, the book hints at lessons in contemporary writing that Pratesi had intuited in his relatively long sojourn in Milan where the bohemian writers of the *Scapigliatura* movement had made their effects felt.[6] Guidotti refers to it as Pratesi's acknowledgment of the influence of the Decadent poets and writers, like Gabriele D'Annunzio, also in vogue at the time. Not full acceptance of Decadence, according to Guidotti, but vague outlines behind whose ornate leaves and branches remains the solid trunk of the earlier Pratesi altered by attempts at thematic innovation and a larger repertoire of stylistic features, updated to reflect the literary sensibilities of readers as one century came to an end and another began.[7]

Alessandro Gherardi remained wholly unconvinced by the new inclination. Writing to his friend soon after the book was released, he complimented the simple, flowing style, the imagery, the descriptions, but at the same time felt disheartened by the "general impression that remains in the minds and hearts of the readers." Namely, he felt that the novel lacked any sense of redemption that might attenuate the sordid elements. He expressed deep disappointment with the story's failure to teach any moral behaviour, and he accused Pratesi of actually enjoying some of the negative aspects too much, especially in the realistic description of the character Palmira, the artist's model: "You insist too strongly, I think, on her legs, her breasts, her shoulders, her curves, her accoutrements, and the flexibility of that beautiful body; and it seems that you take pleasure in it; the reader can feel this pleasure, and that's where the evil lies. [It would be] less dangerous and more efficacious to hint and let the imagination think rather than have you describe."[8] Gherardi also gathered support for his opinion from what Abba had related to him about the novel, although the latter's letter has not been preserved. Both appear to be acting out their own insecurities and anxieties over the changing social environment reflected in the *Perifidie del caso*. In a letter of the previous Christmas, Gherardi had commented sadly on his growing concerns about the future; to read in the novel his close friend's utter disregard for redemptive possibilities of the times weighed heavily on Gherardi.[9] Furthermore, Gherardi also lamented that Pratesi had not availed himself of a historical framework for his novel. Abba and Gherardi, of course, were Pratesi's most conservative and probably most innocuous critics. If they were upset in their personal considerations of the novel, Pratesi must have indeed strayed from his usual literary practice. Such an opinion can also be inferred from the muted criticism of one of Pratesi's faithful female readers and supporters, Adelaide Maraini. Always a barometer of taste for his readers, she delicately skirted around making comments about the novel itself, preferring to point out that the reviews she read had been positive ones. But at one point, she too revealed her anxieties about Pratesi's new novel: "I read with pleasure the review in the *Rassegna* [*settimanale universale*], and I think it points out well and sincerely the numerous merits of your novel; if you lived in an environment enlivened by family and friends, who knows what kinds of more serene themes you might analyse, with that subtlety and perspicacity that distinguishes you."[10]

Pratesi must have awaited Barzellotti's opinion with some trepidation. Barzellotti usually voiced much more detailed and much harsher judgments of his friend's work than did Mrs Maraini or Abba or Gherardi, but on this occasion his review stands out for its enthusiasm:

> As far as I'm concerned, one of your best works, perhaps the best (among novels); well written, as usual, but here the style takes on sobriety, a

vigorous determination, and here and there, a poetic warmth that give the book a character all its own. Given the world you describe ... a world that is certainly very perverse, perhaps viewed only and too much in its perversity, the characters you depict could not be more vivid or more true, they could not have a more clearly delineated physiognomy ... I can see that as far as the art of observing reality you have made great progress. For those who look to true unadorned artistry and those who above all have a feeling for the vivacity and spontaneity of the Tuscan tongue ... this should be an appealing book.[11]

He too, then, had noticed something different about Pratesi's approach to writing, attributing it to the vivid appropriateness of the language, despite the depravity of the world described in the story. In pointing out the excellent descriptions, on the other hand, Barzellotti also implicitly diminishes the plot, and in this, echoes the voices of other critics. By this time, Pratesi had also received a lengthy letter from Ernesto Masi, who had previously reviewed *Il Mondo di Dolcetta* and had found it old fashioned.[12] But this time Masi reacted diversely writing that "the catastrophe [in the plot] belongs to a romance drama. But it surprised me. At least, I did not expect it ... It appears that you have dealt with a problem of art and of psychology."[13] Again, it is the plot of the novel that appears lacking. Masi closed the letter with "heartfelt wishes that the novel will enjoy the fortune it deserves."[14] He also marvelled at how contemporary the work was; it had to have been written before the revolt against the onerous grain tax and subsequent strikes that had unsettled Milan in the spring of 1898, yet it reflected the zeitgeist of that period extraordinarily well.

At the time, Masi could not have known the importance of the formal review of the novel he would subsequently write, and which would appear in the *Nuova Antologia*, in guaranteeing the success of the novel. As a marketing strategy, Masi's book review certainly fulfilled its role. On the other hand, Pratesi, too, had himself made two fundamental decisions regarding the marketing of his work that also supported its success. First, his failure to secure a spot in the *Nuova Antologia* for an initial serialized version of the novel actually worked in his favour for it allowed the novel to seem more fresh and new when it appeared in book form; his loyal readers did not consider the book a rereading of a story already familiar to them. Second, in sending the book to Treves for publication, Pratesi also benefited from the enormous marketing machine represented by the *Illustrazione italiana*, another Treves publication, which boasted a substantial readership.[15] In addition to a regular long review signed Renato in the *Illustrazione italiana*, Pratesi's work also enjoyed two further references, one in the summer of 1898 and the second in early January 1899.[16] Perhaps not as ubiquitous as his earlier fortune of having *Jacopo e Marianna* advertised daily for a year in *Il Diritto*, the mentions of the book in the *Illustrazione* nonetheless reached a significant number of potential readers. The *Nazione* (Florence) as well announced the book shortly after its publication, with a positive nod.[17]

Ironically, the *Illustrazione italiana* published the first review of the book together with a review of the novel *La Verginità*, written by Pratesi nemesis Enrico Corradini. According to the reviewer, the latter pales in comparison to *Le Perfidie del caso*. Even the space allotted to Corradini (a dismissive half-column compared with one-and-one-third columns for Pratesi) supports the critic's approval. The review of Corradini's novel basically summarizes the plot, while Pratesi's novel is presented through a critical lens. The opening statement of the *Perfidie* review indicates the direction the critic will take: the novel, he writes, "signals a great progress over the previous novels of this refined, conscientious Tuscan writer who for many years has waged a noble battle for Italian literature ... [which is] truly enriched by this new thoughtful work, profound and polished in all its parts ... and which allows the psychologist-novelist to examine attitudes that till now have remained uncaptured [in strong literary works] such as this one by Pratesi."[18] He continued with favourable comparisons to both Alessandro Manzoni and Émile Zola, lauding Pratesi's *Perfidie* for its language and for its mastery of a theme where the artist protagonist predominates (saying it could have been called *The Story of an Artist*). He noted that in this novel "the psychologist comes to the fore on every page: his arrows hit their mark."[19]

In August, Ernesto Masi's official review article appeared in the *Nuova Antologia*, covering five pages. Again, as he had in his personal letter to Pratesi, Masi praised the work for how it depicted the psychology of a society; the whole novel, he affirms in his laudatory conclusion, is

> a psychological study of great strength in small proportions, a profound analysis of its characters but that gathers and portrays them as if in great proportions; in the misery in which certain moral and social conditions of our time are scrutinized, in the passionate efficacy with which this intimate drama develops, and in the vivid power of the landscape [we have confirmation] once again that Mario Pratesi possesses that singular

temperament of thinker and artist that makes him one of the most notable and ingenious among Italian writers.[20]

Masi's comment above reappeared in the *Illustrazione italiana* on 4 September 1898; the review obviously pleased Pratesi for he included it as the preface to the second edition of the novel in 1900.

Pratesi's archives also include two manuscripts (one incomplete) of a review which appeared in the *Rassegna settimanale universale* in December of 1898, and which later served as the basis of the promotional quote in the *Illustrazione italiana* of January 1899. Here again the praises abounded; the critic, Van Winkle, felt that "above all this story is notable for its clarity of perspectives, its purity of plot line, a noble and truly artistic elegance of style, which give the author the right to take his place on the front lines of the best novelists, ours and foreign. We do not know who among living writers might boast a more sure mastery of language, a style so noble and so pure, a palette so rich and effective."[21] The review clearly pleased Pratesi for he sent handwritten copies to his friends. He received replies from both Adelaide Maraini and Gherardi agreeing with the tenor of the review despite their initial hesitation upon reading the novel.[22] He must have been somewhat puzzled by the person behind the name Van Winkle. Pratesi's incomplete manuscript copy of the piece conserved in his archives has a tentative "critico olandese" ("Dutch critic") beside the reviewer's name; the manuscript of the full review contains an added note beside the name: "The article I have transcribed is signed by Van Winkle, perhaps of Dutch origin, a person who, as we see, is good and kind, completely unknown to me and who appears to me quite different from our own bitter, envious, and boorish critics."[23] Pratesi must have suspected that Van Winkle was a pseudonym (and there are in the review several linguistic clues that the reviewer is Italian and not Dutch at all), but he was unable to discover who the author was.

Given the predominantly positive reviews of *Perfidie*, whom did Pratesi intend with his derogatory remark about boorish Italian critics in his comment above? None other, it appears, than Enrico Corradini, who once again used the pages of his *Il Marzocco* to denigrate Pratesi's work. An unmerited ad hominem attack that completely contradicted the clear warning against such egregious behaviour that Bonghi had placed in his preface to the book review journal *La Cultura* in the early 1880s. Corradini began his tirade with a pointed reminder of his opinion of *Il Mondo di Dolcetta*, followed by the immediate regret that Pratesi, in terms of bad novels, was a recidivist: "Now he has published the *Perfidie del caso* with Treves and he comes along to tell us about … perfectly useless things ... And yet, despite everything, Pratesi has talent … He has a smooth and flowing style, with good [use of] language, and he shows affection and respect for our Florence, which is to his credit. He should, however, develop the good taste not to write useless things. Perhaps he would write less, but it would be so much better for him and for his readers."[24]

The *Perfidie del caso* represents a sort of experiment for Pratesi, a break from his usual way of narrating, and an acknowledgment that literature in Italy had veered far from the Manzonian exemplar. Guidotti felt that it had not completely succeeded as a full literary endeavour. For him the novel "allows hints of success to peek through its fabric but the shadows still dominate the light, and the contrasts of style remain evident. The best of the novel is found in the vignettes, which are juxtaposed discordantly to Dannunzian emulations and French-type psychological reflection to realism that is crude and, in Pratesi, unusual. This novel is a commonplace book filled with excellent pages, but still a commonplace book."[25]

Perhaps Pratesi himself felt some anxiety about his different approach to writing because in the months following the publication of the work, he decided to step back from penning another full-length novel, returning instead to previous work in a genre in which he excelled: travel writing. He gathered and corrected the articles of the series *Ricordi veneziani*, which had originally been published in the *Illustrazione italiana* in 1889, and then had formed part of the book *Di paese in paese* in 1892. His intention now was to follow his regular practice and dedicate a volume specifically to these articles; the book appeared in 1899 through the Milanese publishing house of Baldini and Castoldi. It was soon followed by a second edition, also through Baldini and Castoldi.[26] Pratesi's health at this time had begun to deteriorate notably; he was plagued by gastrointestinal problems and despite the fact that years earlier he had professed to Abba that he did not believe in doctors, he now took the advice of the Maraini family to see their doctor, Virginio Pensuti, who specialized in conditions affecting the stomach.[27]

Even with the positive reaction to the previous publications of the *Ricordi veneziani*, the two editions by Baldini and Castoldi did not attract the attention of critics, nor even of Pratesi's usual cadre of patient and praising observers, a curiously untypical response. When the edition by Sandron appeared in the early summer of 1901,[28] Abba, contrary to his usual procrastinations, sent his reaction to the book almost immediately. He particularly noted Pratesi's use of a more contemporary tone in the piece, reflecting Pratesi's attempts at a more au courant literary style. Abba wrote:

> What a master of form you have become! Your style has become limpid and flowing ... and how measured your thoughts are, even where you denigrate the world! A kindness always remains in that denigration ... You offer images of a new and surprising simplicity. You must have been truly happy while composing some of the pages, even some of your sentences, happy I say to have felt them develop inside of you, and then to come forward and give us your thoughts with such charm ... Will other readers appreciate you the way I do? Many certainly, the best ones. But something that amazes me ... is the freshness of these pages.[29]

Alfredo Panzini, the critic of the *Vita Internazionale* concurred in his brief overview, numbering the *Ricordi veneziani* among the books that he had read with the greatest pleasure, claiming he had savoured almost every single page. He admired the near perfect evocation of the historical Venice, and the vivacity and movement of the description of life in that city. He claimed the superiority of Pratesi's volume over travel books written about Venice by foreigners. He found some fault with the chapters on the Venetian artists (Titian, Veronese, and Tintoretto) because they seemed hurried and not seamlessly integrated into the whole. On the other hand, the style had admirable elegance, reflection, and clarity.[30] A much longer review by Giulio Natali expressed similar sentiments. Natali, a professor at the Scuola normale in Belluno, had met Pratesi in 1901 and considered him a respected mentor for his own work. He remembered that Pratesi was "a handsome man, with vivacious eyes and a pointed grey beard, dignified in his comportment and dress, severe and friendly at the same time, and who had taken his boring job as school superintendant for the greater good."[31] In his review of the *Ricordi*, Natali began with a comparison to the abridged version of John Ruskin's *Stones of Venice* (1853–55), which had just been published in its Italian translation.[32] Of the two, he much preferred Pratesi's work. In his opinion, the *Ricordi veneziani* brought forth Pratesi "the thinker, the man of good taste, the acute observer, and the productive writer ... who knows how to depict the image of a monument or of a glorious testimony of the past in a few words ... Equally sharp is his psychological scrutiny of the citizens of Venice ... I will leave others to point out some of the technical imperfections [of the book]. I wanted to highlight the originality and the brilliance of the observations."[33]

The positive reviews delighted Pratesi. At that time he was already intent on his next literary project, a novel entitled *Il Peccato del dottore*. For this novel, Pratesi returned to his practice of releasing the work first in serial form, and then as a single volume. By early 1901, even before Natali's review of the *Ricordi veneziani*, Giuseppe Chiarini, editor of the *Rivista d'Italia* had received the first three parts of the latest novel; confirming his pleasure at the chapters, he promised that he would begin including the story in the April issue of the journal. He also suggested that Pratesi himself determine a reasonable fee for the work, rather than have the administration of the publication do so.[34] How disappointing for Pratesi, just a few months later, to remain without the monies owing, and at the point of threatening legal action.[35] Furthermore, the publisher Pratesi had found for the eventual release of the novel as an independent volume insisted on publishing the work only on the basis of paying a percentage from future sales. Nonetheless, the *Peccato del dottore* proved perhaps the most successful, certainly the most contemporary, and perhaps even most daring of Pratesi's works. It enjoyed several editions: the first by Baldini and Castoldi of Milan (1902), then Roux and Viarengo of Turin (1905), another by the original publisher in 1911, and finally, in the year prior to the author's death, by Vitagliano, also of Milan (1920).

The work, which was Pratesi's last full-length novel published as an independent volume, hit close to home. By August of 1900, as the writing progressed always in the moments stolen from his official duties as superintendant of schools, Pratesi overtly recognized its dark underpinnings, confessing to his friend Countess Maria Ponti Pasolini (1857–1938) that despite being beset by physical and spiritual pain, he continued writing. He admitted that his latest effort (*Il Peccato del dottore*) was certainly not a work that might present the world through a rose-coloured lens.[36] In all the years that his friends had strongly hinted at the overly pessimistic tone of his works, Pratesi himself had never openly agreed with them. To have him admit this now was a new writerly comportment for him.

Critic Mario Guidotti found himself somewhat perplexed in commenting on *Il Peccato del dottore*; he suggested that it reflected the literary taste of the day, a predilection lasting only briefly according to Guidotti. He acknowledged its demonstration of Pratesi's new attitude to writing, calling it a book of interesting content as well as of a rather precious Dannunzian hedonism; this, he added, was the element that attracted contemporary readers, but that diminished its literary impact. Guidotti also inadvertently revealed why the novel is so problematic: it is a novel of painful closures in which protagonist and author coalesce rather uncomfortably. Indeed, the roman à clef that had characterized *Da fanciullo: Memorie del mio amico Tristano* seemed somehow more acceptable, even in its darkest descriptions; it was a work that marked the beginning of a promising career. But a roman à clef at the end of an author's career is fraught with knotty aspects. The career no longer seems promising, the author's best work and efforts lie behind him. Guidotti writes that "the man is in his sixties, now, close to the end of an unsuccessful life; a man continually unfulfilled, ever more alone and pessimistic; he is a sincere man but bound to a hypocritical social environment; he fights in vain against the fact that he has been condemned to live among falseness."[37] Guidotti intends here the protagonist of *Il Peccato*, but his words describe Pratesi's situation as well. As in the story itself, a certain heavy sadness accompanies the realization that this would be a work of closures. Pratesi, in this novel, intended to exorcise the demons that had plagued him throughout his writing career, but without penning his own autobiography. How more appropriately to do this than to trace the life of a fictional educated professional (here, a doctor, a healer who himself remains a broken man)! Guidotti notes that, after *Il Peccato del dottore*, Pratesi wrote only works of minor importance.[38] It may be more prudent to say instead that after 1902, having vicariously bared his soul in *Il Peccato*, Pratesi no longer wished to commit himself to the onerous demands of full-length novels.

Pratesi inscribes his own life in *Il Peccato del dottore*, including the existence of a daughter. Most certainly he foresaw the havoc the work might effect once published. Giuseppe Chiarini, publisher of the serialized version warned him that he would not likely be able to stay in Belluno after the work was fully released.[39] Pratesi expressed his awareness of the situation to Gino Bandini, a distant relative and most kindred of spirits, the man whom he would trust as heir, and as friend and confidante in the years remaining to him. To Bandini, Pratesi confided that his unworthy Bellunese colleagues would all see themselves "photographed" in the novel.[40] However, quite to the contrary, Pratesi later had to admit that he was taken aback by the complete silence surrounding the publication. Writing again to Gino Bandini some months later, he revealed that with the exception of one of the school principals, no one among his colleagues had even acknowledged the work, treating it instead as if it did not exist.[41] His friends also remained silent. For example, from Barzellotti there initially came a brief postcard saying how much he had enjoyed the descriptions of the protagonist's dog and cat, with a promise of more detailed observations later.[42] By the end of March of the following year he had still not commented on the work, but sent another letter excusing his silence because of his work commitments.[43] And only the following September did Barzellotti finally read the novel in full. His comments praised the work for the flow, style, and mastery of language. But ultimately, he opined, the characters were not engaging to the reader, and while the book left a good impression, he remained unsatisfied and disappointed by the rigidity and insistence of the pessimism in the book.[44] His comments echoed those of Abba, who wrote in late July that Pratesi's world must indeed have been miserable: "Was it really like that? It must have been because your voice in those pages rings true … Ah, my dear Mario, there exist many more worthy virtues to depict in art, more worthy than the ones you focus on. Seek them, seek them as only you know how to do because depicting those [negative] characters brings nothing positive, they remain such as they are, and since they are often successful in life, you risk giving vulnerable readers the impression, that between good and evil, the latter is preferable."[45]

Alessandro Gherardi chided Pratesi in a similar manner, saying that the characters were depicted as real but the pervasive pessimistic attitude undermined the book. With more edificatory optimism, he wrote, "You would probably be a more interesting read, your book would end with more openness towards beauty and goodness, to which, in the end, should be what every artistic and literary production aspires."[46]

Pratesi had been beset all through the early part of 1902 by unsuccessful attempts to publish the novel in a single volume. He must have become anxious about its public critical reception, given the silence of his colleagues, the hesitations of the publishing houses he had approached, and the gentle censure of his friends. Having anticipated negative reactions, he had asked to be transferred from his position in Belluno. But then, although positions first at Pesaro and also at Porto Maurizio were offered, he changed his mind in view of the lack of reaction.[47] Pratesi had also complained to Abba about it in a letter of 14 February 1902, writing, "One should not hope to find *generosity* and *loyalty* in Italy, the classic land of envy and lies. Few are the admirers of superior things, and when they note that you are superior, they hide you away. What pettiness! What vanity! From '88 on, that is, since *Eredità*, *Mondo di Dolcetta* etc. I have given my country six books and I can say without vanity or arrogance that they are at least as [worthy] as those books that were well publicized. But instead, who has spoken well of [my work]?"[48] His lament revealed a raw vulnerability, perhaps unexpected at this point in his life and writing career. Likely to alleviate his anxiety, he began to guide potential official reviews. He asked Gino Bandini to review *Il Peccato del dottore*, without naming a periodical where it might appear. Bandini's first draft did not please the elderly author, and he asked for revisions, especially an attenuation of the exuberant praise so that the article might appear more objective.[49] Some weeks later, he urged Bandini to consider in his review also Barzellotti's initial reaction to the novel, and he copied for him verbatim a part of Barzellotti's letter.[50] Bandini's review was completed by March of the following year, but again Pratesi asked for revisions, both general and more detailed, suggesting now that the critique be sent to a fairly new journal, *Medusa*, rather than elsewhere.[51] When the review finally appeared in the 23 March 1902 issue of the periodical, Pratesi wrote to Bandini immediately to express his thanks and his pleasure. He also voiced his great dismay that no publisher had yet shown an interest in publishing the story in an independent volume.[52] Once the book did appear, sometime in the late spring, Pratesi's anxiety over finding good reviews increased. Sidney Sonnino received a copy of the novel and passed it on to Domenico Oliva for a critique in Sonnino's *Giornale d'Italia*, as he confirmed in a letter of 6 July 1902, despite the fact Oliva had previously offered a decidedly unenthusiastic review of *Il Mondo di Dolcetta*.[53] Pratesi must have suggested to the *Giornale d'Italia* the possibility of using Bandini's review, but Sonnino felt it more prudent to assign another reviewer, namely, Oliva. However, by the end of August, Oliva had not yet written his critique. In the meantime, Raffaello Barbiera, in quite a nasty mood, wrote in the *Illustrazione italiana* that he hoped the book would have many readers, but "let's get over all this sinning. Pratesi is a careful narrator, endowed with a beautiful pure language … but he just isn't interesting even though he copies from reality, as he has done [here]."[54] Paltry words of back-handed praise, more harmful than helpful, and certainly, since book reviews served also as advertisements, no incentive to the thousands of subscribers of the magazine to procure the book for themselves. Pratesi must have wondered if anyone would appreciate his work, and so he again contacted Sonnino about a review; the latter reconfirmed that the book had indeed been passed on to Oliva, who, however, was on holiday at that time.⁵⁵ But Oliva, for reasons unknown, decided to withdraw from the assignment. The book was then passed on to Ernesto Masi, who had written so positively of Le Perfidie del caso a few years before.⁵⁶ Masi must have contacted Pratesi to inform him that he would review the book; Pratesi, encouraged by Masi's apparent enthusiasm for Il Peccato del dottore, saw an opportunity for another laudatory review. Consequently, with Masi he openly vented his anger and frustration in a letter ten pages long: "Dear Friend, the gracious way you speak of my book has consoled me, because (let me tell you right away), it has been welcomed as if it were a foreign guest, with a cold, false smile for the sake of courtesy."⁵⁷ In the rest of the letter Pratesi provided the framework for the eventual review, as he had done for Gino Bandini, pointing to the stronger points of the novel, describing his intentions in writing, and also lamenting the misguided reactions to a work that was *"carefully considered*, rational, and *sincere*."⁵⁸ No record remains of whether Masi submitted drafts of his review for pre-publication approval by Pratesi, as had Bandini. The critique appeared in the *Giornale d'Italia* on 8 April 1903.

Both Bandini and Masi wrote generous reviews: generous in columnar space and generous in attitude. At the same time, both eschewed the bias of Pratesi's behind the scenes guidance. Consequently, their assessments are positive but measured. Bandini is the more philosophical of the two reviewers, recalling previous works by Pratesi and assuring that *Il Peccato* meets the same high literary standard. Pratesi "gathers within his book a study of the many diverse passions of the human heart; he knows how to depict hate and love, how to express irony and pain, how to analyse human psychology with exquisite nuances, how to investigate and portray the tastes and feelings of humans and animals ... as if he were a perfect humorist whose smile also reveals a deep sadness."⁵⁹

Masi, on the other hand, provides many more details about the plot and characters of the novel, but also pauses to express his astonishment at Pratesi's literary reception:

> It happens that we've read some of the latest assessments of Pratesi's work, and we were surprised to see how overlooked and forgotten, both in criticism and praise, are the nature and character of this author's works, many of which have earned recognition since his earliest essays. Almost no one recognizes in this writer a philosopher artist who uses his art to

probe social and psychological problems ...We don't want to run the risk of praising this novel as a deliberately forgotten masterpiece. Not at all! In our opinion this book has faults, nor are some of these trifling or light. But [the novel] remains nonetheless the profoundly human study of an exceptional individual whom the world ... affects in a sinister way, and who provides a view of present day Italian life in its public and private ramifications; this is a work that has been proposed and described with passion, with originality and with sincerity.[60]

In his (feigned) surprised reaction to other opinions of the novel, Masi may have intended not only the barbs of the *Illustrazione italiana* but also the brief critique of *La Lombardia*, published on 14 November 1902, in which the volume was described as elegant in presentation, correct in terms of Italian language, but monotonous. Other reviews were scarce, even as Pratesi noted.

Il Peccato del dottore merits more notice, and it is regrettable that subsequent editions did not attract the attention of book reviewers. Certainly, the volume represented a relatively successful commercial venture (although not for Pratesi, personally). Ultimately, the novel may have been impeded not because of monotony as Raffaello Barbiera and the anonymous critic of *La Lombardia* asserted, but because in its fictional world it represents a chillingly decadent zeitgeist. It is the story of a defeated man, by a defeated man. The use of a first person narrator (a first for Pratesi) heightens the pervasive defeatism of the novel because, in the end, the narrator dies. Even his dog, named Speranza (which narrator and author shared), significantly, disappears after the death of the doctor. The cat (also shared by narrator and author), with his evocative and symbolic name, Camuffi (from the Italian *camuffare*, to disguise or to hide), who displays a cynical deference to all in order to profit personally from the situations in which he finds himself, thrives and prospers in this novel where sarcasm, satire, and cynicism play main roles.[61] How diametrically opposed he is in character to the first noble cat of Pratesi's writing which had enchanted the reviewer of *Da fanciullo: Memorie del mio amico Tristano*.[62]

In *Il Peccato del dottore*, Pratesi has produced an extremely complicated work, despite the simple story. While his characters serve as open books even from their very names (Cav. Ronzoni, il segretario Candore, il commendatore Tummistufetti, il capo usciere Fiscaroli, and, of course, Donna Angioliera),[63] Pratesi seems to remain painfully and bitterly true to his early literary intention, that of depicting experiences and feelings that he had personally observed and felt. His layered approach juxtaposes present and past, and then past with a nearer present, and then the future. Despite his extreme sensitivity, enhanced by his awareness of Dannunzian aesthetics, Pratesi does not use his work as a vehicle for self-justification or self-vindication. The doctor had committed a sin (actually many sins) for which there was no expiation, and which left in its wake several victims, including the most innocent of all, his natural daughter Maria. Of his transgressions he is fully cognizant, as the novel makes clear.[64]

In speaking of the protagonist, Dr Fabio Stellini, Abba had written that Pratesi was "that doctor in part, or maybe completely,"[65] but his consternation comes from the negative and even evil environment in which the protagonist must live. Does the negativity serve as warning or enticement? In a later letter, Abba elaborated on this idea: "I enjoyed those pages, written by a Master, and most of the book was thus; but for me there is a matter of principle, perhaps antiquated but that I retain as just, and that is that the ignoble aspects of life should not be assumed into art, because it doesn't shame the wretched and it doesn't help the good who see enough evil in their reality. Or should art reveal evil?"[66] Pratesi, in his letters to friends and relatives, always remained personally detached from Dr Stellini. Yet, beyond doubt, with the doctor, he succeeded in portraying the most intimate pain of human existence, that of a man fighting alone in a hostile world. He felt that this was his own portrait as well.

In the thirty years that separate Tristano and Fabio Stellini, Pratesi consistently acted as the keen observer of human deportment. His predilection was clearly for the more difficult problematic characteristics of human behaviour, as his literary works readily attest. He wanted his readers to recognize that the stuff of life is not always beautiful; it is also ugly. To succeed in his intentions, Pratesi had struggled to attract the Muse of Poetry. As a young author, he had reprimanded her for her reticence and elusiveness, but she indeed accompanied him faithfully. How significant then that, in *Il Peccato del dottore*, the figure of Poetry should appear to Stellini in his last moments of life insisting that she is no illusion but instead she is "the reality of things and facts transformed into rhythm, into flight, in an all-knowing voice. [She understands] all nature that breathes with intelligence and divine spirit; [she is] the mystery of the universal soul, the most intimate force that connects hearts, making them feel life; through harmony, imagery, and eternal knowledge, [she gives] mankind all the stuff of their dreams, all the horror of their catastrophes, all the giddiness of their infatuations, all the compassion of their sobs, and mankind takes pleasure in this."[67]

Through this personification, Pratesi makes Poetry hold a mirror to us, the readers. We shall not see reflected therein Mario Pratesi dressed in the guise of the young Tristano or the elderly Stellini. We shall not hear a metaphorized version of Pratesi's story. If Pratesi has been of value as author, if he has truly presented the "intimacy and greatest profundity in the human truth of character,"[68] as he had written in his final testament, then we will see reflected therein our own stories and our own selves. The shock, or at least aversion, of such a realization may indeed explain the critical silence that caused Pratesi so much anguish. But, even if the work has artistic weaknesses, it deserves a place in Italian literary history nonetheless, as Guidotti notes, for it "anticipates the restlessness and anxieties of the early 20th century," as it moved towards the inevitability of further world crises.[69] Pratesi was a sensitive and intuitive writer; he had learned a hard lesson from transferring the angst of his own social milieu backwards in time, as he had done in *Il Mondo di Dolcetta*. In *Peccato*, on the other hand, he digs deep into the contemporary world, elucidating the irony that his readers would recognize in their own daily travails and battles of existence. He responds to their ennui, their tiredness, to their awareness of a world propelled towards unnamed changes, for it is also his own.

After the publication of *Il Peccato del dottore*, Pratesi began to think seriously of retiring from his position as school superintendant. In the summer of 1905 he announced that he would leave Belluno by November, hoping to find a quiet port "after so many storms."[70] The letter contains his increasingly bitter and hostile reactions to the critical opinions of his works. To his credit, he did not lay down his pen despite his acrimonious attitude, but continued to prepare works for publication. He gathered several articles and poetry previously published in *Di paese in paese* (1892), and added several more recent pieces for the volume *Figure e paesi d'Italia*, which the publishing house Roux and Viarengo undertook, along with a new edition of *Il Peccato del dottore*. *Figure e paesi d'Italia: Impressioni e ricordi* was ready by mid-December 1904, as Barzellotti noted eagerly; it contained Pratesi's laudatory comments on Barzellotti's studies of the tragic preacher and visionary David Lazzaretti (1834–1878).[71] With this volume, Pratesi returned to his "safe mode," as it were: successful articles, some allowing him to exploit his excellent skills in the travel writing genre, others focusing on his talent in describing people, including beloved Italian composer Giuseppe

Verdi (1813–1901), English poet Percy Bysshe Shelley (1792–1822), and the previously mentioned David Lazzaretti.[72] Barzellotti assured Pratesi that such a volume would most certainly sell well.[73] Barzellotti was correct in his assumptions, and taking advantage of the new publicity garnered for it by Pratesi's work, he himself began to prepare another edition of his study of Lazzaretti.[74] However, he sent no comments regarding Pratesi's *Figure e paesi*. Nor did other friends: Adelaide Maraini thanked Pratesi for dedicating the volume to her husband Clemente in a long note that concerned itself primarily with her health and that of her husband.[75] Francesco Sclavo sent a promise of a faithful future read to be followed by a discussion,[76] as did Luisa Anzoletti.[77] Paolo Savj-Lopez of the University of Catania requested permission to use some of the pages in a new anthology intended for secondary schools, lauding the work as fresh and alive, capable of instilling in young readers a love for their country.[78] But if Pratesi had complained to Bandini and to his brother Dante of the silence of his "informal" critics, he erred in suggesting that formal critics did not care about his book.[79] Although not many, they generally expressed much praise for the book. The *Pro-Caltanissetta e Provincia* (which likely inspired Savj-Lopez's request), declared *Figure e paesi* "one of those few excellent and useful books which should be suggested for our schools to educate aesthetic taste and critical acuity so that students might learn to love their country better, its history and its pure and genteel language." Pratesi, according to this critic, had produced a work of art, in which the places and people described appear as if right before the reader's eyes. It was a book of enviable precision and true genius.[80] Emilio Treves personally gave it his blessing in his regular column in the *Illustrazione italiana*. Calling Pratesi a respected veteran of teaching and writing, he noted that Pratesi's pages should be anthologized in other works for they were filled with excellent representations of reality, new imagery, and melodic verses.[81] He felt that Pratesi proved once again that his real talent lay in writing descriptive travelogues rather than fictional prose. This back-handed compliment enraged Pratesi and provoked him to write a letter of protest in which he acknowledged, with indignant and deliberately feigned humility, those "defective" works of his whose sincerity had proven a literary impediment. He added that he did not appreciate having his descriptive writing lauded at the expense of his fictional works.[82] Another critic, Laura Gropallo, writing in *La Cultura*, noted Pratesi's deep sensitivity to places and persons, a sensitivity resulting in pages that were tenderly and emotionally evocative. For her, the volume embodied delightfully cultured pages dictated by a spirit open to Beauty, and enhanced by a varied and richly supple language.[83] Pratesi's former colleague at Belluno, Giulio Natali, concurred, repeating almost word for word for this volume the praise he had written in his review of *Ricordi veneziani*; Pratesi was "the thinker, the man of taste, the keen observer, the prolific writer gifted with extraordinary linguistic dexterity" to whom the Italian reading public owed much gratitude for his works.[84] Natali also commented on Pratesi's essays of literary criticism, writing that "the value of the critic and essayist explains the intellectual and noble literary wealth of the novelist."[85]

But perhaps most unexpected, and consequently most personally satisfying, were the words of the usually deprecatory *Il Marzocco*. Enrico Corradini who had nursed his personal grudge against the *Nuova Antologia* into an anti-Pratesian tirade, was not the reviewer on this occasion; instead, poet and critic Giuseppe Lipparini (1877–1951) dedicated almost a full page to Pratesi's volume, even though much of the review concerned itself with his own travails as a professor beset by the ignorance of his high school students during final oral examinations. The gist of his jeremiad is this: if Lipparini's young charges had read Pratesi's work, they would be considerably more knowledgeable about Italian geography and more appreciative of their native land. While he found fault with the inclusion of Pratesi's poetry in the volume, feeling that it detracted from the volume's success, he affirmed that Pratesi was one of the most serene and honest of Italian writers, whose fresh outlook on life in little towns and in the countryside expanded not only lungs but also horizons. He found the book to be an intimate travelogue that welcomed the reader into the nooks and crannies of the author's trips along the peninsula, and he wished for more similar works.[86]

The *Rivista d'Italia* wrote similarly. Its unnamed reviewer pointed out the originality of thought, the detailed descriptions, and the attraction of its chapters; the reviewer admired how Pratesi could probe the souls of his subjects, right into their most intimate corners, "whether he studies the complex and well-known figure of Massimo d'Azeglio, or the humble and proud character of the Calabrian peasant girl."[87] This critic, like Giulio Natali, also noted that the book contained chapters of excellent literary criticism, adding however that these pieces were hobbled somewhat by the fact that Pratesi was not objective enough.[88]

By the fall of 1905, Pratesi's volume had become old news, and he returned to his final year as superintendant at Belluno. Barzellotti had written to him, congratulating him on his unwavering commitment to writing and publishing. Perhaps his own family troubles had prevented him from noticing that despite continued literary activitiy, Pratesi had by now fully embodied the defeat he had described in *Peccato del dottore*. He did write, but no longer did his works attract critical attention. Even friends and acquaintances were silent. After *Figure e paesi*, none of his subsequent new works was reviewed in any major periodical, although the re-edition of *Il Mondo di Dolcetta* brought a few accolades in 1916; his nomination as a member of the prestigious Accademia della Crusca, in June 1916, may also have attracted a new readership.[89] Some of his regular informal reviewers, including his beloved friends Abba and Gherardi, had passed away by the time the new edition of *Il Mondo di Dolcetta* was published in 1916, but younger contacts such as poet and writer Luisa Anzoletti, and Nella Mazzoni, daughter of his former publisher Giuseppe Chiarini, wrote to him to express their positive reactions.[90] In addition, the *Rassegna nazionale* published a laudatory letter from poet Alfonso Conte, who said he hoped to read more similar stories by Pratesi in the future.[91] Only one formal review appeared, requested on Pratesi's behalf by Luisa Anzoletti, who had by this time become a close friend of his.[92] Written by Giuseppe Fanciulli for *La Perseveranza*, the review noted the frank and noble literary artistry of Pratesi. For Fanciulli, the book succeeded because it was not simply a novel propelled by plot development; it is also a work where the Sienese countryside played a major role, and a work, moreover, with admirable mastery of the Tuscan language.[93] Nonetheless, Enrico Corradini's negative and spiteful review of the novel's first edition still rankled. It haunted the book's re-edition, indeed, it had actually acted as a prime motivator for the re-edition because, as Pratesi wrote to Bandini in 1916, the original version, "although deeply reflected upon and written at a time of unspeakable difficulties, was met with silence or attracted the unworthy poisonous comments of people like Mr Corradini."[94] Not unexpectedly, Pratesi likely realized the critical unreliability of Fanciulli's review. Solicited by Luisa Anzoletti, who had been trying to find publishers for some of Pratesi's other works, Fanciulli's praise must have seemed like an honourable mention rather than a prize. Pratesi had read Anzoletti's letter informing him that publishers preferred only war stories, and in recommending his works, she had received only negative replies, despite her personal attempts. While she assured him once again that Corradini's review was an act of disrespect towards the *Nuova Antologia* (using the word "hate" to describe it) and not an attack on his excellent writing, she inadvertently also added advice that Pratesi likely remembered with some irony when he read Fanciulli's review: "It would be useful if you were to begin some exchanges with authors here [in Milan] who might possibly have access to being published in the newspapers. In that case, if you cared to comment on their books, by writing your reviews [of them] for important papers, they could return the favour so that publishers would keep you in mind."[95] Fanciulli, of course, was himself a writer; that his review of *Il Mondo di Dolcetta* might have been the result of similar advice from Anzoletti to him about Pratesi could not have been lost on the latter.

In the years after his retirement, Pratesi returned to shorter individual pieces. For the most part, he set aside the travel writing, success notwithstanding, and retreated into the past through novellas set in previous centuries. Happiness eluded him there as well; his pessimism and general cynical dissatisfaction with his life weighed his pages down to a greater degree than previously, but as Guidotti justly notes, there remained in Pratesi the restlessness to write; he deeply desired to try new ways of using language, to assert his moral and aesthetic honesty through literary works.[96] He did not always succeed in the former, but certainly did so in the latter, according to Guidotti. For the most part, Pratesi's short stories appeared in the *Nuova Antologia*, and were edited by Giovanni Cena (1870–1917), with whom Pratesi developed a friendship based on deep mutual respect. The two had begun their publishing collaboration in 1903, and when Cena died, his passing in December 1917 devastated Pratesi, who felt he had lost the last of his friends in a year in which he had reached a personal nadir.[97] Cena oversaw the completion of three stories that occupied Pratesi as he prepared for and then began his retirement years: "La Dama del minuetto" (December 1905), "La Dote di Marcellina" (June 1906), and "La Barba di Meleagro di Bagnaia" (June 1907). Even before the publication of the latter in the *Nuova Antologia*, Pratesi was eagerly searching out a publisher who might collect his latest stories into a single volume which he intended to title *Novelle italiane*,[98] but more than a year passed before he announced the publisher, Sandron. The volume, now called *La Dama del minuetto*, contained the three new stories mentioned above, as well as the previously published stories "Catuzza (Una iettatura)," and "Il Dottor Febo."[99] In addition, he included the article that had appeared in the *Illustrazione italiana* in 1905, "Canto toscano d'autunno." Seven illustrations by the notable artist Gustavo Rosso added visual interest to the work. But, when no one reviewed the volume formally in the weeks just after its publication in 1910, an absence Pratesi felt keenly, he blamed Sandron for a lack of commitment to publicizing the work. The publisher replied that, quite to the contrary, the book had been sent to numerous periodicals, and had been advertised *long and widely* (emphasis in the letter). Exhorting Pratesi to be more patient, he assured him that eventually the book would have its reviews.[100] But there were none.

In the meantime, while preparing the collection *La Dama del minuetto*, Pratesi had also undertaken a longer work of fiction, "La Follia del Marchese Roberto," not a short story but not quite the length of a novel.[101] The plot focused on the inability of the protagonist to deal with a rapidly changing world on the threshold of a new century, so different from the one he had hoped to pass on to future generations of his family. As Guidotti has noted, the Marquis slowly realizes that he has become a disappointed anachronism.[102] Pratesi had already dealt with the theme in "Padre Anacleto di Caprarola" in 1882, but approached it now from the perspective of the secular world alone. Giacomo Barzellotti remained unusually reticent after reading it, and commented only that he found the title character well portrayed.[103] The playwright Gerolamo Rovetta (1851–1910), whom Pratesi had known since his days in Milan, praised the story for its veracity, despite the decadent atmosphere, calling its truth singularly attractive. He noted the believable atmosphere and the strong and clear style.[104] Cesare Abba was more eloquent, observing that the story offered stupendous pages, where plot became perspicacious psychological analysis:

> Marquis Roberto is perfectly rendered. Perhaps [the evil governess] is somewhat exaggerated, but only at certain points; all things considered she, too, is well depicted. The young girl is truly noble, her love like a ray of sunlight ... And that lesson on Dante and Petrarch ... I believe that few pages about the two great authors have been written with such clear vision and with such eloquent and noble understatement. They will certainly be remembered by your readers. And will appear fresh. You actually believe I didn't like the work? You jest ... And I'm sure that this is one of your favourite pieces.[105]

But formal reviewers held back, presaging the silence that would later also surround the volume *Dama del Minuetto*, a year and a half later. Undeterred, Pratesi forged ahead with new stories. Just after "Le due figliuole dell'ostessa" had appeared in the *Nuova Antologia* in early 1910, he even proposed another new anthology of short stories to the publisher Remo Sandron, who gently refused, justifying his decision by pointing out that it would not be financially prudent to publish a book on the same theme by the same author so quickly after the release of the *Dama del minuetto*. Pratesi withdrew the proposal for the time being, but it remained always in his thoughts. Even a decade later, towards the end of his life, his letters to former student Firenze Santandrea indicate that he still hoped to publish new collections of his work. He reiterated this desire in his last will and testament as well.

In 1906, Pratesi, relieved to abandon a teaching career he had considered an encumbrance, moved to lodgings in a house overlooking the city of Florence. The city lay at his feet, the lazily meandering Arno separating him from the hustle and bustle below. Directly across from him he could see the windows of Niccolò Tommaseo's house, now belonging to someone else. Tommaseo and his wife Diamante had died many decades before; their son had become a medical doctor in Spalato (Split) on the Dalmatian coast. Caterina, with whom the young Pratesi had fallen so painfully in love, had become a cloistered nun. He must have remembered Tommaseo's abject poverty as he calculated his own meagre resources. Prudent as he was, his financial situation demanded careful attention to every coin. From 1908 on he supported a housekeeper, Felicità (Cice) Bianchi, and at times also her daughter Annina, in order to help them distance themselves from an abusive family situation.[106] The people who surrounded him were kind and loyal, among them the children of his friends, and also former students. Although he lived alone, he enjoyed regular contact with his brother Dante, now retired from the military, and, like Pratesi, unmarried. Dante lived with the Bandini family: the journalist Gino (1881–1948) who would later become vice-mayor of Rome and who was a founder of Italcable, Amalia (Liuccia) his wife, their two sons, and Augusta Farulli, Gino's mother. Gino, of course, was particularly close to Mario Pratesi, and even when mobilized in the years of the Great War, wrote to him whenever he could.

Pratesi's age and infirmities wore him down. It seems that his Muse had also grown tired. After *La Dama del minuetto* in 1910, there were to be no more volumes of fictional prose, excepting the re-edition of *Il Mondo di Dolcetta* (1916). Nonetheless, he wrote steadily, and in the years before, during, and after the Great War his name appeared regularly in print, in newspaper articles and letters to local papers, but most notably in the *Nuova Antologia* (a longish novella "Armonie e dissonanze" (1913), and short stories "Il Capitano delle corazze" (1911),

"Don Angelo e la sua nipote" (1914), "Troppa grazia Sant'Antonio" (1915), "Acque passate" (1917), "Un povero militare" (1918), and "Il sogno del vecchio Benvenuto" (1920). His non-fictional work, mostly brief essays or obituaries, appeared in the *Rassegna nazionale*. He mentored young writers. Some of his works received perfunctory acknowledgment from friends who received extracts from the periodical. As for published reviews, however, his stories passed unnoticed; even his friends commented only in personal correspondence, praising the masterful stylist, but criticizing him for the dark view he held of the world – a recurring observation that had been made throughout Pratesi's writing career. Luisa Anzoletti used an apt and eloquent metaphor in her reflections on the story "Acque passate." She remarked that the work reminded her of the literary equivalent of Michelangelo's *Last Judgment*.[107] Poet Giuseppe Manni (1844–1923) and dear and old friend Sofia Bertolini Guerrieri Gonzaga (1873–1961) echoed the sentiment.[108] Pratesi read the same comment repeated also for his story "Un povero militare," which focused on the contemporary tragedy of the First World War; only the poet Luisa Santandrea (1890–1963) sent detailed comments in a personal letter, especially praising Pratesi's ability to write so realistically, choosing truth of representation over other literary goals. She wrote that Pratesi had "recognized a great truth with Tolstoyan frankness, even in admitting the necessity of fighting weapons with weapons."[109] The story had been published even as the Great War dragged itself to an end, an event that inspired his friend Sienese sculptress Luisa Mussini (1865–1925) to see in Pratesi's story an example not only of good writing but also of the need for hope in a consolatory Christian faith.[110] How much credence Pratesi gave to the opinions of the three Luisas, Anzoletti, Santandrea, and Mussini, is difficult to judge. He had acted as literary mentor, and also editor, for all three women and would not have expected negative criticism from them. All three also staunchly maintained the rigid optimisim that derived from their unwavering Christian faith. Nonetheless, ill, frustrated, and ever more irascible and lonely, Pratesi must have appreciated their attention to his work, and his letters indicate that he was grateful to be remembered by them.

One story remained for Pratesi: "Il sogno del vecchio Benvenuto." After several delays, it appeared just as the illness that would end his life began to make itself ineluctably and incurably manifest. At the same time, he also worked on the final edition of *Il Peccato del dottore* (Vitagliano, 1920). This was also the moment he composed his last will and testament, which he used not only as a further opportunity to review his career and his works, but also to announce the contents of a possible posthumous book.[111]

Again, with the exception of some perfunctory nods, Pratesi received no critical acknowledgments of the work. In commenting on "Il sogno," Guidotti downplays Guido Mazzoni's opinion, expressed in a memorial tribute after Pratesi's passing, that the the story has some literary merit. For Guidotti, this final novella "seems, in truth, not to go much beyond a good antique print: with its rich shading, bursting with episodes and emotions and turned into mediocre prose."[112] However, Guidotti perhaps had overlooked an essential aspect of the story. "Il sogno del vecchio Benvenuto" is an elegy, a mournful reflection, a regretful lament for a career that had started brilliantly and then had petered out inexorably. Not surprisingly, then, the plot deals with an elderly Benvenuto Cellini, master sculptor, but not appreciated by his patron Cosimo de' Medici who prefers flashy excess to exquisite mastery. He dreams one final masterpiece but dies before he can complete it. Trapped by personal demons, he is beset by problems including aging; his earlier fame has diminished. But Cellini's artistic temperament, his Muse, is a cruel mistress with her tenacious grasp on him, increasing his impatience with those who do not understand art, increasing his isolation. This is also clearly Pratesi's self-portrait, one he describes in a letter to Bandini in 1920 as if he were his own book: "last summer saw the start of my epilogue, or the dark tragedy of old age. It is providential because it makes one desire and even invoke death."[113]

That the story appeared just weeks before he penned his final testament,[114] and during the time he was correcting the final edition of *Il Peccato* should not be overlooked. "Il sogno ..." is, consequently, all the more worth reading and appreciating for its psychological depth, its examination of an excruciating encounter with one's old age, and the feeling of helplessness it instils in battling its inevitable onset. In ontological terms, Pratesi confirms himself as his own archaism in this story, in complementarity with *Il Peccato del dottore*, the story that marked the onset of his end-of-life writing. The realization of this attitude may explain the silence of the reviewers: confronted with narration of the inevitable ravages of time presented over and over after the experimentation of *Il Peccato del dottore*, the reviewers could not offer their readers new enticements to attract public attention for Pratesi's works. Such, after all, is their role as reviewers.

Pratesi was right: old age for him was terrible, it was dark and painful and isolating. But even if he reiterated this in the most elegant of styles, even if he remained the Tuscan perfectionist of language, reviewers could not find original or different aspects to add to the observations they had already made about his writing many times years before. As well as his age, infirmity had added to his naturally pessimistic disposition to lock him personally and in his writing into a reiterative spiral.

Theodor Adorno or Edward Said would refer to this period between 1906 and 1920 as Pratesi's late-style writing. Certainly, like most artists in their late style, after his final full-length novel, Pratesi focused on profound, unornamented work. He concentrated on his literary expertise, which lay in his masterful verbal portraits that poignantly reflected the everyday routines and frustrations familiar to all his readers.

In speaking of Beethoven's late style, Theodor Adorno comments that the composer's "late work still remains process, but not as development; rather as a catching fire between extremes, which no longer allow for any secure middle ground or harmony of spontaneity."[115] After 1906, Pratesi unquestionably corresponded to this description. He remained staunchly enamoured of a Muse that spoke to him of situations more typical to Romantic narrative rather than to contemporary realities. He preferred an almost fetishistic attachment to decay, denouement, and death. He just could not let go of repeated typologies, and responded with intellectualized hostility in justifying his literary stagnation. Hostility, and according to critic Giorgio de Rienzo, also aggressivity, crept in – betraying "Pratesi's awareness of the precise historical context of the problems in his social environment and of which he provides the detailed chronicle."[116] Edward Said has elucidated in his work on late style the restless underpinnings of what, for readers of Pratesi's late fiction, may have seemed an elegant but useless exercise. Said writes: "The actuality of reading is, fundamentally, an act of perhaps modest human emancipation and enlightenment that changes and enhances one's knowledge for purposes other than reductiveness, cynicism, or fruitless standing aside ... Otherwise, why bother at all?[117] For Pratesi, reading and writing had been an emancipation even at the beginning of his life. Hand in hand with this came the deep desire that his works be read and intelligently written about. His correspondence clearly shows his disappointment and discomfort in the face of critical silence.

Said's "otherwise why bother at all?" would have been an important question for Pratesi, and his answer would include the idea that concomitant with changing and enhancing one's knowledge is the idea of bequeathing the knowledge to new generations of readers. This is Pratesi's clear intent in his last will and testament for, in composing the document, he called for a full re-edition of all his works, many of which had already seen several iterations through serialization and then publication as a single volume.

But the future is not the purview of critical reviewers, whose job is to synthesize and comment on a recently published work. Intuitively, they reacted to the lack of vital dynamism in Pratesi's literary corpus, especially after *Il Peccato*: his main protagonist, no matter what his name, had ceased developing and had taken on a defeatist attitude of someone who will never achieve happiness, who will find this crucial piece of his Weltanschauung to be ever elusive. What is left when the wisdom of age and the despair of age catastrophically collide is a simple, stripped-down refrain: man against unbeatable forces unreconciled to his inevitable fate yet paradoxically desiring it and invoking it, as Pratesi told Bandini. This is the essence of Pratesi's late, unreviewed works. Said's "why bother at all?" rings too dismissively for Pratesi who, after all, had won the respect of Italian readers and critics alike, who had been given a place by them among the three major writers of Italian realism or *verismo*, together with Giovanni Verga and Luigi Capuana. But when the reviewers read his post-retirement works, they confronted page after page of the pathos informing the inner turmoil and unquietness of his characters, page after page mirroring his own rapid physical deterioration and which he also described over and over in his correspondence with friends and colleagues.

And it would not be inappropriate to say that out of respect for a literary master, the elegant painter of verbal pictures, but who had become a pathetic old man, the literary reviewers, perhaps with some embarrassment, put down their pens and silently looked away.

Conclusion

Mario Pratesi's relatively long writing career evolved at a pivotal moment for Italian literature. Together with major geopolitical changes that affected the citizens of Italy, intellectual and cultural pursuits also underwent revolutionary upheavals. For example, the search for a new literary reality with its concomitant claim on a national Italian literary identity that Alessandro Manzoni had propelled forward, saw major developments at the very time that Pratesi's career as a writer began. His early employment under the mentorship of statesman and poet-philosopher Niccolò Tommaseo provided an auspicious start, even though Pratesi worked only as a secretary, and for a relatively brief time. Encouraged by a host of new mentors with close and powerful connections to publishers, including Giacomo Barzellotti, Clemente Maraini, Luigi Luzzatti, Vernon Lee, Emilia Peruzzi, Sidney Sonnino, and even Giosuè Carducci, Pratesi answered the invitation of the Muse he felt called to him; he followed his Muse despite initial familial objections, and continuing financial difficulties. As he wrote, he depended on his mentors, and on his admirably wide circle of friends and acquaintances. In his letters to them, which allow us to take a peek into his workshop, following the approach of *critique génétique*, he always asked for comments and suggestions. He listened to advice, though he did not always take it. There were exceptions to this way of proceeding, at the beginning and then again at the end of his career. His first prose narrative, *Da fanciullo: Memorie del mio amico Tristano*, seems to have been the product of psychiatric therapy while he was hospitalized in Siena in 1868–69, a plausible explanation for why it appeared fully elaborated in *Il Diritto* in 1870. In the years after 1906, when he retired from teaching and school administration, his letters once again reveal a paucity of comments on his continuing projects. In the latter case, it is not difficult to surmise that this was due in part to technological advances like the telephone and more rapid travel by train which made conversation easier and letter writing less preferred. But it was also due to the fact that most of his informal reviewers and mentors had onerous positions elsewhere, or more sadly, had passed away.

From his first prose narrative, brief as it was, Pratesi's works found public prominence and acclaim through book reviews. At first indistinguishable from literary criticism, book reviewing came into its own as a genre during the years of Pratesi's writing career. Especially in the latter half of the nineteenth century, book reviews took on the format still familiar to authors today offering full bibliographical information about the book and a short synopsis or description of the contents enhanced by a brief critical appraisal of the book's merits and weaknesses. Unlike a critical review, which provided exegetical or analytical perspectives to an exclusive learned community, book reviews appeared also in more popular periodicals and served to entice (or warn) the reading public. The genre developed throughout Europe almost simultaneously. Pratesi's first attempt at a review, focused on Giuseppe Cesare Abba's *Arrigo* (1866), was probably never published; the critical analysis of the poem betrays a clear bias for the work of a close personal friend. Both Pratesi and Abba knew the value of positive review; it meant better sales and more exposure for the writer, and a better relationship with the publisher. "For all book sellers and publishers," Pratesi wrote to Abba in 1887, "a book is only as good as its sales. A rejection from [a publisher] does not depend on whether a book lacks merit, but on the trends in the [reading] taste of the public which [a publisher], modern and market wise, follows."[1] This Pratesi perceived as a difficult reality, and in his later years he regularly railed against it. Much later in life, Pratesi described the characteristics of a bad book review, implying that a good book review would reveal opposite virtues:

> The critiques [of the reviewers in periodicals], as is customary in Italy, offer either tepid praise, conceded with difficulty and redolent with little censures (sometimes nonsensical) which don't incite anyone to buy the book and are more detrimental than helpful because they make the book appear mediocre. Sometimes they go overboard in praise that no one believes because the words are the same ones used to advertise [medicinal products]. A review that captures the most characteristic and salient aspects of the book, that touches on its profound thought, is hardly ever seen

in our periodicals. Book reviews generally lack any awareness of balanced critique, and not only rarely does one sense the reviewer's envy [towards the author].[2]

Pratesi, too, at times felt envious of younger authors, of their popularity, as his correspondence shows.

A critique génétique approach allows an interdisciplinary study of an author and his or her works. Inevitably, it leads to considerations on how the author's life events affected, shaped, and biased the written pages produced. A study using this approach almost by necessity becomes a type of biography. Pratesi's lifelong battle against depression with its inescapable physical debilitations played a fundamental role in his works. Publication after publication is an excursus into the heart and soul of a sensitive and easily discouraged man, who through his friends, and also through his Muse, found the energy to continue writing. But it also means that the same dour, gloomy themes pervaded his works. This can also be said for his deep conviction that he was somehow being disadvantaged. This aspect appears in his correspondence and in his fictional characters as cynicism. On the other hand, he filled his travel pieces with the joy and sheer pleasure of the destination, of its detail, of his discovery of it. And rightly, Pratesi was an acclaimed success in these pieces. Critics confirmed this again and again, and he sometimes felt slighted by the praise for the travel articles, feeling it detracted from the value of his fictional prose. Whether fiction or travel piece or essay, all critics noted and eloquently praised Pratesi's mastery of language, of the nuances and effects of Tuscan words, phrases, and cadences. But, in the end, the language was not enough to sustain his popularity before a quickly changing social and literary environment. Milanese poet Luisa Santandrea, and her husband, Firenze, a former student of Pratesi's, tried to change the sad reality of their mentor's rejection by the readers of the early twentieth century. Writing to her friend Gina Lombroso Ferrero in Florence, Luisa Santandrea summarizes the trying circumstances of Pratesi's life in the brief months before he passed away. Financial difficulties, added to physical torment caused by his cancer, and yet, as always, there was the enduring hope that perhaps his writing could be valued again. Santandrea writes:

> In little more than a year we have supported him with 2,000 lire. Pratesi himself can also tell you, because we always send him the letters, that on various occasions, we have tried a number of publishers: Treves, "Sten" of

Torino, Bemporad, Casa Varietas, etc., always including copies of books, but our attempts have all been *in vain*! All the publishers say that Pratesi's books are very well conceived and written, but they just are not the type that suits today's tastes … They don't want to take any risks [by publishing him], much less offer him an advance.

But since it doesn't hurt to keep trying, we three can continue doing so: I in Milan, you in Florence, and Trigona in Rome.

… the most suitable *novels* are: *L'Eredità*, *Il Mondo di Dolcetta*, *Jacopo e Marianna*, *Le Perfidie del caso*, and the *novellas* "La Follia del Marchese Roberto," "Troppa grazia Sant'Antonio," "Acque passate," and others, and some of the [other] *volumes* such as *Figure e paesi d'Italia*, *Ricordi veneziani* (this last is beautiful, among his best along with *L'Eredità*).

Let's keep in touch … and not bait Pratesi with vain hope because (and I know this *from personal experience*), he is really prone to *illusion*, and also feels *entitled*; as long as his friends act on his behalf with the publishers, he is calm and even too kind – but once the publishers enter the picture directly, even as a far-off hope, he loses the serenity of patience, and believes they exploit him …, finding injustices and villainy and so on.[3]

Luisa Santandrea is not Pratesi's book reviewer here, nor is her letter a review. But in her words, we can understand her genuine affection for the Tuscan author, her mentor. We can sense her desire to alleviate some of the psychological pain of his last days. We can read her own confirmation that he had been a writer of some literary worth, a notable contributor to the development of Italy's literary identity. Literary critics, including Benedetto Croce, began to notice Pratesi's works after his death. But it was the book reviewers, his contemporaries, who applauded him first and in this way acknowledged how fundamentally he participated in the late nineteenth-century world of Italian letters, even as he felt in his youth he had wanted to do. Even as his Muse had demanded he do.

Notes

Introduction

1 Opening line of *A Tale of Two Cities* by Charles Dickens (1859).
2 Jessie Laussot Hillebrand to Pratesi, 11 Oct. 1889. The book is the *Manuale di musica all'uso degli insegnanti ed alunni* by Giovanni Alibrandi (Turin: Loescher, 1881).
3 Nicola Abbagnano, "Positivism," in *Encyclopedia of Philosophy*, edited by Donald M. Borchert (Detroit: Macmillan Reference USA, 2006), vol. 7, 2nd ed., 710–17.
4 The quote "Having made Italy, it is now necessary to make the Italians" is generally attributed to statesman Massimo Taparelli, Marquis of Azeglio (1798–1866), although controversy exists as to its exact source.
5 But one example is Emilia Peruzzi's use of *pastetta* in the sense of political or electoral imbroglio in her letter of 22 Feb. 1882. Italian dictionaries generally attribute its etymology to a much later date.
6 Louis Hay, "Genetic Criticism: Origins and Perspectives," in Jed Deppman, Daniel Ferrer, and Michael Groden, eds., *Genetic Criticism: Texts and Avant-textes* (Philadelphia: University of Pennsylvania Press, 2004), 23.
7 Jean Bellemin-Noël, "Psychoanalytic Reading and Avant-texte," ibid., 28.
8 See Edward Said, *On Late Style: Music and Literature against the Grain* (New York: Pantheon, 2006). A fuller discussion follows in the last chapter.
9 Hay, "Genetic Criticism," 22.
10 Bonghi continued to visit the Salotto until political differences after the 1876 fall of the right-wing government divided their friendship irreparably. Edmondo de Amicis, *Un salotto fiorentino del secolo scorso* (Florence: Barbèra, 1902), 29.

11 Ruggero Bonghi, "Prefazione," in Nicola Bernardini, *Guida alla stampa periodica italiana* (Lecce: Editrice Salentina, 1890), iii.
12 Tullio De Mauro, in *Storia linguistica dell'Italia unità* (Bari: Laterza, 1970), indicates that in the period beginning the Italian unification process (1861), the peninsula had a population of 25 million people. Only 2.5% (some 600,000, living mostly in Tuscany or near Rome, could communicate in Standard Italian). Comparative statistics for the time show that in fact the rate of illiteracy in Italy stood at 77.7% in 1861, and had decreased to 67.2% by 1880. The statistics for England in these years are 31% and 14%, respectively. See http://cronologia.leonardo.it/analfa1.htm
13 The novella , written in 1869, was first published in instalments in *Il Diritto* (19, 20, and 21 March 1870). It appeared as an extract later that year in a small booklet published by Civelli in Florence and later in book form together with the poem *La tarantella sul Lido*, published by Le Monnier in Florence in 1872 entitled *Da fanciullo: Memorie del mio amico Tristano*.
14 Advances in printing techniques and machinery were numerous in this period, and included the introduction, in 1840, of wood pulp paper (rather than rag paper) which, while of lesser quality, was far less expensive. This in turn allowed more supply for a market that had clearly increased its demand for periodicals. For a full discussion, see Mario Lombardo and Fabrizio Pignatel, *La stampa periodica in Italia: Mezzo secolo di riviste illustrate* (Rome: Editori Riuniti, 1985), 7–37.
15 Giovanni Bardazzi, "Lettori e critici: '*Il Conciliatore*' e Manzoni; Foscolo e Leopardi; Mazzini, Cattaneo, Tenca; Tommaseo," in *Storia della letteratura italiana*, vol. XI, *La critica letteraria dal Due al Novecento*, edited by Enrico Malato (Rome: Salerno, 2003), 648.
16 Edward A. Bloom, "'Labors of the Learned': Neoclassic Book Reviewing Aims and Techniques," *Studies in Philology* 54/4 (1957), 537.
17 Evelina Orteza y Miranda, "On Book Reviewing," *Journal of Educational Thought* 30 (Aug. 1996), 191.
18 Bloom, "'Labors of the Learned,'" 537.
19 Virginia Woolf, *Reviewing*, with a Note by Leonard Woolf (London: Hogarth Press, 1969 [1939]), 7.
20 Roger Philip McCutcheon, "The Beginnings of Book-Reviewing in English Periodicals," *PMLA* 37/4 (1922), 698.
21 *Perfect Diurnall* 270 (25 Sept.–2 Oct. 1648), 2175, as quoted in McCutcheon, "The Beginnings," 701. Diodati (1576–1649), a Protestant theologian whose family had fled from Lucca to Switzerland because of religious beliefs, translated the Bible into Italian in the first years of the seventeenth century. He used Greek and Hebrew sources for his work. The publication

referred to here is *Annotationes in Biblia* (1607) whose English title was *Pious and Learned Annotations upon the Holy Bible*.
22 Ruggero Bonghi, "Concetto e ragioni di questa pubblicazione," *La Cultura* 1/1 (1882), 1.
23 Derek Roper, *Reviewing before Edinburgh, 1708–1802* (London: Methuen, 1978), 19.
24 Bonghi, "Concetto e ragioni," 1. The phrase *La Republique des Lettres* is found in Sallo's preface to the *Journal*.
25 Enrico Malato, in *Storia della letteratura italiana*, vol. XI, *La critica letteraria dal Due al Novecento*, edited by Enrico Malato (Rome: Salerno, 2003), 564. Bonghi does not mention Bacchini.
26 Bonghi,"Concetto e ragioni," 1.
27 Malato, in *Storia*, 565.
28 The information for this section on Baretti is from a summary by Malato, in *Storia*, 570–4.
29 Roper, *Reviewing*, 26. The five reviewing journals were (in order of importance) *Monthly Review, Critical Review, English Review, Analytical Review,* and *British Critic*.
30 Enzo Bottasso, *Storia della biblioteca in Italia* (Milan: Editrice Bibliografica, 1984), 199.
31 Bruce Macphail, "Book Reviews and the Scholarly Publisher," in James O. Hoge, ed., *Literary Reviewing* (Charlottesville: University Press of Virginia, 1987), 104.
32 James O. Hoge, "Introduction," in *Literary Reviewing*, ibid., viii.
33 Bonghi, "Concetto e ragioni," 24.
34 Ibid.
35 *Hamlet*, Act I, Sc. v, 166–7.
36 "Tutti i libri troveranno ricetto ed accoglienza purché mostrino un coscienzioso lavoro di mente, ed un leale desiderio di cogliere il bello nell'arte o il vero nella scienza. A questo leale desiderio per parte degli autori risponderà un leale annuncio per parte dei critici." Bonghi, "Concetto e ragioni," 8.
37 Bardazzi, "Lettori e critici," 649.
38 Anthony Curtis, *Lit Ed: On Reviewing and Reviewers* (Manchester: Carcanet, 1998), 2. Nicola Bernardini has identified a large number but not all of the pseudonyms used in contemporary Italian journals. He also recounts how jealously guarded the real names of the writers were, starting from the refusal on principal of the publisher of *Antologia*, Giampietro Vieusseux, to reveal the names of the authors who had criticized the Russian czar in his journal.

39 Notice in *La Cultura* 2/1 (1 May 1882), title page.
40 Clemente Maraini to Pratesi, 21 Nov. 1872.
41 *Diary of Virginia Woolf*, 5 vols., edited by Anne Oliver Bell and Andrew McNellie (London: Hogarth Press, 1975–80). Quote taken from entry on 18 Feb. 1922, found in vol. 2, 69.
42 Virginia Woolf, *Reviewing*, 5.
43 Ibid, 14.
44 Ibid, 22.
45 Note by Leonard Woolf, in ibid., 28–31.
46 In Italy, the first bibliographical compendium of periodicals held in Italian libraries dates to 1885. The *Elenco delle pubblicazioni periodiche ricevute dalle biblioteche pubbliche governative d'Italia nel 1884* (Rome: Presso i principali librai, 1885), includes 26 libraries; among them they subscribed to 1,890 Italian and foreign periodicals. For an excellent study on the rapid growth of public libraries, see Bottasso, *Storia della biblioteca*.

Chapter 1: Florence

1 Mario Pratesi to G.C. Abba, 26 Oct. 1872. The correspondence between Pratesi and Giuseppe Cesare Abba is quoted with the kind permission of the heirs of Pratesi, unless otherwise indicated. All translations are my own, unless otherwise indicated.
2 Pratesi to Abba, 27 Nov. 1872.
3 He also uses it to describe *Jacopo e Marianna* in a letter to Emilia Peruzzi of 14 Nov. 1872. Letter conserved in Biblioteca Nazionale Centrale di Firenze (BNCF), Fondo Peruzzi, Cassetta 158, ins.16–21.
4 Brothers Tito and Priamo (deceased in infancy) were the sons of Igino Pratesi and Caterina Meoni (died 1836), while Dante and Mario's mother was Edda Bandini (died 1846). The mother of siblings Plinio and Corinna was Anna Maria Galletti, who died in 1857. Igino died in 1891.
5 Pratesi to Abba, 16 Apr. 1872.
6 Pratesi to Abba, 17 Nov. 1867: "Tu sapessi poi quanto dolga anche a me di non essere stato di quel pugno di generosi che provarono primi i fucili Chasspot a Mentana! Ieri sera saliva la costa di Belvedere per recarmi da un pover'uomo, mio conoscente che gli muore la moglie ed è disperato. Credeva che non sarei arrivato in cima, tanto il cuore batteva e mi faceva affannoso. Che avrei fatto, diceva, a Mentana e a Monterotondo? Ah! Se non fossi distrutto qual sono farei altra figura da questa che io fo miserissima!"
7 Mario Pratesi Archives, Victoria University Library, Toronto.

8 Pratesi to Abba, early June 1867.
9 Pratesi to Abba, 2 June 1870.
10 Pratesi to Abba, Aug. 1867.
11 Gino Bandini, "Giuseppe Cesare Abba e Mario Pratesi. Mezzo secolo di amicizia in un carteggio inedito," *Pegaso* 4/7 (1932), 20. The letter is erroneously dated 27 Jan. 1867 instead of 1868; Pratesi was hired in the late summer or early fall of 1867 as indicated in his letter to Tommaseo of 14 Apr. 1868 (Carteggio Tommaseo, Tomm Cass 117, ins 17 now in BNCF).
12 Pratesi to Niccolò Tommaseo, 14 Apr. 1868 (Tomm Cass 117, ins 17).
13 Pratesi to Abba, 22 Aug. 1874, and also Pratesi to Giosuè Carducci, 22 Dec. 1869, letter now preserved in the Casa Carducci Archives, Cartone XCIII.42 (26.243).
14 Igino Pratesi a Mario Pratesi 8 Dec. The letters reveal a much more empathetic man than biographical information published to date presents.
15 Mario Pratesi, *Per una morta fanciulla; La chiesuola di Ponte alle Grazie; L'Angelo custode* (Siena: Tip. Mucci), 1869.
16 Throughout his correspondence but especially in his letter to Carducci noted above (Pratesi to Carducci, 22 Dec. 1869).
17 Other pieces published in 1869 included the poems *A Caterina Benincasa*, *In Morte di Giovan Battista Bertossi uno dei Mille*, *Ai colli di Firenze – Ricordanze*, and *La tarantella sul lido*. Besides these, he had also published various articles in this period including "Dialogo de' morti del Camposanto della Misericordia al giungere delle ceneri di Quinto Settano" (*Volontario di Siena*), "Le glorie e le gioie del lavoro di Paolo Mantegazza" (*Il Diritto*), and "D'una academia musicale offerta dalla Società Cherubini" (*Il Sistro*). Letter to Abba, 15 Apr. 1870. The latter two articles are of biographical importance because they confirm his acquaintance and friendship with Clemente Maraini (publisher of *Il Diritto*) and Jessie Laussot Hillebrand (founder of the Società Cherubini), both of whom supported him with encouragement and financial help. The original title, *Le Memorie del mio amico Tristano* was subsequently changed to *Da Fanciullo: Memorie del mio amico Tristano*. See Mario Pratesi, *Da fanciullo: Memorie del mio amico Tristano; Edizioni 1883 e 1872*, ed. C.A. Madrignani and G. Bertonicini (Pisa: ETS Editrice), 1991.
18 Mario Guidotti, *Un'aurora dall'Amiata* (Siena: Maia, 1956), 35, and also in *Il romanzo toscano e Mario Pratesi* (Florence: Vallecchi, 1983), 38.
19 Pratesi to Abba, 13 May 1869: "Ed io l'arte mia che avrei desunta dal mio proprio sentire, la mia propria maniera non d'altri, l'avrei avuta. Ed era d'ispirarmi nei fatti minuti e semplici della vita, di cercare l'idealità nel reale dei fatti comuni, di porre in luce quanto v'è di più recondito di meno curato e pregiato nel mondo, di mostrare il senso estetico delle cose più

naturali che accadono tutti i giorni, di far vedere le lagrime di certe situazioni sociali, certe apparenze sia della natura, sia della umana esistenza, arte casalinga, semplice, passionata, lirica e satira insieme che riflettesse tutti i colori del prisma sociale, tutte le armonie della vita e della natura."

20 Livi, inspired by Goethe's *The Sorrows of Young Werther*, was highly interested in studying suicide and crimes of imitation. Suicide, he felt, was not always an act of madness. Later he also urged the abolition of capital punishment. A more detailed study can be found in Paolo Francesco Peloso and Tom Dening, "The Abolition of Capital Punishment: Contributions from Two Nineteenth-Century Italian Psychiatrists," *History of Psychiatry* 20/2 (2009), 216.

21 The Pratesi archives contain the first version *La vita dell'infanzia: Memorie dell'amico Tristano* (Florence: Civelli, 1870; this booklet was an extract of the instalments published in *Il Diritto*, The last page ends with the following information: Florence 26 Feb. 1870, Mario Pratesi, a date which anticipates the appearance of the story in *Il Diritto*. The archives also contain a copy of *Da Fanciullo: Memorie del mio amico Tristano; La Tarantella sul Lido* (Florence: Le Monnier, 1872; with no date or signature on last page). In the 1883 version of the story, Pratesi indicates on the last page that the book was written in 1869.

22 The brief novella was republished in 1872 as indicated above, but also as part of *In Provincia* (Florence: Barbèra, 1883), then in *Letture italiane tratte da opere recenti e annotate da Sofia Heim*, 2nd revised and expanded ed. (Zurich: F. Schulthess, 1892), and more recently in M. Pratesi, *Racconti*, edited by G. Luti and J. Soldateschi (Rome: Salerno, 1979).

23 Madrignani and Bertonicini, *Da fanciullo*, 7. The book underwent a title change. I will refer to it as *Da Fanciullo* (later title) or *Le Memorie* (earlier title).

24 Ibid., 8–10.

25 Ibid., 12

26 Ibid., 11.

27 Ibid., 9. Pratesi's article was a harbinger of the theme of the cemetery which would fascinate him all his life: "Dialogo dei morti del Camposanto della Misericordia al giungere delle ceneri di Quinto Settano," firmato Tristano *Il volontario: Periodico settimanale della giovine democrazia* 1/32 (8 Sept. 1869), 2–3.

28 In the same review, he also considered two other volumes, neither of which is even remotely similar to Pratesi's work; one dealt with new plans for a railway between Porto-Civitanova and Foligno, and the other was a report on financial support awarded in 1871 to artisans and workers.

29 Diogene (Attilio Brunialti), review of *Da fanciullo: Memorie del mio amico Tristano* in *La Tarantella sul Lido* (Florence: Le Monnier, 1872) and in *Il Diritto*, 7 Feb. 1872.
30 Pratesi to Abba, 23 June 1869.
31 Guidotti, *Un'aurora dall'Amiata*, 40, and also in *Il romanzo toscano e Mario Pratesi*, 43.
32 Guidotti, *Un'aurora dall'Amiata*, 41, and also in *Il romanzo toscano e Mario Pratesi*, 44.
33 Pratesi to Abba, 15 Sept. 1870: "Io ho finito il mio racconto. Sono 28 capitoli che mi sono scoppiati dal cuore. Ci ho messo l'anima mia, le mie lagrime, la mia bile, e la mia lingua di Siena; tuttavia non credo d'aver fatto nulla di buono."
34 Pratesi to Abba, 18 Dec. 1870: "Ho troppo rispetto per l'arte che io adoro, perché mi possa mettere a lavorare quando mi sento incapace di trarre dal mio animo l'ispirato concetto. Oh Dio quanto sono infelice! Che spasimo, che tortura è mai questa! E non posso più piangere!"
35 Abba to Pratesi, 31 Aug. 1871.
36 Ibid.
37 All known in their French versions; *Madame Bovary* appeared in Italian in 1881 (translated by Oreste Cenacchi), *Thérèse Raquin* in 1880 (translated by L. Rocco). Baudelaire's *Fleurs* were known but not translated until 1893.
38 Abba to Pratesi, 31 Aug. 1871: "narra come fanno le nonne, che procedono diritte nel loro racconto." Here Abba may have been reflecting contemporary research and appreciation of the oral tradition. Pratesi would have known of these through his work with Tommaseo, always deeply attached to the authentic voice of the populace, as his treatises on language, and in particular *Della bellezza educatrice* (1838), describe.
39 Giacomo Barzellotti to Pratesi, 24 Dec. 1880: "Il mio discorso al Circolo filologico sull'importanza dello studio delle letterature straniere nel presente stato della cultura nazionale andò bene. Parlai con franchezza e senza timore del pubblico per un'ora e qualche minuto e mi parve che il pubblico non si nojasse."
40 All quotes above from Abba to Pratesi, 22 Oct. 1871.
41 Pratesi, however, had not completely forgotten the situation, and in 1873, asked Giacomo Barzellotti to seek Tommaseo's assurance that no misunderstandings remained between them regarding a possible marriage to Caterina. Tommaseo replied that no proposal had ever been specifically made for his daughter's hand, and none would have been accepted. Barzellotti to Pratesi, 3 Mar. 1873.
42 Tommaseo to Pratesi, 27 Sept. 1871.

43 Tommaseo to Pratesi, 15 Nov. 1872.
44 Tommaseo to Pratesi, 7 Feb. 1872: "E perché prende Ella sempre a ritrarre preti ridicoli, come se non ce ne fosse tra' laici di ridicoli e peggio? Lo scherno non ammaestra, il disprezzo non ispira valore: un raggio di bene rischiara lunghe miglia di buio. Scriva, come fa, sempre schietto; si riguardi da qualche locuzione che dal popolo non avrà intesa."
45 Barzellotti to Pratesi, 2 Aug. 1872: "pur in questo anzi è segno del gusto che tu hai per l'armonia e le proporzioni di un lavoro d'arte; e del resto in un tempo in cui di descrizioni, fitte e rifitte di particolari minuti, ne abbiamo fino agli occhi, io te ne lodo di molto."
46 Barzellotti to Pratesi, 19 Dec. 1872
47 Barzellotti, review of *Jacopo e Marianna* in *Nuova Antologia* 22 (Jan. 1873), 246–53.
48 C. Corsi to Pratesi, 18 Sept. 1872.
49 S. Sonnino, *Lettere di Sidney Sonnino ad Emilia Peruzzi, 1872–1878*, edited by Paola Carlucci (Pisa: Scuola Normale Superiore, 1998).
50 Sofia Bertolini Guerrieri-Gonzaga to Pratesi, 5 Apr. 1905.
51 A. Brunialti to Pratesi, 22 Nov. 1872: "Ho insistito un po' troppo, gli è vero sopra una, che m'è parsa *linea pura* del suo Jacopo. Ma, che vuole? Lei sa che animali sono i lettori, non parlar vero di aver nella mangiatoja tutto fieno di quello scelto e ci vogliono dentro qualche fil di paglia. Per me, a dir del libro suo quello che ne sentivo, ci avrei detto ancor meglio, ma per togliere qualsiasi dubbio, ho dovuto cercar fuori con la mia lanterna una qualche pecca, foss'anco lieve, tanto da temperar la lode così che apparisse vera anche a' più scettici."
52 The other two authors reviewed are Salvatore Farina and Anton Giulio Barrili.
53 The student wrote: "Il signor Pratesi, adunque, sia bene attento, è un sant'uomo, più santo del prof. Santa Maria, più immacolato del *vergine e martire* Rozza, che i signori della Deputazione, guidati dal patriarca Villari ed ispirati dallo Spirito Santo, come anello di congiunzione tra i due poteri [militanti?] in Pavia, rappresentati da Don Lucido e Bargoni, scelsero a docente di lettere italiane nell'Istituto Tecnico. E le lettere hanno in costui un valente campione, e gli studenti dell'Istituto Tecnico un ottimo insegnante.

"Basta solo il dire che spende l'intera ora della lezione nello spiegare o la verginità di Maria, o la infallibilità del pontefice, o il miracolo di Sant'Antonio e del suo porco ... il sig. Pratesi, saprà in mezzo a tanta corruzione e in mezzo all'ateismo ... condurre la gioventù per la retta via ed insegnare loro la vera morale, ed alla fine il sentiero che conduce al paradiso."

The pages are undated, but Pratesi's correspondence about the matter suggests the issue was published of the end of January. My sincere thanks to Dr Marianna Bruschi of the newspaper *Provincia pavese* who patiently and tenaciously searched for this document in the archives of the newspaper.

54 Pratesi to Abba, 3 Feb. 1873.
55 Pratesi to Abba, 12 Mar. 1873.
56 Ibid.
57 Pratesi to Abba, 23 Apr. 1873: "quello adolcinato inutile e frivolissimo romanzucolo il quale hanno voluto strombazzare non so per qual dirizzone. Il pensiero di dover lasciare quell'orma vana dietro di me, quell'aborto, quel minuzzolo, quell'ala di moscerino, il quale ne' tre mesi che sopravviverà [sic] al padre suo non potrà che attestarne il fiacco, gretto e misero ingegno mi tormenta molto più dei tubercoli."
58 Pratesi to Abba, 30 May 1873.
59 Anonymous reviewer in *L'Opinione* (Turin), 15 Mar. 1873.
60 Giuseppe Solimbergo, review of *Jacopo e Marianna* in *Gazzetta d'Italia* (Florence), 11 Apr. 1873.
61 G.L. Piccardi, review of *Jacopo e Marianna* in *Gazzetta del Popolo* (Rome), 11 July 1873.
62 *Vita Nuova* (Siena), 27 Apr. 1873. In the original letter, Carcano also advises Maraini to send a copy of the novel to Alessandro Manzoni, which Pratesi apparently did. He received a note of thanks from Manzoni.
63 *Historisches Lexikon der Schweiz/Dictionnaire historique de la Suisse/Dizionario storico della Svizzera*. http://www.hls-dhs-dss.ch/textes/i/I30530.php
64 Clement Maraini to Pratesi, 13 Feb. 1872.
65 Maraini to Pratesi, 7 Feb. 1873.
66 Maraini to Pratesi, 10 Nov. 1872.
67 Nicola Bernardini, *Guida alla stampa periodica italiana* (Lecce: Editrice Salentina, 1890), 625.
68 Alessandro Gherardi to Pratesi, 26 Mar. 1872.
69 Maraini to Pratesi, 19 Apr. 1872: "Spero che la tosse colla buona stagione sarà calmata, e insieme alla tosse scacci anche quella cattiva compagna che è la melanconia. Ella è giovane, ha ingegno, e, se ciò può avere un valore, ha un'amico che vorrebbe vederlo contento, felice ed operosamente tranquillo. Le parrà la mia forse una contradizione nei termini: ma non è. Io pure ho un temperamento malinconico e chiuso; ma per vincere gli altri nella battaglia della vita, ho dovuto prima abituarmi a vincere me stesso. Ella che ha tanto valore di mente e di carattere, se vorrà vincerà. E di ciò sarebbe lieto come di fortuna sua il di Lei amico sincero e leale Maraini."
70 Maraini to Pratesi, 24 June 1874.

71 Luzzatti Luigi (to Pratesi 30 May 1873) copied for Pratesi his letter to the Minister of Education Ferraris justifying the request for a transfer from Pavia: "Pratesi è pieno di gentilezza, di onestà, e di poesia. È un alto poeta inornato[?] della sventura! Languirebbe nelle aure e bassure uliginose di Pavia. Portalo a *Terni* o a Viterbo promuovendolo a *titolare*."
72 Pratesi to Abba, 30 May 1873.
73 Pratesi to Abba, 1 Aug. 1873.

Chapter 2: Milan

1 For an in-depth study of the habitués of the salotto, see Lucille Mary Fortunato De Lisle, "The Circle of the Pear: Emilia Toscanelli Peruzzi and Her Salon – Political and Cultural Reflections, Issues and Exchange of Ideas in the New Italy, 1860–1880" (1 Jan. 1989), *Boston College Dissertations and Theses*, Paper AAI9015796.
2 Mario Pratesi to G.C. Abba, 9 Apr. 1873. The correspondence between Pratesi and Giuseppe Cesare Abba is quoted with the kind permission of the heirs of Pratesi, unless otherwise indicated.
3 Pratesi to Abba, 28 Oct. 1873.
4 Giacomo Barzellotti to Pratesi, 1874, before Apr.
5 Ibid.
6 It was following this visit that Pratesi misinterpreted the friendly letter from Giulia Maraini as a demonstration of her romantic interest in him.
7 Pratesi to Clemente Maraini, 6 Apr. 1874: "Io questi ultimi giorni ho scritto un altra umile novelluccia la quale avendola prima pensata molto, è compita ora del tutto per ciò che riguarda i caratteri, l'orditura, la partizione; insomma il concetto non rimane che l'opera della lima. Alla fine di questo mese spero che sarà in punto, ed io gliela manderò perche Ella la pubblichi nel *Diritto*. S'intitola: *Una rissa* ovvero *corruzione ed amore*. Titolo un po' patriarcale e alla carlona, ma che corrisponde al mio concetto. Son proprio contento di poterle dare qualcosa."
8 Ibid.: "Questo lavoro mi venne fatto con molta facilità[?]: e nell' animo mi [illeggibile] un pò di fiducia che a scrivere racconti del genere popolare, non mi manchi affatto la vena. Ad alimentare questa vena, impedita da tanto perversa fortuna, giova il desiderio grande che è in me che il nostro popolo abbia lettura, delle quali, in mezzo a tante frivolezze, a tante indifferenza e a tanto materialismo, sia raccomandata la fede operatrice di miracoli come dicono il Guicciardini ed il Goethe: la fede, non quale la giudica il Vaticano ma quale era sentita dal Manzoni e dal Mazzini, le anime più grandi che abbia avuto la penisola in questo secolo."

9 Ibid.: "Quando mi metto a scrivere, non tollero più nessun altra faccenda, la lezione mi riesce insoffribile, perdo il sonno, e la mia irritabilità cresce in modo da non soffrire intorno a me che voli una mosca. Tortura grande davvero! Basta pazienza! e avanti ancora!"
10 He had previously admitted this to Giosuè Carducci in a letter of 22 Dec. 1869 (letter now preserved in the Casa Carducci Archives, Cartone XCIII.42 (26.243).
11 Pratesi to Abba, 22 Aug. 1874.
12 Barzellotti to Pratesi, 20 Aug. 1874.
13 Fatini suggests, in "Un romanziere amiatino, Mario Pratesi (Lettere a Giacomo Barzellotti)," *Annuario 1931–32 del Liceo Ginnasio Carducci Ricasoli*, that they may have met in Florence or Pisa. Guidotti confirms Pisa.
14 Giacomo Barzellotti, *Delle dottrine filosofiche nei libri di Cicerone: Tesi di Laurea di G. Barzellotti* (Florence: Barbèra, 1869).
15 Pratesi to Lina Trigona, 20 Sept. 1917: "La triste notizia m'ha tolto il sonno stanotte, e ora m'impiglia la parola in una specie di singhiozzo muto dell'anima che ricorda, e che più non riavrà quello che ricorda: 59 anni di amicizia! Un'eguale passione degli studi ci univa: passione che animò, e da giovani e da vecchi, tanti nostril colloqui che ora son finiti per sempre … Parve poco sensibile perché soffrì il dolore delle sue sventure domestiche celatamente, fortemente da filosofo e da cristiano."
16 Barzellotti to Pratesi, summer 1866: "trovasti nella infelicità che ti opprimeva tante forze (forse non quanta avresti potuto) per condurre alcuni studj, e ti esercitasti nell'italiano e nel latino: quest'ultimo ti aprì la via di una nuova letteratura, di una nuova storia, di un nuovo ordine di studj. Cerca in te stesso e non ti troverai tanto povero."
17 "Belisario," *Nuova Antologia* (Mar.–Apr. 1876), and later in the volume *In Provincia* (Florence: Barbèra, 1883 and 1884).
18 Barzellotti to Pratesi, Jan. 1875-A: "Ritrovo il tuo solito fare naturale, parco, semplice; il tuo modo di osservare e di descrivere. Le prime due o tre pagine mi sono parse anche questa volta quello che ti dissi costì, un po' studiosamente lavorate; ci si sente stridere un po' le pulegge classiche nel movimento dello stile; ma poi la forma piglia (mi pare) un andamento più piano, quale tu le hai volute dare. Via via che leggevo, ho notato (in margine con puntini impercettibili che non hanno significato se non per me solo, e che una ditata cancella) i particolari che o mi dispiacciono, o vorrei mutati; e che tu, se vuoi, potrai mutare sulle bozze; ma son cose da nulla. Per notartene qualcuno."
19 Barzellotti to Pratesi, Jan. 1875-C.

20 Barzellotti to Pratesi, Jan. 1875-B.
21 Barzellotti to Pratesi, Jan. 1875-C.
22 Ibid.
23 Clemente Maraini to Pratesi, 4 May 1875.
24 Barzellotti to Pratesi, 29 May 1875: "Ma perché hai lasciata la Novella? Perché, ricreata, come di dicevi, che l'hai nei mesi passati, non la mandi di nuovo all'Antologia, invece di tenerla nel cassetto? Anche così com'era prima poteva essere pubblicata con moltissimo tuo onore; ora poi sono certo che farebbe tutt'altra figura anche per qualche lato in cui prima era meno bella, perché la pratica che ho del tuo modo di correggere e di limare i lavori mi assicura che tu le avrai certamente mutato faccia. Deciditi dunque, e non ti scoraggiare ora che sei in porto."
25 Pratesi to Abba, 20 May 1876.
26 Ibid.
27 Abba to Pratesi, 25 Aug. 1876.
28 Ibid.
29 Barzellotti to Pratesi, May 1876: "tu vuoi che te ne dica schiettamente il mio parere ed eccotelo. Mi è piaciuta, perché ci ho trovato verità di disegno e di colorito, senza esagerazione, molti affetti, benissimo descritti a tratti principali dei caratteri e anche acutamente analizzate parecchie situazioni; buonissima e artisticamente delicata, come al solito, la forma, sicché, come si diceva anche coll'Hillebrand di novelle scritte a quel modo l'Antologia non ne aveva avute finora; e non sembra finora possa averne da altri che da te. Il fatto, la favola, l'intreccio rimane come ti dissi un po' tenue e un po' smilzo; ... perché forse l'azione si affretta poco e ha pochi incidenti; poco movimento. Bada potrò ingannarmi; fai conto di questo giudizio come di un'impressione affatto individuale."
30 Ibid.: "A ciò ti gioveranno molto gli studii faticosissimi che ora sostieni e che io benedico, ammirandoti perché dopo tanti dolori e tante fatiche hai avuto la forza e il coraggio di sobbarcarteli."
31 Adelaide Maraini to Pratesi, 30 May 1876: "Io l'ho letto, e vi trovai bellezze impareggiabile [sic] di sentimento critico, di conoscenza del cuore umano, di finezze di dettaglio – Ciò che io vi trovai, è forse un pò di analogia con Jacopo e Marianna ... perché il soggetto e l'intreccio non riescono nuovi. Ecco la pura verità."
32 "Un vagabondo," *Nuova Antologia* (15 Nov., 1 and 15 Dec. 1878), and later in *In Provincia*.
33 Fatini, "Un romanziere amiatino," 20.
34 Pratesi to Abba, 1 Jan. 1877.
35 Fatini, "Un romanziere amiatino," 19.

36 Pratesi to Abba, 1 Dec. 1877.
37 Alessandro Gherardi to Pratesi, 25 Dec. 1877.
38 Pratesi to Abba, 23 Dec. 1878. Abba did not reply until 22 Mar. 1879; his letter, however, reiterated his opinion that Pratesi had a natural talent for writing. He called the novella one of the best of the genre.
39 Igino Pratesi to Pratesi, 20 Dec. 1878.
40 Atto Vannucci to Pratesi, 30 Dec. 1878.
41 Gherardi to Pratesi, 8 Jan. 1879: "Eppure tante altre cose potrei dirti, e più in lode che in biasimo sicuramente; perché tra li [sic] scrittori di novelle e romanzi non so davvero quanti ti possano oggi avanzare non che stare accanto per dignità di concetti, per vero e profondo senso dell'arte e per eleganza di forma."
42 "Dal Monteamiata a Sovana," *La Rassegna settimanale* (1 July 1879) and later in *In Provincia*.
43 Leopoldo Franchetti to Pratesi, 25 Apr. 1879. For a more thorough discussion on how the *Rassegna* shaped Pratesi's tendencies to *verismo*, see Roberto Bigazzi, *I colori del vero: Vent'anni di narrative, 1860–1880* (Pisa: Nistri-Lischi, 1969), 285–9. In their study *Letteratura e paesaggio in Toscana: Da Pratesi a Cassola*, Iolanda Fonnesu and Leonardo Rombai also point to the ineluctable influence of the *Rassegna* in informing an Italian literary sensibility for *Verismo*, not only for Giovanni Verga, but for Pratesi as well. Ibid., 21.
44 "Un Corvo tra i selvaggi," *La Rassegna settimanale* (14 Dec. 1879).
45 Leopoldo Franchetti to Pratesi, 6 Dec. 1879: "Se hai altri argomenti in testa scrivili, scrivili, scrivili. È capace che quelli assicurino la tua carriera. Il bozzetto che ci hai mandato prova che i tipi li trovi anche a Terni e contorni. Quando tua abbia fatto un certo numero di quei lavori, puoi pubblicarli in volume."
46 Karl Hillebrand to Pratesi, 8 Dec. 1879: "Ho letto e riletto con sommo piacere il vostro bozzetto e vengo a congratularvene. Ecco precisamente il genere, la forma e la cornice che convengono al vostro ingegno. Vi rammentate che ve l'ho sempre detto ed il gran successo che ha riscontrato cotesto vostro quadretto viene a confermare la mia prima impressione. Perché romanzi lunghi, novelle a gran intreccio, se questo genere più semplice, più naturale è più nella vostra natura? ... Spero che questa vittoria vi farà coraggio e che presto vedremo qualch'altro caso di cotesto genere."
47 Jessie Hillebrand to Pratesi, 16 Dec. 1879: "Sono diversi giorni che io mi rimprovero di non aver ancora risposto alla vostra lettera, che mi fece, al solito, assai più piacere che non ne avete un' idea. Ieri fui però <u>scossa</u> talmente dal vostro 'Corvo' che non voglio tardare a dirvi quanto mi ha

incantato questa lettura Io trovavo la Rassegna di Domenica fra le mie carte principiai a leggere il 'Corvo' e ne fui talmente sorpresa ed incantata che lo lessi due volte di seguito ... [Karl] Ne dirà lui stesso suo avviso e ne farà la sua critica assai più importante della *mia*, ma io aveva proprio bisogno di dire a Messer Mario che, non solamente quando vedo un bel paesaggio mi viene la voglia di scrivergli, ma anche quando leggo qualchecosa di bello, e così oggi avevo proprio bisogno di dirgli che il "Corvo" è ciò che ho letto di più bello e di più artistico da molto tempo. Scusine [sic] le lodi. Non ne faccio spesso, ed il mio entusiasmo non cresce come le patate, può tener l'uno e le altri [sic] per sincerissimi e non interamente senza valore."

48 Ibid.: "Di questo numero della Rassegna andranno a passeggiare in Europa una 20na d'esemplarii; per far conoscere e stimare nostro Messer Mario al suo vero valore."
49 Barzellotti to Pratesi, 26 Dec. 1879.
50 Barzellotti to Pratesi, 29 Sept. 1880: "L'altro giorno io rileggevo il 'Corvo' che è veramente una delle cose più belle e ingegnose che siano state scritte in Italia da molti anni ed è forse unica nel suo genere. Daccene qualcun'altra."
51 Pratesi to Angelo De Gubernatis, 11 Feb. 1880.
52 Pratesi to Abba, 13 Mar. 1880.
53 "Quaresima e carnevale," *La Rassegna settimanale* (20 Feb. 1880), later as "Il dottor Febo" in *In Provincia*, then as "Il carnevale del cieco" in *La Dama del minuetto* (Milan-Palermo: Sandron, 1910).
54 Abba to Pratesi, 16 Apr. 1881.
55 "Dopo una lettura del Cantico dei Cantici," *La Rassegna settimanale* (9 May 1880), and later in *In Provincia*.
56 "Un ballo nel monastero," *La Rassegna settimanale* (25 July 1880), then as "Un ballo nel convento" in *In provincia* and then retitled "La mummia" in *La Dama del minuetto*. Translated into French by G.D. and published as "Un bal dans un monastère toscan" in *Revue Britannique* 10 (Oct. 1880).
57 Sidney Sonnino to Pratesi, 31 Aug. 1880.
58 The *Rassegna settimanale* continued until the end of Jan. 1882 (when Sonnino's collaboration came to an end) and was superseded by *La Rassegna*.
59 Sidney Sonnino to Pratesi, 27 Oct. 1880.
60 Igino Pratesi to Dante Pratesi, 13 Nov. 1880.
61 Vannucci to Pratesi, 21 Jan. 1881.
62 "A Raven amidst Savages," *Cornhill Magazine* 44 (1881).
63 Barzellotti to Pratesi, 24 Dec. 1880.

64 From the translation of the English review, which I have been unable to find. The German translation of "Corvo" to which the critic alludes seems not to exist. Perhaps Jessie Hillebrand had intended to translate the story into German as well, or had asked her husband to do so. The mention of this non-existent translation indicates that perhaps the review was ghostwritten by an English acquaintance of the Hillebrands, or even by Mrs Hillebrand herself. One of the three copies of the translated review seems to be in her hand. One is written by Barzellotti, the third hand is unknown. The three translations are similar, with minor variations. Pratesi Archives, Victoria University Library Special Collections.
65 See correspondence with Firenze Santandrea.
66 Barzellotti, *Delle dottrine filosofiche*.
67 Augusto Conti to Pratesi, 3 Jan. 1872, and also 28 Dec. 1872.
68 Such was the case of the travel pieces "L'Isola di Pianosa" and "L'Isola d'Elba" written at this time and intended for the volume *In Provincia*. These were not included among his works until the publication of *Figure e paesi d'Italia* (Turin: Roux and Viarengo, 1905). See letter from Igino Pratesi to Pratesi, 19 Apr. 1883. Just how carefully Pratesi sought a realistic portrayal in his travel pieces can be surmised in his request for photographs of Pianosa made to the painter Stefano Ussi (1822–1901) who had accompanied him on the trip to Pianosa. See letter of Stefano Ussi to Pratesi, circa 1882.
69 Sidney Sonnino to Pratesi, 7 June and 16 July 1881.
70 Vernon Lee (Violet Paget) to Piero Barbèra, 20 Oct. 1881: "Mi valgo del vantaggio di essere in relazioni letterarie colla di Lei notissima Casa Editrice per presentarle il mio amico toscano di bellissimi e molto caratteristici doni, i cui bozzetti 'Un corvo fra i Selvaggi' e 'Un ballo nel monastero' fecero molta impressione l'anno scorso nella *Rassegna Settimanale*. Il Signor Pratesi è in ricerca di un Editore per uno suo raccolto di racconti e 'bozzetti' i quali se deve giudicarsi dagli altri suoi lavori dovrebbe riuscire molto grato al pubblico letterario. Credo di fare in ciò atto utile non solo al Signor Pratesi ma pure a Lei ed alla sua Casa."
71 Gherardi to Pratesi, 29 Dec. 1882.
72 Gherardi to Pratesi, 5 Dec. 1881: "Non ti ci affaticar per tanto a limare e correggere. Tutto è perfittibile ma la perfezione non si tocca; e non sempre a furia di correggere si migliora: spesso si finisce per perdere l'impronta originale del primo getto."
73 Giuseppe Martinozzi to Pratesi, 23 Dec. 1881: "io sento che i quadri tuoi hanno una potenza di vita, una carnalità così soda e vera, un rilievo così naturalmente animato, che la maggior parte degli altri artisti italiani mi

sembrano acquerellisti paragonati a te. Ho smesso da qualche tempo di tener dietro alla letteratura così detta amena, ma non mi ricordo d'aver mai visto nulla di così terribilmente e *originalmente* (mi spiego come posso!) vivo e penetrante, come le tue indimenticabili figure."
74 Barzellotti to Pratesi, 12 Mar. 1882: "Caro mio, i tuoi ultimi lavori (vorrei che tu sentissi gli elogi che ne fanno quà varii miei amici) sono tutt'altro che gli scritti di una mente e di un'anima che deperisce. Sono anzi, per molti aspetti, le tue cose migliori."
75 Pratesi to Piero Barbèra, 27 Nov. 1882.
76 Preface to *The Countess of Albany* (London: W.H. Allen 1884), viii, also available at http://www.gutenberg.ca/ebooks/lee-albany/lee-albany-00-h-dir/lee-albany-00-h.html
77 Pratesi to Barbèra, 27 Nov. 1882: "In tutti que' lavori ho posto molto pensiero, che non apparirà ai lettori superficiali, ma io non ho scritto nè per le donne nè pei ganimedi plebei, che non cercano se non la curiosità e quello che chiamano l'*interesse* del racconto. Veda dunque di fare il meglio che può." Pratesi's reaction likely reflected his own discomfort with the growing prominence of the decadent Scapigliati artists and writers. Further discussion will be found in chapter 4.
78 Cesare Guasti to Pratesi, 17 June 1883.
79 Cesira Siciliani to Pratesi, 18 June 1883; Enrico Panzacchi to Pratesi, 28 June 1883; and Adelaide Maraini to Pratesi, 15 June 1885 (she refers to having received a copy of the second edition). Strangely enough Pratesi omitted the Maraini family in sending complimentary copies of the first. Cf. Igino Pratesi to Pratesi, 23 May 1883.
80 Gherardi to Pratesi, 5 July 1883.
81 G[iuseppe] D[epanis], review of *In Provincia* in *La Gazzetta Letteraria* 7/24 (16 June 1883). Depanis (1853–1942) was a well-known music critic and, at this time, the editor of the *Gazzetta*.
82 Vernon Lee, review of *In provincia*, in *The Academy: A Weekly Review of Literature, Science and Art* (14 July 1883), 28.
83 Alice Werner to Pratesi, 8 Aug. 1883.
84 Alice Werner, *The Humour of Italy* (London: Walter Scott Ltd, 1892), 338–9.
85 Aristodemo B****, review of *In Provincia* in *La Rassegna nazionale* (1 Nov. 1883), 462–4. He is listed in several bibliographies as B. Aristodemo.
86 Ruggiero Bonghi, review of *In Provincia* in *La Cultura* (Oct. 1883), 322–6.
87 B.A.T, review of *In Provincia* in *L'Illustrazione italiana* (8 July 1883), 22–3. The pseudonym may be a playful reference to the French expression *Bon à tirer* (ready to be printed) often written BAT, which had been used in publishing since 1835.

88 *I migliori libri italiani consigliati da cento illustri contemporanei* (Milan: Ulrico Hoepli, 1892), 162.
89 Although as usual he complained about his situation as his letters to Emilia Peruzzi show. Letters conserved in Biblioteca Nazionale Centrale di Firenze, Fondo Peruzzi, Cassetta 158, ins.16–21.
90 Vernon Lee, "Un italiano dalla natura Nordica: A proposito delle novelle di Mario Pratesi," *Il Fanfulla della domenica* (28 June 1885).
91 Adelaide Maraini wrote to express her agreement with Vernon Lee, lamenting however that Pratesi wrote too little. Adelaide Maraini to Pratesi, 2 July 1885.
92 M. Pratesi, "Catuzza," *Nuova Antologia* (1 Mar. 1885), with the title "Una iettatura," in *Di paese in paese* (Milan: Galli, 1892) and in *Figure e paesi d'Italia*.
93 Barzellotti to Pratesi, 12 Mar. 1885: "È una delle tue più rigorose, e in cui la descrizione della natura e certi tratti, che dipingono i caratteri delle persone, sono più fortemente scolpiti ... Lo stile è bellissimo e credo che hai fatto bene a non correggere troppo. In somma vai avanti, ché non solo sei il solito Mario, ma sei progredito, e il Carducci ... parlando, tempo fa degli scrittori di cose letterarie attuali metteva te in prima linea, additandoti tra quelli su cui l'Antologia deve fare più fondamento. Dovresti tentare di mettere in qualche novella anche qualche questione del giorno, qualche cosa che oggi si discute etc." Carducci (1835–1907) was Italy's foremost poet, revolutionary in his attitude and approach, and well known for his criticism of Italian literature. He and Pratesi enjoyed a close friendship.
94 Gherardi to Pratesi, 16 Mar. 1885: "Ma perché, mio caro, non ti stacchi una volta, qualche volta, da queste dolorose immagini della società inferma o perversa? Tu che veneri così altamente la virtù e la integrità del carattere, che ti scaldi a ogn'idea generosa, che così fortemente senti l'affetto della famiglia e l'amicizia, perché non cerchi qualche soggetto da far vibrare anche queste corde della tua mente e del tuo cuore, e non sempre quelle che in te rispondono al dolore, all'orrore al disprezzo, forse soverchio, che provi per tutte le malvagità e le miserie degli uomini? Tu possiedi l'arte di scrivere, fai che quest'arte dia i maggiori e migliori frutti che può."

Chapter 3: Belluno

1 "Riva Calabra" appeared in the *Domenica del Fracassa* on 13 Dec. 1885. Other poems published at this time included "Campagna milanese (Lungo il Naviglio)," *L'Illustrazione italiana* (19 Dec. 1886), "Certosa di Garignano,"

L'Illustrazione italiana (6 Feb. 1887), and "Tarantella sul lido," *L'Illustrazione italiana* (3 Apr. 1887).
2 Mario Pratesi, "Santi, solitari e filosofi," *L'Illustrazione italiana* (28 July 1886).
3 Mario Pratesi, "La Saffo della Signora A. Maraini e l'arte di moda," *Il Rosmini* (1 Apr. 1887) republished as "Arte vecchia e arte nuova" later *in Figure e paesi d'Italia* (Turin: Roux and Viarengo, 1905). He had previously written about the statue in "Saffo: Statua della signora Adelaide Maraini," *L'Illustrazione italiana* (22 Apr. 1877).
4 Alessandro Gherardi to Pratesi, 13 Apr. 1887.
5 Pratesi to Igino Pratesi, 20 June 1888; also Pratesi to Giacomo Barzellotti, 22 June 1888, in Fatini, "Un romanziere amiatino, Mario Pratesi (Lettere a Giacomo Barzellotti)," *Annuario 1931–32 del Liceo Ginnasio Carducci Ricasoli*, 34.
6 Mario Guidotti, *Un'aurora dall'Amiata* (Siena: Maia, 1956), 62, and also in *Il romanzo toscano e Mario Pratesi* (Vallecchi: 1983), 64.
7 *Giovanni Verga scrittore fotografo*, edited by Roberto Mutti, with introduction by Guido Bezzola (Novara: De Agostini, 2004).
8 Vernon Lee, to Pratesi 17 Mar. 1889: "Il suo nuovo libro mi pare, in quanto allo stile, anche superiore all'altro, e di tempra più maschia. Ma non vorrei che il suo senso di tutte le sudicie strettezze di questa vita le facesse perdere il suo sorriso di umorista. Sarà così la vita di campagna presa in esempi separati; ma nell'insieme, nella media è possibile che tutto sia così luridamente triste?"

   Later, another English researcher, Alice Werner, in her volume *The Humour of Italy* (1892), would also point to Pratesi as humorist in this same sense of someone who has grasped the temperament of Italy. Pratesi and Barzellotti also discussed the topic, and it is striking how closely the latter anticipates the work of Luigi Pirandello in *Sull'umorismo* (1908) in a letter to Pratesi in which he observes the natural pessimism of Italians, elaborating that interpreting the comic or the ridiculous depends on the consideration of other perspectives. Giacomo Barzellotti to Pratesi, 26 Dec. 1874.
9 Barzellotti to Pratesi, 16 Apr. 1889: "chi gusta l'arte e la tradizione nostra, e la vuol vedere messa in armonia con le nuove forme della letteratura d'oggi in quello che esse hanno di buono e di vero, non può non riconoscere, nel tuo libro uno dei più notevoli che si siano scritti in Italia da parecchi anni."
10 Jessie Hillebrand to Pratesi, 29 Aug. 1889b.
11 Antonio Fogazzaro to Pratesi, 1 Dec. 1893.
12 Guidotti, *Un'aurora dall'Amiata*, 62–3, and also in *Il romanzo toscano e Mario Pratesi*, 64–5.

13 Mauro Bolognini, 1961.
14 A.A., review of *L'Eredità* in *Lettere e Arti* (16 Feb. 1890), 14–15.
15 Y., review of *L'Eredità* in *La Rassegna nazionale* (1 Mar. 1890), 206. The review is listed as being the work of B. Aristodemo (*sic*) in some bibliographies. Luigi Coppola often signed his reviews Ypsilon, as Nicola Bernardini indicates in his extensive list of reviewer pseudonyms, but he wrote for the *Fanfulla della domenica* and *Pasquino* and had passed away before the publication of Pratesi's novel. Nicola Bernardini, *Guida alla stampa periodica italiana* (Lecce: Editrice Salentina, 1890), 235–46.
16 Pratesi to G.C. Abba, 22 Apr. 1887. The emphasized words are veiled references to his love affair, now nearing its end.
17 Pratesi to Barzellotti, 8 Feb. 1888, in Fatini, "Un romanziere amiatino," 32. Again, the emphasized words are veiled references to his affair, now nearing its end.
18 Mario Pratesi, "Ricordi veneziani," *L'Illustrazione italiana* (17 Mar., 19 May, 2 and 30 June, 28 July, 4 Aug., 10 Nov., and 8 Dec. 1889), republished in *Di paese in paese* (Milan: Galli, 1892), and later in a single volume published in 1899 (Milan: Baldini and Castoldi), then republished in Milan-Palermo by Sandron nel in 1901. A German edition appeared, translated by Mrs Müller-Roder (Berlin-Leipzig: Lüpeden-Merron, 1905).
19 Luigi Morandi to Pratesi, 14 Jan. 1890. The volume, *Antologia della nostra critica letteraria moderna*, compiled by Luigi Morandi (Città di Castello: S. Lapi) was published in 1891.
20 Unsigned review in "In Biblioteca," *Il Diritto*, 17 June 1892.
21 Domenico Oliva to Pratesi, 9 May 1892. I have been unable to ascertain whether or not the *Corriere della Sera* reviewed the book.
22 G[erolamo] R[ovetta], "Un libro d'arte," *Vita moderna*, 31 July 1892.
23 Aramis, "Di paese in paese," *Corriere di Palermo*, 7 Oct. 1892.
24 Unsigned review in *L'Avvisatore Alessandrino*, 27 June 1892. The other titles mentioned were all by women: *Addio, Amore!* (Matilde Serao), *Mater Lachrymosa* (Sofia Bini), *Sennio* (Neera), and *Solo al mondo* (Maria Savi Lopez).
25 Unsigned review in "La nostra biblioteca," *La Sentinella bresciana*, 30 June 1892.
26 A. Ricchetti, "Note letterarie," *L'Adriatico*, 18 July 1892.
27 Nevio, "Le poesie di Mario Pratesi," *La Fortuna* (Fano), 2 Sept. 1892.
28 Colin, Jämes-Ed., review of *Di paese in paese* in *Bulletin: Société neuchâteloise de géographie* 7 (1892–93), and Dr. Franz Söhns, review of *Di paese in paese* in *Neuphilologisches Centralblatt* 10 (Oct. 1892). Söhns quotes line 343 from the *Ars poetica* of Horace.

29 See discussion in the introduction to this book.
30 Telegram from Ferdinando Martini to Pratesi, 28 Sept. 1892.
31 Emilia Peruzzi to Pratesi, 10 Nov. 1892. See also his letters to her of 17 Oct. and 14 and 19 Nov. 1892. Letters conserved in Biblioteca Nazionale Centrale di Firenze (BNCF), Fondo Peruzzi, Cassetta 158, ins.16–21.
32 Pratesi to Barzellotti, 22 Aug. 1893 in Fatini, "Un romanziere amiatino," 36.
33 "Il Mondo di Dolcetta, Racconto," in *Nuova Antologia* (16 Sept., 1 and 16 Oct., 1 and 16 Nov., 1 and 16 Dec., 1894, and 1 and 16 Jan., 1 and 16 Feb., and 1 and 16 Mar. 1895). Published as a single volume (Milan: Galli, 1895). Later it appeared serialized in the *Rassegna nazionale* (1 Jan. to 16 Oct. 1916), and again in a separate volume published by the *Rassegna nazionale* in 1916.
34 Pratesi to Barzellotti, 18 Oct. 1894, in Fatini, "Un romanziere amiatino," 37–8: "Non sai in mezzo a quali difficoltà e travagli di mente e di corpo fu scritto ... quindi io del lavoro non ne sono contento. Ma tu vedrai con quali concetti e intenti fu scritto: la vita italiana e il carattere italiano avrei voluto ritrarli, ma forse ho fatto un buco nell'acqua."
35 Barzellotti to Pratesi, 31 Dec. 1891.
36 Barzellotti to Pratesi, 14 Jan. 1895.
37 Adelaide Maraini to Pratesi, 29 Mar. 1895.
38 Jessie Hillebrand to Pratesi, 16 Aug. 1896.
39 Abba to Pratesi, 8 Aug. 1895.
40 E[rnesto] M[asi], review of *Il Mondo di Dolcetta* in *L'Arte* 9 (1 Mar. 1896). Emphasis in original.
41 Silvius, review *of Il Mondo di Dolcetta* in *Il Pallano* (Lanciano) 11(13 Mar. 1896): "E pure le trecento fitte pagine del volume, in verità un po' troppo toscaneggianti e non sdegnose del ribobolo, si fanno leggere con vero interesse ... Romanzo, come si può immaginare che sia, come si vuole che i romanzi siano, come se ne fanno, come se ne sono fatti veramene non è ... E se il Pratesi, che certo prepara alla letteratura un nuovo lavoro, con uno sforzo di condensione, saprà da un centro unico dar moto al mondo della sua fantasia, avremo, senza dubbio, in tempo non lontano, un romanzo che farà onore a lui e al paese."
42 Unsigned review of *Il Mondo di Dolcetta* in *La Stella di Mondovì* (28 Mar. 1896).
43 Unsigned review of *Il Mondo di Dolcetta* in *La Provincia: Giornale politico-letterario* (Teramo) (29 Mar. 1896).
44 D[omenico] O[liva], review of *Il Mondo di Dolcetta* in *Corriere della Sera* (24 Mar. 1896).
45 Domenico Oliva to Pratesi, 9 May 1892.

46 Enrico Corradini, "A proposito d'un ... Romanzo," review of *Il mondo di Dolcetta* in *Marzocco* (23 Feb. 1896).
47 Pratesi Archives, Victoria University Library Special Collections. One copy was likely sent to the poetess and author Luisa Anzoletti, who admired the novel greatly when it was republished in 1916. She reminded Pratesi that Corradini's venom was actually directed at the *Nuova Antologia* rather than at him. Luisa Anzoletti to Pratesi, 5 Jan. 1917. Critic Renato Bertacchini concurs, noting also that even the beginning of Corradini's review, with the ellipses in its title was already indicative of Corradini's intent to "make fun of [Pratesi's] style, of his heavy prose, heaping public scorn on a rather simple, humble plot." Renato Bertacchini, "Pratesi tra due secoli," in Mario Pratesi, *L'Eredità*, edited by Vasco Pratolini (Milan: Bompiani, 1965 [1942]), 25.
48 Perhaps in an ironic dig at the fact that Pratesi was one of the authors chosen by Alice Werner as a representative of Italian humour. See Alice Werner, *The Humour of Italy* (London: Walter Scott, 1892).
49 Unsigned review of *Il Mondo di Dolcetta*, in *Fanfulla della domenica* (Mar. 1896; before 14 Mar.).
50 Quoted in Pratesi to Antonio Fogazzaro, 14 Mar. 1896.
51 The letter sent from Naples and dated 1 Mar. 1896 is conserved in the BNCF in the Fondo Peruzzi, Cassetta 11, ins. 24: "Ha ella veduto il *Mondo di Dolcetta* del nostro amico Pratesi? A me, suo amicissimo, che lo stimo tanto, duole dover dire che non è la sua cosa migliore; causa sempre tutto il terribile pessimismo che ha messo nella rappresentazione d'una società, che a' suoi occhi, non ha in sè che male e che, quindi, ritratta così da lui, produce non altro che un'impressione di aridità penosa e di disgusto. Sono molto dispiacente che proprio nel *Fanfulla della domenica* di oggi ... ci sia anche una recensione severissima sul libro di Mario. Me ne duole perché so quanto egli sia suscettibile. Ma è anche, bisogna dire, ostinato troppo nel voler rappresentare le cose del mondo solo dal loro lato peggiore, il quale, oltre a non esser l'unico, non è il più vero. Io mi persuado, ogni giorno più, che il *realismo* pessimistico (che oggi però comincia a dar giù [sic] è, oltrecchè noioso, un *grande errore*, e che l'Arte dev'essere *vera* ma non riproduttrice dell'arida realtà positiva, altrimenti non è arte."
52 Emilia Peruzzi to Pratesi, 12 Mar. 1896.
53 Pratesi to Emilia Peruzzi, 16 Mar. 1896. Letter conservato in BNCF, Fondo Peruzzi, Cassetta 158, ins.16–21.
54 The opera had its debut at the Teatro Regio of Turin (beginning of Feb. 1896), moved to the Teatro San Carlo in March 1896, and by November was at the Teatro Comunale di Bologna. It seems that Leoncavallo's opera

of the same name also suffered because of overexposure of the storyline (1897).
55 Pratesi Archives, Victoria University Library Special Collections. There are two manuscript copies of the review, one heavily annotated is followed by a letter in draft form. Anzoletti's reply to Pratesi of 5 Jan. 1917 would indicate that she was the recipient of the letter: "Il sig. Spencer non vede nulla di questo ... Eppure è in questo, e nella pittura dei costumi toscani dell'ultima età granducale, l'essenza del romanzo la sua realtà e la sua verità che critici e lettori, o nemici, o orbi, o superficiali tacquero sempre. Per non parlare di articoli indegni come quello del Sig. Corradini, anche i giudizi troppo angusti o incompleti come quello del Sig. Spencer nocciono a un libro, in quanto ne rendono l'immagine troppo rimpiccolita, e senza le note più caratteristiche e più essenziali."
56 Joseph Spencer Kennard, *Romanzi e romanzieri italiani*, 2nd ed., vol. 1 (Florence: Barbèra, 1905), 244.
57 Pratesi Archives, Victoria University Library Special Collections.
58 Pratesi to Barzellotti, undated letter, in Fatini, "Un romanziere amiatino," 37.
59 G.C. Abba to Pratesi, Ceppo [Christmas Day] 1896: "E del tuo romanzo? Non mi stupisce nè di quel che ne dissero i critici, nè dell'accoglienza che esso ebbe dal pubblico dei così detti lettori. Maschi o femmine, troppi si sentono ciascuno un po' nella pelle di quei personaggi che tu rappresenti."
60 Unsigned review of *Il Mondo di Dolcetta* in *Minerva: Rassegna internazionale e rivista delle riviste* 11 (May 1896): "Leggete il libro del Pratesi e più d'una vi farà battere il cuore e vi farà spuntar sulle labbra quel sorriso che anche fra i drammi più angosciosi sa intrecciare un autore dalla tavolozza ricca e svariata. Certamente perdonerete all'autore anche certe prolissità che in qualche punto avreste voluto risparmiate, e anche qualche crudezza di immagini che non aggiunge forza, e forse riesce pesante alla sveltezza del complesso del bellissimo lavoro."
61 Mario Pratesi, *Il Mondo di Dolcetta*, edited by Renato Bertacchini. Bertacchini's introduction presents a very detailed comparison of the three editions; his edition is a republication of Pratesi's 1916 edition. Even the latter contains many typographical errors, which Bertacchini corrects; some, as noted by Bertacchini, were corrected by Pratesi in an autographed copy offered to Gino Bandini (now in the Thomas Fisher Rare Book Library of the University of Toronto); most of the corrections in the latter are pencilled in by another reader, however, not Pratesi himself. Observations similar to those of Guidotti and Bertacchini are also made by Jole Soldateschi in her study of the variants of Pratesi's *In Provincia*, in her volume *Il laboratorio della prosa: Pratesi Palazzeschi Cicognini*.

62 Mario Guidotti, *Un'aurora dall'Amiata*, 90–1, and *Il romanzo toscano e Mario Pratesi* (Florence: Vallecchi, 1986), 92–3.
63 Barzellotti a Pratesi, 28 Aug. 1915: "Ho molto piacere che tu ripubblichi Dolcetta. E sono sicuro che ora sarà più gustata."
64 Guidotti, *Un'aurora dall'Amiata*, 92, and also in *Il romanzo toscano*, 93.
65 Renato Fucini to Pratesi, 31 Aug. 1896: "Quando penso di esserti, qualche volta, paragonato a te per il modo di osservare, di sentire e di scrivere, faccio il viso rosso dalla vergogna. E non ti dico altro – Lavora, amico mio, perché il tuo bozzolo non è finito; e della seta in buzzo mi pare che tu debba avercene a matasse."
66 Testament of Mario Pratesi, dated 19 Oct. 1920, with codicil dated 20 Mar. 1921.
67 Susan Cheever, *Louisa May Alcott: A Personal Biography* (New York: Simon and Schuster, 2010), 198.

Chapter 4: Florence Once More

1 For a description of Pratesi's daily life in Belluno, with his dog Nicchi Nacchi and thieving cat Camuffi, see his letter to Giacomo Barzellotti, 27 July 1897, cited by Fatini, "Un romanziere amiatino, Mario Pratesi (Lettere a Giacomo Barzellotti)," *Annuario 1931–32 del Liceo Ginnasio Carducci Ricasoli*, 39.
2 Telephone service was officially inaugurated in Italy after 1880 and began to operate more fully by the late 1890s. Telephone connections (including infrastructure) began on a national scale after 1903. Mario Lombardo and Fabrizio Pignatel, *La stampa periodica in Italia: Mezzo secolo di riviste illustrate* (Roma: Editori Riuniti, 1985), 26.
3 Pratesi to Barzellotti, 23 July 1897, in Fatini, "Un romanziere amiatino," 39.
4 Barzellotti to Pratesi, 11 and 12 June 1897.
5 Sidney Sonnino to Pratesi, 24 Aug. 1898.
6 The *Scapigliati* (literally, the dishevelled) represented a movement of late nineteenth-century Italian artists, writers, and musicians whose anti-Romantic attitudes led to works in which the conventional bourgeoisie and traditional literary themes were pronounced old fashioned and provincial. Themes of dissolution and social dissatisfaction informed their works. Physical illnesses or defects for them represented psychological fragility and moral decrepitude in a quickly changing social environment. While a similar aesthetic movement, Decadentism was particularly prominent in highly industrialized countries, Italy's Scapigliati represented analogous attitudes of inquietude and social disenfranchisement in a less industrialized but still problematic society. For further discussion, see Barbara

Spackman, *Decadent Genealogies: The Rhetoric of Sickness from Baudelaire to D'Annunzio* (Ithaca: Cornell University Press, 1989) for a European perspective, and for more emphasis on the aesthetic aspects of the movement in Italy, see Massimo Arcangeli, *La Scapigliatura poetica milanese e la poesia italiana fra Otto e Novecento: Capitoli di lingua e di stile* (Rome: Aracne, 2003).

7 Mario Guidotti, *Un'aurora dall'Amiata* (Siena: Maia, 1956), 93–6, and also in *Il romanzo toscano e Mario Pratesi* (Vallecchi: Florence, 1983), 95–8.

8 Alessandro Gherardi to Pratesi, 29 June 1898: "Ma tu ritorni e insisti troppo, mi pare, sui fianchi, sul seno, sulle spalle, sulle curve, sugli appicchi, sulla plasticità di quel bellissimo corpo, e pare tu te ne compiaccia: questo compiacimento si comunica al lettore, e qui sta il male. Meno pericoloso, è talvolta, e più efficace, accennare e lasciar pensare che descrivere."

9 Gherardi to Pratesi, 24 Dec. 1897: "un saluto e un augurio per l'anno che verrà: benché pur troppo, e da un gran pezzo oramai, gli anni incalzino gli anni via via più tristi e sconsolati. Certo anche alla nostra età, e più che a tant'altri, si addice *l'in pejus precipitant* d'Orazio. Un'altra certo dovrà servire[?] a cui non s'addica, se prima non torna il caos ma noi non la vedremo. Pazienza!"

10 Adelaide Maraini to Pratesi 15 Dec. 1898: "Ho con piacere letto l'articolo sulla Rassegna [settimanale universale], e mi pare che abbia rilevato bene e con cuore i grandi pregi del suo romanzo se lei vivesse in un ambiente riscaldato della famiglia e dell'amicizia chissà quali soggetti più sereni ella potrebbe analizzare, con quella delicatezza e penetrazione che la distingue."

11 Barzellotti to Pratesi, 3 July 1898: "A me una delle tue cose migliori, forse la migliore (tra le narrazioni continuate); è benissimo scritta, come tu, del resto, scrivi sempre, ma in questa lo stile ha una sobrietà e una determinazione vigorosa di linee, e, qua e e [sic] là, un calore poetico, che danno al libro un carattere tutto suo. Dato quel mondo, che tu dipingi, e di cui e in cui vivono i tuoi personaggi – mondo certo, molto perverso, forse veduto solo e troppo dal suo lato perverso – le figure da te ritratte non potrebbero essere più vive e più vere, non potrebbero avere linee e fisonomie più spiccate ... si sente che tu nell'arte dell'osservare il vero hai fatto molti progressi. Il libro a chi guarda all'arte vera e non imbellettata, a chi soprattutto, ha il sentimento della vivezza e della spontaneità della lingua toscana, ... dovrebbe piacere."

12 E[rnesto] M[asi], review of *Il Mondo di Dolcetta* in *L'Arte* 9 (1 Mar. 1896).

13 Ernesto Masi to Pratesi, 21 June 1898: "La catastrofe è di dramma romantico. Ma mi ha sorpreso! Io almeno non me l'aspettavo ... Mi pare che ti sei proposto un problema d'arte e di psicologia."

14 Ibid.: "Auguro di cuore al tuo libro la fortuna che merita."
15 About 15,000 copies per run according to Nicola Bernardini, in *Guida alla stampa periodica italiana* (Lecce: Editrice Salentina, 1890), 518.
16 Renato, review of *Le Perfidie del caso* in *L'Illustrazione italiana* (19 June 1898), 430.
17 The column "Biblioteca della Nazione" is unsigned and undated.
18 Renato, review.
19 Ibid.
20 Ernesto Masi, review of *Le Perfidie del caso* in *Nuova Antologia* (16 Aug. 1898), 737: "uno studio psicologico di molta forza, una profonda analisi di caratteri e nell' insieme un quadro di piccole proporzioni bensì, ma che ne compendia e raffigura di maggiori assai, e nella tristezza, con cui sono scrutate certe condizioni morali e sociali del nostro tempo, nella passionata efficacia, con cui tutto quest' intimo dramma avvolge e si svolge, nella pittoresca potenza delle descrizioni e del paesaggio, riafferma anche una volta in Mario Pratesi quel singolare temperamento di pensatore e d'artista, che ne fanno uno dei più notevoli e più geniali scrittori italiani."
21 Van Winkle, review of *Le Perfidie del caso* in *Rassegna settimanale universale* (4 Dec. 1898): "Ma soprattutto è notevole questo racconto per una chiarezza di vedute, una purezza di linee, una signorile, e veramente artistica, eleganza di forma, le quali da sole danno diritto all'autore di essere collocato in prima fila fra i migliori novellieri nostrani e stranieri. Noi non sappiamo quale fra gli scrittori viventi possa vantare una più sicura padronanza di lingua, uno stile così puro e così nobile, una tavolozza così ricca e così efficace."
22 Adelaide Maraini to Pratesi, 15 Dec. 1898, and Gherardi to Pratesi, 23 Dec. 1898.
23 Pratesi's manuscript copy of Van Winkle's review, 3: "L'articolo, che ho trascritto, è firmato da Van Winkle, forse d'origine olandese; persona, come si vede, molto buona e gentile, a me affatto ignota; se non che essa m'apparisce molto diversa dagli acerrimi, invidiosi e grossolani critici nostri."
24 Enrico Corradini, review of *Le Perfidie del caso* in *Il Marzocco* (24 July 1898): "D'un altro romanzo del Pratesi, certo *Mondo di Dolcetta*, mi ricordo di aver detto un gran male in questo stesso giornal. Ahimè, il buon Pratesi è recidivo! Ora pubblica presso il Treves *Le perfidie del caso* per raccontarci ... cose perfettamente inutili a sapere; ... E dire, che il Pratesi, non ostante tutto, ha ingegno. Basterebbe a provarlo quella macchietta del conte Ranieri. Ha anche una prosa facile e scorrevole con discreta lingua e dimostra per la nostra Firenze un affetto e una riverenza, che veramente gli

fanno onore. Soltanto dovrebbe acquistare il buon gusto di non dire cose inutili. Forse scriverebbe meno; ma sarebbe tanto di guadagnato per lui e per i lettori."

In commenting on Corradini's reviews, Renato Bertacchini recalls once again the critic's polemical attitude towards Pratesi, overtly chastising Corradini for not being able to distinguish between his personal discontent with the *Nuova Antologia* and the work of the writers it published. Renato Bertacchini, "Pratesi tra due secoli," in Mario Pratesi, *L'Eredità*, edited by Vasco Pratolini (Milan: Bompiani, 1965 [1942]), 23–4.

25 Guidotti, *Un'aurora dall'Amiata*, 99–100, and also in *Il romanzo toscano e Mario Pratesi*, 102. In the latter, Guidotti omits his conclusion that the novel is no more than a commonplace book.

26 Besides a listing in the holdings of the Sormani Library in Milan, I have been unable to find any additional information about the 1899 editions. Alessandro Gherardi refers to the 1901 edition as Pratesi's "new book." Gherardi to Pratesi, 2 Jan. 1901. After a problematic start (see Taddeo Wiel to Pratesi, 23 Nov. 1903), the book was also published in a German edition (Berlin-Leipzig: Lüpeden-Merron, 1905, translated by Emma Müller-Röder). The edition did not please Pratesi at all. Cf. Pratesi to Gino Bandini, 20 July 1905.

27 Adelaide Maraini to Pratesi, after 15 Dec. 1898, and Mimi Maraini to Pratesi at the beginning of 1899.

28 Carlo Chiesa to Pratesi, 17 June 1901.

29 G.C. Abba to Pratesi, 23 June 1901: "Come ti sei fatto maestro di forma! Il tuo stile è divenuto così terso e mobile … E il pensiero come viene misurato, anche là dove tu lo volgi a disprezzo del mondo! C'è in quel disprezzo un non so che di benevolo sempre … Hai poi delle immagini d'una novità semplice e sorprendente. Devi esser stato ben lieto nel momento che finivi certe pagine, certi periodi persino, lieto dico d'averli sentiti volgersi in te, e affacciarsi, e uscir con la grazia che avevano pigliato nel tuo pensiero … Ti gusteranno i lettori come ti gusto io? Molti certamente, e i migliori. Ma una cosa che mi stupisce … è la giovanilità di queste pagine."

The correspondence between Pratesi and Giuseppe Cesare Abba is quoted with the kind permission of the heirs of Pratesi, unless otherwise indicated.

30 Alfredo Panzini, review of *Ricordi veneziani* in "Tra Libri e Riviste, *Vita Internazionale* (5 July 1901).

31 Giulio Natali, "Mario Pratesi (Con sette lettere inedite," *Ricordi e profili di maestri e amici* (Rome: Edizioni di storia e letteratura, 1965), 56.

32 John Ruskin, *Venezia (Il Riposo di San Marco, La Cappella degli Schiavoni, L'Accademia, Paolo Veronese e gli Inquisitori, Sant'Orsola, Il Tintoretto e*

Michelangelo), translated with comments by Maria Pezzé Pascolato (Florence: Barbèra, 1901).
33 Giulio Natali, review of *Ricordi veneziani* in *Rassegna nazionale* (15 Aug. 1901): "il pensatore, l'uomo di buon gusto, l'osservatore arguto e lo scrittore fecondo ... Il Pratesi con poche parole sa ritrarre al vivo l'immagine d'un monumento, di un glorioso testimonio del passato ... Non meno acute sono le osservazioni psicologiche sul popolo veneziano ... Ad altri notare in questo libro alcune imperfezioni formali. A me è sembrato meglio rilevare la novità e genialità delle osservazioni."
34 Giuseppe Chiarini to Pratesi, 1 Mar. 1901.
35 Pratesi to Barzellotti, 16 Mar. 1902, in Fatini, "Un romanziere amiatino," 41, and also to Sabato Santo [29 Mar.] 1902, in ibid., 42.
36 Pratesi to Maria Ponti Pasolini, 24 Aug. 1900: "Io in mezzo a molte angosce corporali e sprituali scrivo a pezzi e bocconi, cioè quando posso, un mio racconto dove son tutti i colori, tranne il color di rosa."
37 Guidotti, *Un'aurora dall'Amiata*, 101, and also in *Il romanzo toscano e Mario Pratesi*, 103.
38 Ibid.
39 Chiarini to Pratesi, 1 Mar. 1901.
40 Pratesi to Gino Bandini, 12 July 1901.
41 Pratesi to Bandini, 30 Jan. 1902.
42 Barzellotti to Pratesi, 1 Aug. 1901.
43 Barzellotti to Pratesi, 24 Mar. 1902.
44 Barzellotti to Pratesi, 29 Sept. 1902.
45 Abba to Pratesi, 21 July 1902: "come è triste tutto quel mondo! Proprio tale fu dunque quello che conoscesti? Deve essere stato perché la tua voce in quelle pagine è tutta sincerità ... Ah! Caro Mario quante virtù vivono ben più degne di essere riflesse dall'arte, che la materia cui tu concedi i tuoi sguardi. Cercale, cercale ed esaltale come tu sapresti fare: già ritraendo quei tipi non si fa nulla di bene, essi rimagono quali sono; e siccome di solito son fortunati si rischi di additar in essi agli incerti ai sospesi tra il bene e il male che la via di questo è da preferirsi.
46 Gherardi to Pratesi, 1 Aug. 1902: "Ti farai leggere non con più interesse, ma con più edificazione; farai chiudere i tuoi libri col cuore più largo, con la mente più fresca con l'aspirazione al bello ed al buono che dev'essere il fine ultimo (o io m'inganno) d'ogni produzione artistica e letteraria."
47 Barzellotti to Pratesi, 1 Apr. 1903, and Pratesi to Barzellotti, 10 July 1903. The latter is found in Fatini, "Un romanziere amiatino," 44.
48 Pratesi to Abba, 14 Feb. 1902: "Non bisogna sperare di trovare della generosità e della lealtà in Italia, la terra classica dell'invidia e della menzogna. Pochi gli ammiratori di ciò che è alto, e se vedono che sei alto,

ti nascondono. Oh che meschinità! e che vanità! ... Io, dall'88 in poi, cioè dall'Eredità, il Mondo di Dolcetta etc., ho dato sei libri al mio paese e posso dire, senza vanità e presunzione, che valgono per lo meno quanto quelli che furono così strombazzati ... Invece, chi ne parlò?"

49 Pratesi to Bandini, 12 July 1901.
50 Pratesi to Bandini, 1 Aug. 1901.
51 Pratesi to Bandini, 2 Mar. 1902. Bandini's review, entitled "Il Nuovo Romanzo di Mario Pratesi," appeared in *Medusa* 1/8 (23 Mar. 1902).
52 Pratesi to Bandini, 23 Mar. 1902.
53 D[omenico] O[liva], review of *Il Mondo di Dolcetta* in *Corriere della Sera* (24 Mar. 1896).
54 R[affaello] B[arbiera], Comment on *Il Peccato del dottore* in *L'Illustrazione italiana* (6 July 1902).
55 Sidney Sonnino to Pratesi, 28 Aug. 1902.
56 *Nuova Antologia*, 16 Aug. 1898.
57 Pratesi to Masi, 4 Jan. 1903.
58 Ibid.
59 Gino Bandini, "Il Nuovo Romanzo di Mario Pratesi": "che riunisce in sè lo studio di tante passioni diverse del cuore umano, che ci sa dare l'odio e l'affetto, esprimere l'ironia e il dolore, che può analizzare casi psicologici con finezza squisita, investigare e ritrarre i gusti e i sentimenti degli uomini e degli animali come se uscisse dalla penna di un perfetto umorista che asseconda sotto il sorriso il pensiero triste e profondo."
60 Ernesto Masi, review of *Il Peccato del dottore* in *Il Giornale d'Italia* (8 Apr. 1903): "C'è capitato di leggere qua e là qualche giudizio dell'ultimo libro di Pratesi e ci ha sorpreso veder tanto dimenticate e trascurate, e nei biasimi e nelle lodi, l'indole e la particolare fisonomia di questo scrittore, state già tuttavia riconosciute l'una e l'altra fino dai primi suoi saggi. Quasi nessuno sembra riconoscere in lui il filosofo artista, il quale si vale dell'arte a studio di problemi psicologici e sociali ... Non vorremmo essere a nostra volta fraintesi e che ci si attribuisse il proposito di vantare il libro del Pratesi per un capolavoro, su cui la critica fosse passata senz'accorgersene o deliberatamente malevole. Mai più! Secondo noi anzi il libro ha pecche non scarse nè lievi. Ad ogni modo però resta uno studio umano e profondo non solo d'un'individualità eccezionale, su cui il mondo, che l'attornia, agisce con effetti sinistri, ma di tutto un aspetto di vita italiana attuale nelle sue ramificazioni pubbliche e private, pensato e descritto con passione, con originalità, con sincerità."
61 Pratesi himself owned a cat named Camuffi whom he described to Barzellotti as "un gatto rosso intelligentissimo e ladrissimo." Pratesi to Barzellotti, 27 July 1897, in Fatini, "Un romanziere amiatino," 40.

62 Diogene (Attilio Brunialti), review of *Da fanciullo: memorie del mio amico Tristano; La Tarantella sul Lido* (Florence: Le Monnier, 1872), in *Il Diritto* (7 Feb. 1872).
63 In Pratesi's correspondence she is always referred to as Donna Angiolina.
64 Pratesi, *Il Peccato del dottore*: "Tuttavia sono sempre io il più colpevole. Io dovevo rispettare e compatire di più una fragile donna; non dovevo innamorarmene troppo; non dovevo negarle da ultimo la parola di perdono e di pace che ella voleva da me prima di partire, e d'immolarsi per la figliuola. Come prima l'egoismo sensuale, così l'orgoglio ferito, e infine sempre lo stesso egoismo soffocò in me ogni voce della coscienza e della pietà. Questo è il mio peccato, questo il mio rimorso" (295–6).
65 Abba to Pratesi, 21 July 1902: "Quel Dottore sei tu in parte, fors'anche quasi in tutto."
66 Abba to Pratesi, 1 Jan. 1903: "io vi aveva gustato delle pagine da Maestro, le più anzi mi erano sembrate tali; ma per me sta sempre un principio che sarà forse antiquato e che tuttavia credo giusto, e sta in ciò che la parte ignobile della vita non vuol essere assunta dall'arte, perché non fa vergognare i tristi d'esser tristi, e non giova ai buoni che di trovarsi a vedere il male hanno anche troppe occasioni nella realtà. O vogliamo che l'arte si faccia rivelatrice del male?"
67 Pratesi, *Il Peccato del dottore*: "Io sono ... la realtà delle cose e dei fatti trasformata in ritmo, in volo, in voce sovrano. Io comprendo tutto quanto palpita d'intelligente e divino nella natura: io sono il mistero dell'anima universale; la forza più intima che lega i cuori e fa sentir loro l'unità della vita; io rendo agli uomini in numeri armoniosi, in immagini d'aquila, e nei detti dell'eterna sapienza, tutta la materia dei loro sogni, tutto l'orrore delle loro catastrofi, tutta l'ebbrezza dei loro amori, tutta la pietà dei loro singhiozzi, e ci hanno piacere" (314).
68 "Pensiero intimo e più profondo, nell'umana verità dei caratteri." Testament in *Carteggio Inedito di Mario Pratesi*, edited by Anne Urbancic and Carmela Colella, Victoria University Library, Toronto, 2009. http://pratesi.vicu.utoronto.ca/index.html
69 Guidotti, *Un'aurora dall'Amiata*, 108, and also in *Il romanzo toscano e Mario Pratesi*, 110.
70 Pratesi to Bandini and Dante Pratesi, 20 July 1905.
71 "Il profeta di Montelabbro" in *Figure e paesi d'Italia* (1905). Barzellotti to Pratesi, 15 Dec. 1904.
72 Several chapters had been previously published elsewhere including "Una iettatura," "La villa di Massimo D'Azeglio," and the more recent "L'idea religiosa dopo il 1815 e il *Prometeo* di Shelley (*Nuova Antologia*, 1 Sept. 1903), and "*I Cenci:* Dramma di Shelley" (*Nuova Antologia*, 16 June 1904).

73 Barzellotti to Pratesi, 15 Dec. 1904.
74 Giacomo Barzellotti, *Monte Amiata e il suo profeta* (Milan: Treves, 1909).
75 Adelaide Maraini to Pratesi, end of Mar. 1905. Clemente, who was too ill to write, died in the following month.
76 Francesco Sclavo to Pratesi, 18 July 1905.
77 Luisa Anzoletti to Pratesi, 30 June 1905.
78 Paolo Savj-Lopez to Pratesi, 7 Nov. 1905: "pagine fresche e vive, atte a suscitar l'amore del Paese nostro facendolo ben conoscere ai giovani." Pratesi's work can be found in Paolo Savj-Lopez, *Dalla vita e dall'arte: Letture moderne di Prosa e Poesia per le scuole secondarie* (Turin: Paravia, 1906). There is no evidence that Pratesi's career as teacher shaped or influenced his travel pieces, which though anthologized in school texts, had always been primarily intended for a wider reading public. Nor did educational reforms that came into effect during his teaching years appear to influence his work.
79 Pratesi to Bandini and Dante Pratesi, 20 July 1905.
80 N. Di Maria Mulé, "Un bello ed utile libro," review of *Figure e paesi d'Italia* in *Pro-Caltanissetta e Provincia* 1/3 (6 May 1905).
81 [Emilio Treves], "Movimento letterario," review of *Figure e paesi d'Italia* in *L'Illustrazione italiana* (28 May 1905). For a further brief discussion, see Massimo Grillandi, *Emilio Treves* (Turin: UTET, 1977). By that time, Treves was no longer the publisher of the magazine, but did contribute as journalist. Emilio Treves to Pratesi, 7 Feb. 1902.
82 Mario Pratesi, "Una lettera di Mario Pratesi," *L'Illustrazione italiana* (18 June1905). It appears that with this letter, Pratesi's collaboration with the popular magazine came to its end. His last contribution of a few months later is a piece that only confirmed Treves' opinion: "Canto toscano d'autunno," appeared in *L'Illustrazione italiana* on 19 Nov. 1905. Some bibliographies indicate that later Pratesi contributed a poem on the occasion of the marriage of Guido Treves with Antonietta Pesenti. *L'Illustrazione italiana* published a special limited edition (400 copies) of the magazine to be distributed to friends and wedding guests, never available to the public. However, Pratesi's name does not appear there, nor in the accompanying book of prose and poetry by eminent contemporary writers offered as a gift to the bride and groom by Emilio Treves. See "Nozze Treves-Pesenti," *L'Illustrazione italiana*, special issue limited to 400 copies, not for public sale,1 July 1909 (now in the archives of Il Vittoriale degli Italiani), and Franco di Tizio, *Antonietta Treves e D'Annunzio: Carteggio inedito 1909–1938* (Altino, Chieti: Ianieri, 2005).
83 Laura Gropallo, review of *Figure e paesi d'Italia* in *La Cultura* 24/6 (1905), 195–6: "Anima mite e gentile, nessun paesaggio, come nessuna figura lo

lascia indifferente, coducendolo a confondere figure e paesaggio in una evocazione piena di tenerezza e di commozione ... Insomma un libro di piacevole cultura, dettato da un animo aperto al Bello ... Una lingua viva nella varietà de' suoi vocaboli come nella sua ricca flessuosità."
84 Giulio Natali, "Un pensatore artista," review of *Figure e paesi d'Italia* in *L'Avvenire: Giornale della provincia di Pavia* (25–6 July 1905). Pratesi was "il pensatore, l'uomo di buon gusto, l'osservatore arguto, lo scrittore fecondo e di straordinaria ricchezza di lingua."
85 "Il valore del critico e del saggista spiega la signorile plenitudine anche intellettuale del romanziere." I have been unable to trace the original review; Natali summarizes it in his article: "Mario Pratesi (Con sette lettere inedite," in *Ricordi e profili di maestri e amici* (Rome: Edizioni di storia e letteratura, 1965), 61–2.
86 Giuseppe Lipparini, review of *Figure e paesi d'Italia* in *Il Marzocco* (30 July 1905).
87 Unsigned review of *Figure e paesi d'Italia* in *Rivista d'Italia* 8/7 (July 1905), 151.
88 Ibid.: "In questo volume conosciamo il Pratesi anche sotto il nuovo aspetto di critico letterario: ... che rivela gusto estetico molto fine, ma forse non abbastanza possesso della qualità critica per eccellenza che consisteva, secondo il De Sanctis, nel saper trasfonder se stesso nella personalità dei vari autori. Invece anche nella critica il Pratesi resta soprattutto *se stesso*, dandoci talvolta più un'esposizione delle idee proprie che un esame di quelle dello scrittore."
89 Barzellotti to Pratesi, 17 June 1916.
90 Luisa Anzoletti to Pratesi, 5 Jan. 1917, and Nella Mazzoni to Pratesi, end of 1916.
91 Alfonso Conte, letter in *La Rassegna nazionale* (16 Nov. 1916).
92 Luisa Anzoletti to Pratesi, 5 Jan. 1917.
93 Unsigned [but Giuseppe Fanciulli] review of *Il Mondo di Dolcetta* in *La Perseveranza* (25 Feb. 1917).
94 Pratesi to Bandini, 5 Dec. 1916: "Al libro meditato e sentito e scritto in mezzo a dolori indicibili fu opposto il silenzio, o ebbe articoli indegnamente velenosi come quello del Sig. Corr[adini]; ... Vorrei dunque che rivivesse in un nuovo volume."
95 Luisa Anzoletti to Pratesi, 5 Jan. 1917: "Sarebbe poi utile cosa ch'Ella entrasse in rapporti di scambievoli buoni uffici con qualche scrittore di qui, il quale abbia, come dicono, entratura nei giornali. Allora, s'Ella volesse occuparsi dei loro libri, per esempio scrivendone il Suo giudizio in qualche giornale importante, ne sarebbe ricambiato dalle loro penne e verrebbe così richiamata quell'attenzione del pubblico riguardo all'autore, da cui oggigiorno tanto dipende l'interesse dell'editore."

96 Guidotti, *Un'aurora dall'Amiata*, 109, and also in *Il romanzo toscano e Mario Pratesi*, 111.
97 In addition to Cena, his brother Dante, Giacomo Barzellotti, and Adelaide Maraini also passed away in 1917 as did Oskar Bullé, Eugenia Karo, Raffaello Fornaciari, Leopoldo Franchetti, Domenico Oliva, Leopoldo Pullè, and Pasquale Villari, all long-time friends or colleagues whose deaths affected Pratesi profoundly.
98 Pratesi to Maggiorino Ferraris, 18 Feb. 1907.
99 Pratesi to Bandini, 11 Nov. 1908.
100 Remo Sandron to Pratesi, 16 June 1910.
101 Pratesi to Ferraris, 22 Mar. 1908. "La Follia del Marchese Roberto," *Nuova Antologia* (16 Oct., 1 and 16 Nov. 1908).
102 Guidotti, *Un'aurora dall'Amiata*, 110, and also in *Il romanzo toscano e Mario Pratesi*, 112.
103 Barzellotti to Pratesi, 3 Nov. 1908.
104 Rovetta to Pratesi, 11 Dec. 1908.
105 Abba to Pratesi, 26 Dec. 1908: "Nel tuo racconto vi sono delle pagine stupende dove l'azione diventa analisi finissima. Il Marchese Roberto è perfettamente fatto. Passa forse un po' la misura quella druda, ma solo in certi momenti; perché nel tutto insieme anch'essa è riuscita. Nobilissima la fanciulla, nato come la luce del sole il suo amore ... Quella lezione su Dante e sul Petrarca glielo ha creato dentro. Credo che poche pagine sui due grandi siano state scritte con visione così sicura e con parola così eloquente nella loro signorile sobrietà. Devono rimanere ben impresse nella mente di chi legge! E riuscire ben nuove! Tu dubiti che il racconto non mi sia piaciuto? L'hai detto per celia. Oh lo sai che m'è piaciuto, perché sento che piace a te. Sono certo che questa è una delle cose tue che ami di più."

Years later, planning a never realized volume of short stories, Pratesi insisted that the pages on Dante and Petrarch indeed presented an original perspective. Pratesi to Firenze Santandrea, 28 Nov. 1919.
106 Mario Pratesi Archives, Victoria University Library, Toronto.
107 Luisa Anzoletti to Pratesi, 10 Mar. 1918.
108 Giuseppe Manni to Pratesi, 30 Oct. 1917, and Sofia Bertolini Guerrieri Gonzaga to Pratesi, 24 Jan. 1918.
109 Luisa Santandrea to Pratesi, 20 Nov. 1918: "Una verità grande Lei ha rico-nosciuta specialmente, con franchezza tolstojana, pur ammettendo la necessità di combattere con le armi chi con le armi."
110 Luisa Mussini to Pratesi, 22 Nov. 1918.
111 Dated 19 Oct. 1920, with codicil dated 20 Mar. 1921.

112 Guidotti, *Un'aurora dall'Amiata*, 112, and also in *Il romanzo toscano e Mario Pratesi*, 114. Guidotti refers to Mazzoni's comments in the *Rapporto accademico per l'anno 1920–21* in commemoration of Renato Fucini and Mario Pratesi, Atti Accademici della Crusca, 1920–21, 3–20.
113 Pratesi to Augusta and Gino Bandini, 21 June 1920: "dall'ultima estate scorsa, è per me incominciato l'epilogo, o la tragedia nera della vecchiaia, la quale può esser provvidenziale in questo, che ci fa desiderare, e spesso invocare, la morte."
114 Dated 19 Oct. 1920, with codicil dated 20 Mar. 1921.
115 Quoted in Edward Said, *On Late Style: Music and Literature against the Grain* (New York: Pantheon, 2006), 11.
116 Giorgio De Rienzo, *Il poeta fuori gioco: Nostalgia, mitologia e cronaca dell'Ottocento minore* (Rome: Bulzoni, 1981), 249.
117 Said, *On Late Style*, 67.

Conclusion

1 Pratesi to G.C. Abba, 22 Apr. 1887: "come per tutti i librai e gli editori, il libro buono è solo quel che si vende. Il … rifiuto dipende dunque non dal libro che manchi di pregio ma dal gusto comune a cui partecipa [l'editore] che segue, modernissimo e mercantissimo, la corrente."

   The correspondence between Pratesi and Giuseppe Cesare Abba is quoted with the kind permission of the heirs of Pratesi, unless otherwise indicated.

2 Pratesi to Gino Bandini, 20 July 1905: "La loro critica, come si fa in Italia, o è una mezza lode, concessa a stento, tramescolata a piccole censure, spesso cervellotiche, la quale non invoglia certo a comprare il libro, e fa piuttosto male che bene, perché induce l'opinione che si tratti d'un libro mediocrissimo: ovvero è lode a grancassa, a cui pochi credono, e che è la stessa che si usa per il *Tot*, o per le pillole del Bertelli. Un articolo, anche breve, che colga le note più caratteristiche e più salienti del libro, il fondo del suo pensiero, non si ha quasi mai dai nostri giornali. Mancano di coscienza d'equità, e non di rado vi senti la piccola invidiuzza lontano un miglio.

3 "Nel giro di poco più di un anno gli abbiamo sovvenuto due mila lire. (Pratesi stesso glie lo può dire, perché sempre gli mandammo le risposte degli editori.) Noi abbiamo tentato varie volte, anche con invio di copie dei libri, presso Treves, la "Sten" di Torino, Bemporad, Sonzogno, Casa Varieta, ecc ma sempre *invano*! Gli editori dicono tutti che i libri del Pratesi, pur essendo assai ben scritti e pensati, non sono il genere che va

bene per il gusto corrente ... Non vogliono quindi arrischiare, nè tanto meno fare anticipi. Però poichè rifare il tentativo non nuoce, possiamo noi tre: io con gli editori di Milano, lei con quelli di Firenze, e la Trigona con quelli di Roma ... I *romanzi* offribili e liberi sono: *L'Eredità, Il Mondo di Dolcetta, Jacopo e Marianna, Le Perfidie del caso* e poi i *racconti* "La Follia del Marchese Roberto," "Troppa grazia Sant'Antonio," "Acque passate" ed altri, infine parecchi volumi di *Novelle* e *libri vari* come *Figure e paesi d'Italia, Ricordi veneziani* (bellissimi questi, e proprio, secondo me, i suoi *migliori* con *L'Eredità*). Comunichiamoci le risposte reciproche ... [senza] dare esca alle speranze di Pratesi, che (le parlo *per prova*) è facilissimo alle *illusioni*, non solo, ma alle pretese; perché fin che qualcosa fanno per lui gli amici, allora è grato fin troppo, buono e calmo – ma quando c'entrano gli editori, anche come lontana speranza, perde la serenità dell'attesa, e vede uno sfruttamento di terzi in ogni proposta, e trova ingiustizia, infamie e via dicendo."

Gina Lombroso Ferrero (1872–1944), daughter of the criminologist Cesare Lombroso, a writer, was a friend of both Santandrea and Pratesi. The reference to Trigona is to the Marquise Paola (Lina) Farina Trigona di Canicarao-Dainnamara (1880–1964). She was also a writer (pseudonym Paola Stafenda). Her mother Margherita Cini and aunt, Elena Cini French, were old and dear friends of Pratesi. The letter above is quoted with the kind permission of Bosiljka Raditsa, heir of Lombroso Ferrero from correspondence now conserved in the Archivio Contemporaneo "Alessandro Bonsanti," Gabinetto G.P. Vieusseux, Florence, Fondo Lombroso Ferrero, lettera da Luisa Santandrea, 14 maggio 1921.

In writing to Luisa's husband, Firenze Santandrea, who was the Italian literary agent for publishers Curtis Brown of London, Pratesi impatiently urges his former student to present his books for translation into English and possible adaptation to film as quickly as possible (see letters of Pratesi to Santandrea of 31 Dec. 1919, and Jan., 8 Feb., and 21 Mar. 1920). Unfortunately, as the correspondence between Santandrea and playwright Sem Benelli clearly shows, in the same matter of translation and film rights and in the same period, the process was a particularly long and tedious one (over four years in the case of Benelli), and could not respect Pratesi's claim to urgency. The letters between Benelli and Santandrea are preserved in the Archivio Storico del Comune di Prato.

Bibliography

Archives Consulted

Archives of the Biblioteca Nazionale Centrale di Firenze (BNCF).
Archives of the Casa Carducci, Bologna.
Archives of Il Vittoriale degli Italiani, Gardone Riviera, Brescia.
Archivio Contemporaneo "Alessandro Bonsanti," Gabinetto G.P. Vieusseux, Florence.
Archivio Storico, Comune di Prato.
Archivio Storico, Comune di Siena.
Carteggio Inedito di Mario Pratesi. Eds. Anne Urbancic and Carmela Colella, Victoria University Library, Toronto, 2009 http://pratesi.vicu.utoronto.ca/index.html Unless otherwise indicated, all correspondence (except with G.C. Abba) may be found in this collection.
Correspondence between Pratesi and Giuseppe Cesare Abba is quoted with the kind permission of the heirs of Mario Pratesi, unless otherwise indicated.
Mario Pratesi Archives, Victoria University Library, Toronto.

Periodical Collections Consulted

Biblioteca Braidense, Milan.
Biblioteca degli Intronati, Siena.
Biblioteca Nazionale Centrale di Firenze.
Biblioteca Marucelliana di Firenze.
Biblioteca Sormani, Milan.
British Library (periodicals), Colindale Branch, London, UK.
Robert Fisher Rare Books Library, University of Toronto, Toronto.

Works by Mario Pratesi

1863
Agli insorti polacchi. [Poetry.] Florence: Spiombi.

1864
Addio. [Poetry.] Florence: Galileiana.
Alla Gentil Donzella Cleide Bandini nel giorno delle nozze col professore Tommaso Sanesi. [Poetry.] Florence: Galileiana.
In morte di Stanislao Bechi: Canto. Florence: Niccolai.

1866
Alla Gentil Donzella signora Carolina Mayer nel giorno delle sue nozze Col Sig. Dott. Giuseppe Comandi. [Poetry.] Pisa: Nistri, n.d., but 1866.
In occasione che si facevano nella Chiesa di Provenzano triduane preghiere per la vittoria [delle] armi d'Italiane sopra quelle dell'Austria: Carme lirico. Siena: Moschini.
La Notte. Canto di Mario Pratesi a benefizio delle famiglie bisognose dei volontari [For the benefit of families of war volunteers in needy circumstances]. Siena: Mucci.
Vaticinio: Per il Diciassettesimo anniversario di Curtatone e il Settimo Centenario della Battaglia di Legnano. [Poetry.] Pisa: Nistri.

1867
Ode per la festa annuale di Santa Caterina Benincasa nella chiesa della Contrada dell'Oca il 12 maggio 1867. Siena: Mucci.

1869
"D'una academia musicale offerta dalla Società Cherubini" in *Il Sistro*, n.d.
"Dialogo dei morti del Camposanto della Misericordia al giungere delle ceneri di Quinto Settano," signed Tristano, in *Il volontario: Periodico settimanale della giovine democrazia* 1/32 (8 Sept.), 2–3.
"Le glorie e le gioie del lavoro di Paolo Mantegazza" in *Il Diritto*, n.d.
A Caterina Benincasa. Siena: Mucci; extracts from *Letture di Famiglia*.
"A una rondine," extracted from *Giornale illustrato* (1869[?]).
Ai colli di Firenze – Ricordanze. Siena: Mucci.
La Tarantella sul lido. Florence: Le Monnier.
Per le nozze di Lidia Bandini e Gaetano Zanoboni. Florence: Cellini.
Per morti di Custoza e Lissa. In *Morte di Giovan Battista Bertossi uno dei Mille*. Prato: Tip. Contrucci e Soci e Tip. Cellini.
Per una morta fanciulla; La chiesuola di Ponte alle Grazie; L'Angelo custode. Siena: Tip. Mucci.

1870

La vita dell'infanzia; Memorie dell'amico Tristano. In installments in *Il Diritto* 19, 20, and 21 March, and later that year as a small booklet published by Civelli.

1871

"Le viole di Marianna" in *Il Diritto* (Sept.).

1872

Da Fanciullo: Memorie del mio amico Tristano; and La Tarantella sul Lido. Florence: Le Monnier. Reprinted in: *In Provincia* (Florence: Barbèra, 1883 and 1884); in *Letture italiane tratte da opere recenti e annotate da Sofia Heim*, 2nd revised and improved ed. (Zurich: F. Schulthess, 1892); and in M. Pratesi, *Racconti*, edited by G. Luti and J. Soldateschi (Rome: Salerno, 1979).
Jacopo e Marianna. Rome: Civelli.

1873

Necrologio: "Antonietta Pozzolini." *La Nazione* (16 May).
"Noterelle prese a Venezia di M.P." *Il Diritto* (17, 18, 19, 21, 22, 23, 25, 26, 27, and 29 Nov.).

1876

"Belisario" in *Nuova Antologia* (Mar.–Apr.), and later in *In Provincia*.

1877

"Saffo: Statua della signora Adelaide Maraini" in *L'Illustrazione italiana* (22 Apr.).
"Sera d'aprile" in *L'Illustrazione italiana* (6 May).

1878

"Un vagabondo" in *Nuova Antologia* (15 Nov., 1 and 15 Dec.), and later in *In Provincia*.

1879

"Gli Istituti Tecnici" in *Il Diritto* (22 Feb.).
"Dal Monteamiata a Sovana" in *La Rassegna settimanale* (1 June), and later in *In Provincia* as "Sovana." The work also appeared as "Una città etrusca" *in Di paese in paese* (Milan: Galli, 1892) and in *Figure e paesi d'Italia* (Turin: Roux and Viarengo, 1905).
"Un Corvo tra i selvaggi" in *La Rassegna settimanale* (14 Dec.), later translated into English by Jessie Laussot Hillebrand as "A Raven amidst Savages," in the *Cornhill Magazine* 44 (1881).

1880
"Quaresima e carnevale" in *La Rassegna settimanale* (20 Feb.), later as "Il dottor Febo" in *In Provincia*, and then as "Il carnevale del cieco" in *La Dama del minuetto* (Milan-Palermo: Sandron, 1910).

"Dopo una lettura del *Cantico dei Cantici*" in *La Rassegna settimanale* (9 May), and later in *In Provincia*.

"Un ballo nel monastero" in *La Rassegna settimanale* (25 July), then as "Un ballo nel convento" in *In Provincia*, and then retitled "La mummia" in *La Dama del minuetto*. Translated into French by G.D. and published as "Un bal dans un monastère toscan" in *Revue Britannique* 10 (Oct.).

1881
"Il Signor Diego" in *La Rassegna settimanale* (20 Nov.), and later in *In Provincia*.

1882
"L'Isola d'Elba." Written at this time and intended for the volume *In Provincia*, it finally appeared in *Figure e paesi d'Italia*.

"L'Isola di Pianosa." Written at this time and intended for the volume *In Provincia*, it finally appeared in *Figure e paesi d'Italia*.

"Padre Anacleto da Caprarola", in *Nuova Antologia* (1 Oct. 1882) and later in *In Provincia*.

1883 and 1884
"Carlo Hillebrand" in *L'Illustrazione italiana* (16 Nov. 1884).

In Provincia. Florence: Barbèra, 1883 and 1884.

1885
"Catuzza" in *Nuova Antologia* (1 Mar.), then retitled "Una iettatura" in *Di paese in paese* and in *Figure e paesi d'Italia*.

"Il profeta di Montelabbro" in *Pungolo della domenica* (5 May).

"Riva Calabra" [poetry] in *Domenica del Capitan Fracassa* (13 Dec.).

1886
"Santi, solitari e filosofi" in *L'Illustrazione italiana* (28 July).

"Campagna milanese (Lungo il Naviglio)" [poetry] in *L'Illustrazione italiana* (19 Dec.).

1887
"Certosa di Garignano" [poetry] in *L'Illustrazione italiana* (6 Feb.).

"La Saffo della Signora A. Maraini e l'arte di moda" in *Il Rosmini* (1 Apr.), republished as "Arte vecchia e arte nuova" later in *Figure e paesi d'Italia*.

"Tarantella sul lido" [poetry] in *L'Illustrazione italiana* (3 Apr.).

1889
"Ricordi veneziani" in *L'Illustrazione italiana* (17 Mar., 19 May, 2 and 30 June, 28 July, 4 Aug., 10 Nov., and 8 Dec.), republished in *Di paese in paese*, and later in a single volume published in 1899 (Milan: Baldini and Castoldi), then republished in Milan-Palermo by Sandron in 1901. A German edition was translated by Mrs Müller-Roder (Berlin-Leipzig: Lüpeden-Merron, 1905).
L'Eredità. Florence: Barbèra. And *L'Eredità*, edited by Vasco Pratolini (Milan: Bompiani, 1965 [1942]).

1890
"I veneziani di Brera" in *L'Illustrazione italiana* (19 Jan.).
"I grandi pittori veneti del Cinquecento: Paolo Veronese, Tiziano, Jacopo Tintoretto" in *Nuova Antologia* (16 Mar., 1 Apr., and 16 May).
"La Villa di Massimo D'Azeglio" in *Nuova Antologia* (1 Nov.), and later in *Di paese in paese* and in *Figure e paesi d'Italia*.

1892
Di paese in paese. Milan: Galli.

1893
"Per la scuola elementare" in *Fanfulla della domenica* (12 Nov.).
"Ai maestri e alle maestre." In *Calendario Scolastico* (15 Oct.). Belluno: Cavessago.

1894–1895
"Il Mondo di Dolcetta: Racconto" in *Nuova Antologia* (16 Sept., 1 and 16 Oct., 1 and 16 Nov., 1 and 16 Dec. 1894, and 1 and 16 Jan., 1 and 16 Feb., 1 and 16 Mar. 1895. Published as a single volume (Milan: Galli, 1895).
"Agli alunni del Liceo e del Ginnasio di Belluno (in Occasione dell'incarico di Vice-Presidente affidato a Francesco Pellegrini)" in *Bollettino scolastico* (Belluno: Cavessago, 1894).
Sul Feretro del Preside Prof. Francesco de Francesco, 9 aprile 1894. Belluno: Cavessago[?], 1894.

1898
Le Perfidie del caso. Milan: Treves.

1899
"Coscienza: A proposito di un libro" in *La Critica Nuova* 1/2 (14 Jan. 1900). Reviewed in *Coscienza: Liriche di Giuseppe Martinozzi* (Bologna: Zanichelli, 1899).

Di paese in paese. Milan: Baldini and Castoldi.
Ricordi veneziani. 2nd ed. Milan: Baldini and Castoldi.

1900
Le Perfidie del caso, with a preface by Ernesto Masi. 2nd ed. Milan: Treves.
Versi per Nozze Maraini-Guerrieri Gonzaga. Belluno: Tip. Cavessago; at first with the title "Il maggio MDCCCC. Sonetti due con lettera dedicatoria. Nozze Maraini-Guerrieri Gonzaga."

1901
Ricordi veneziani. 3rd ed. revised by the author. Milan-Palermo: Sandron.

1902
"Il monumento a Dante" in *Il Giornale d'Italia* (15 Feb.).
Il Peccato del dottore in *La Rivista d'Italia* (Apr. 1901), then as a single volume (Milan: Baldini and Castoldi, 1902).
"La rovina del campanile di San Marco" in *Medusa* 1/25 (2 July).
"Ricordi fiorentini e romani" in *Il Giornale d'Italia* (6 Sept.).
"Cose vedute e voci interiori" in *Il Giornale d'Italia* (5 Dec.).

1903
"L'idea religiosa dopo il 1815 e il *Prometeo* di Shelley" in *Nuova Antologia* (1 Sept.).

1904
"*I Cenci:* Dramma di Shelley" in *Nuova Antologia* (16 June).

1905
"Jessie Hillebrand" in *L'Illustrazione italiana* (21 May).
"Una lettera di Mario Pratesi" in *L'Illustrazione italiana* (18 June).
"Mozart" in *Il Giornale d'Italia* (2 Sept.).
"Canto toscano d'autunno" in *L'Illustrazione italiana* (19 Nov.).
"La Dama del minuetto" in *Nuova Antologia* (1 and 16 Dec.).
Figure e paesi d'Italia: Impressioni e ricordi. Turin: Roux and Viarengo.
Il Peccato del dottore. Turin: Roux and Viarengo.

1906
"La Dote di Marcellina, novella rustica" in *Nuova Antologia* (16 June).

1907
"Il rimpianto e i ricordi di Giosuè Carducci" in *Il Giornale d'Italia* (22 Feb.).
"La Barba di Meleagro di Bagnaia" in *Nuova Antologia* (16 June).

1908
"La Follia del marchese Roberto, Romanzo" in *Nuova Antologia* (16 Oct., 1 and 16 Nov.).

1909
"Gli orfani" in *Calabria e la Sicilia* (Florence).

1910
"Le due figliuole dell'ostessa, Novella toscana" in *Nuova Antologia* (1 and 16 Feb.).
La Dama del minuetto. Milan-Palermo: Sandron.

1911
"Il Capitano delle corazze: Novella fiorentina del secolo XVII" in *Nuova Antologia* (1 and 16 May and 1 June).
Il Peccato del dottore: Romanzo. Milan: Baldini and Castoldi.

1912
La Canzone in morte di Nullo di G.C. Abba. Turin: STEN.
Prefazione alle *Cose vedute: Novelle di Cesare Abba*. Turin: STEN.

1913
"Armonie e dissonanze, Romanzo" in *Nuova Antologia* (16 Apr., 1 and 16 May and 1 June).

1914
"Don Angelo e la sua nipote, Novella" in *Nuova Antologia* (16 May and 1 June).

1915
"Troppa grazia, Sant'Antonio, Novella" in *Nuova Antologia* (1 and 16 May).
"Alessandro Franchi: Discorso" in *La Rassegna nazionale* (1 June).
"Luisa Anzoletti (*I Canti dell'ora*)" in *La Rassegna nazionale* (1 Aug.).
"Un nobile esempio (Adelaide Maraini)" in *La Rassegna nazionale* (16 Oct.).

1916
Il Mondo di Dolcetta, corrected by the author, serialized in the *La Rassegna nazionale* (1 Jan. to 16 Oct.), again in a separate volume published by the *La Rassegna nazionale* in 1916. This edition was republished with substantial notes on the changes among the editions by Renato Bertacchini ([Bologna]: Cappelli, 1963).
"Gastone Lurini, caduto combattendo il 27 aprile 1916" in *La Rassegna nazionale* (1 Aug.).

"Elia Thesbite: Fantasia su motivi biblici" in *Nuova Antologia* (16 Nov. and 1 Dec.).

1917
"Problemi scolastici" in *La Rassegna nazionale* (16 Apr.).
"Colonello Dante Pratesi (necrologio)" in *La Rassegna nazionale* (16 July).
"Acque passate, Novella" in *Nuova Antologia* (1 Oct.).

1918
"Paesisti" in *La Rassegna nazionale* (1 July).
"Un povero militare, Novella" in *Nuova Antologia* (1 Nov.).

1920
"Il sogno del vecchio Benvenuto, Novella" in *Nuova Antologia* (16 Aug. and 1 Sept.).
"L'anima della donna" in *La Rassegna nazionale* (16 Sept.).
"La loro fede e la loro arte" in *La Rassegna nazionale* (16 Nov.).
Carità cristiana. Florence: Giannini.
Il Peccato del dottore. Milan: Vitagliano.

Published Reviews of Pratesi's Works

Da fanciullo: Memorie del mio amico Tristano
Diogene (Attilio Brunialti). Review of *Da fanciullo: Memorie del mio amico Tristano; La Tarantella sul Lido* (Florence: Le Monnier, 1872), in *Il Diritto* (Rome) (7 Feb. 1872).

Jacopo e Marianna
Diogene (Attilio Brunialti). Review in *Il Diritto* (Rome) (19 Nov. 1872).
Anonymous. Review in *La Perseveranza* (28 Dec. 1872).
Barzellotti, Giacomo. Review in *Nuova Antologia* 22 (Jan. 1873), 246–53.
Unsigned review in *L'Opinione* (Turin) (15 Mar. 1873).
Solimbergo, Giuseppe. Review in *Gazzetta d'Italia* (Florence) (11 Apr. 1873).
Carcano, Giulio. Review in *Vita Nuova* (Siena) (27 Apr. 1873).
Piccardi, G[ian] L[eopoldo]. Review in *Gazzetta del Popolo* (Rome) (11 July 1873).

Un Corvo tra i selvaggi
Anonymous. Review of "The Story of a Raven" in the *St James Gazette: An Evening Review and Record* (10 Feb. 1881).

In Provincia

D[epanis], G[iuseppe]. Review in *La Gazzetta Letteraria* 7/24 (16 June 1883).
B.A.T. Review in *L'Illustrazione italiana* (8 July 1883), 22–3.
Lee, Vernon. Review in the *Academy: A Weekly Review of Literature, Science and Art* (14 July 1883), 28.
Aristodemo B****. Review in *La Rassegna nazionale* (1 Nov. 1883), 462–4.
Bonghi, Ruggiero. Review in *La Cultura* (Oct. 1883), 322–6.
Lee, Vernon. "Un italiano dalla natura nordica: A proposito delle novelle di Mario Pratesi," in *Fanfulla della domenica* (28 June 1885).

L'Eredità

A.A. Review in *Lettere e Arti* (16 Feb. 1890), 14–15.
Y. Review in *La Rassegna nazionale* (1 Mar. 1890), 206.

Di paese in paese

Unsigned review in "In Biblioteca," *Il Diritto* (17 June 1892).
Unsigned review in *L'Avvisatore alessandrino* (27 June 1892).
Unsigned review in "La nostra biblioteca," *La Sentinella bresciana* (30 June 1892).
Ricchetti, A. "Note letterarie," *L'Adriatico* (18 July 1892).
R[ovetta], G[erolamo]. "Un libro d'arte," *Vita moderna* (31 July 1892).
Nevio. "Le poesie di Mario Pratesi," *La Fortuna* (Fano) (2 Sept. 1892).
Söhns, Dr Franz. Review in *Neuphilologisches Centralblatt* 10 (Oct. 1892).
Aramis. "Di paese in paese," *Corriere di Palermo* (7 Oct. 1892).
Colin, Jämes-Ed. Review in *Bulletin: Société neuchâteloise de géographie* 7 (1892–93).

Il Mondo di Dolcetta

Corradini, Enrico. Review in *Il Marzocco* (23 Feb. 1896).
Unsigned review in *Fanfulla della domenica* (Mar. 1896).
M[asi], E[rnesto]. Review in *L'Arte* 9 (1 Mar. 1896).
Silvius. Review in *Il Pallano* (Lanciano) 11 (13 Mar. 1896).
O[liva], D[omenico]. Review in *Corriere della Sera* (24 Mar. 1896).
Unsigned review in *La Stella di Mondovì* (28 Mar. 1896).
Unsigned review in *La Provincia: Giornale politico-letterario* (Teramo) (29 Mar. 1896).
Dottor Pangloss. "Buon tempo antico." Review in *Cacciatore delle Alpi: Foglio settimanale democratico* (19 Apr. 1896).
Dell'A, A.P. Review in *Rivista bibliografica di scienze e lettere* (Naples) (23 Apr. 1896).
Unsigned review in *Minerva: Rassegna internazionale e rivista delle riviste* (11 May 1896).

L.D.S. in *Il Capitan cortese: Periodico settimanale di letteratura, di arte e di vita elegante* (before 30 Aug. 1896).
Spencer Kennard, Joseph. Review in *Romanzi e romanzieri italiani*, vol. 1. 2nd ed. (Florence: Barbèra, 1905), 244.

Le Perfidie del Caso
Unsigned brief review in "Biblioteca della Nazione," *La Nazione* (Florence) (undated, but 1898).
Renato. Review in *L'Illustrazione italiana* (19 June 1898).
Corradini, Enrico. Review in *Il Marzocco* (24 July 1898).
Masi, Ernesto. Review in *Nuova Antologia* (16 Aug. 1898), partially reprinted in *L'Illustrazione italiana* (4 Sept. 1898).
Van Winkle. Review in *La Rassegna settimanale universale* (4 Dec. 1898).

Ricordi veneziani
Panzini, Alfredo. Review in "Tra Libri e Riviste," *Vita Internazionale* (5 July 1901).
Natali, Giulio. Review in *La Rassegna nazionale* (15 Aug. 1901).

Il Peccato del dottore
Bandini, Gino. "Il Nuovo Romanzo di Mario Pratesi," *Medusa* 1/8 (23 Mar. 1902).
B[arbiera], R[affaello]. Comment on *Il Peccato del dottore*, in *L'Illustrazione italiana* (6 July 1902).
Unsigned review in *La Lombardia* (14 Nov. 1902).
Masi, Ernesto. Review in *Il Giornale d'Italia* (8 Apr. 1903).

Figure e paesi d'Italia: Impressioni e ricordi
Di Maria Mulé, N. "Un bello ed utile libro," *Pro-Caltanissetta e Provincia* 1/3 (6 May 1905).
[Treves, Emilio]. "Movimento letterario," *L'Illustrazione italiana* (28 May 1905).
Gropallo, Laura. Review in *La Cultura* 24/6 (1905).
Unsigned review in *Rivista d'Italia* 8/7 (July 1905).
Natali, Giulio. "Un pensatore artista," *L'Avvenire: Giornale della provincia di Pavia* (25–6 July 1905).
Lipparini, Giuseppe. Review in *Il Marzocco* (30 July 1905).

Il Mondo di Dolcetta (1916)
Conte, Alfonso. Letter about *Il Mondo di Dolcetta*, in *La Rassegna nazionale* (16 Nov. 1916).
Unsigned review [but Giuseppe Fanciulli] in *La Perseveranza* (25 Feb. 1917).

References: Secondary Sources

Abbagnano, Nicola. "Positivism," in Donald M. Borchert, ed., *Encyclopedia of Philosophy*, vol. 7, 710–17. 2nd ed. Detroit: Macmillan Reference USA, 2006.

Anzoletti, Luisa. "Per lo studio d'un romanziere." Extracts from *La Rassegna nazionale* (1 Feb. 1907).

Bandini, Gino. "Giuseppe Cesare Abba e Mario Pratesi: Mezzo secolo di amicizia in un carteggio inedito." *Pegaso* 4/7 (1932), 1–32.

Bardazzi, Giovanni. "Lettori e critici: *"Il Conciliatore"* e Manzoni; Foscolo e Leopardi; Mazzini, Cattaneo, Tenca; Tommaseo," in Enrico Malato, ed., *Storia della letteratura italiana*, vol. XI, *La critica letteraria dal Due al Novecento*, 648. Rome: Salerno, 2003.

Bardi, Ubaldo, Mario Casprini, Massimiliano Marchi, and Michele Turchi. *I Peruzzi all'Antella*. Antella: Edizioni C.R.C., 1998.

Barzellotti, Giacomo. *Delle dottrine filosofiche nei libri di Cicerone: Tesi di Laurea di G. Barzellotti*. Florence: Barbèra, 1869.

— . *Monte Amiata e il suo profeta*. Milan: Treves, 1909.

Bellemin-Noël, Jean. "Psychoanalytic Reading and Avant-texte," in Jed Deppman, Daniel Ferrer, and Michael Groden, eds., *Genetic Criticism: Texts and Avant-textes*. Philadelphia: University of Pennsylvania Press, 2004.

Benso, L. Giulio. "Gli amici di Giuseppe Cesare Abba." *La Rassegna nazionale* (16 June 1918).

Bernardini, Nicola. *Guida alla stampa periodica italiana*. Lecce: Editrice Salentina, 1890.

Bertacchini, Renato. "Introduzione" and "Notizie intorno al *Mondo di Dolcetta* e nota al testo," in Mario Pratesi, *Il Mondo di Dolcetta*. Edited by Renato Bertacchini. Bologna: Cappelli, 1963.

— . "Pratesi tra due secoli," in Mario Pratesi, *L'Eredità*. Edited by Vasco Pratolini. Milan: Bompiani, 1965 [1942].

Bigazzi, Roberto. *I colori del vero: Vent'anni di narrativa, 1860–1880*. Pisa: Nistri-Lischi, 1969.

Bloom, Edward A. "'Labors of the Learned': Neoclassic Book Reviewing Aims and Techniques." *Studies in Philology* 54/4 (1957), 537.

Bonghi, Ruggero. "Concetto e ragioni di questa pubblicazione." *La Cultura* 1/1 (1882), 1.

— . "Prefazione," in Nicola Bernardini, *Guida alla stampa periodica italiana*. Lecce: Editrice Salentina, 1890.

Borlenghi, Aldo. "Introduzione a *Il mondo di Dolcetta*," in *Narratori dell'Ottocento e del primo Novecento*, vol. 1. Milan: R. Ricciardi, 1961–63.

Bottasso, Enzo. *Storia della biblioteca in Italia*. Milan: Editrice Bibliografica, 1984.

Bottini Massa, Enrico. *G. Cesare Abba*. Genoa: A.F. Formiggini, 1915.

Castronovo, Valerio. *La stampa italiana dall'Unità al Fascismo*. Bari: Laterza, 1970.

Cattaneo, Giulio. "Prosatori e critici dalla Scapigliatura al verismo: I veristi," in Emilio Cecchi and Natalino Sapegno, eds., *Storia della letteratura italiana*, vol. VIII, *Dall'Ottocento al Novecento*. Milan: Garzanti, 1976 [1969].

Cattanei, Luigi. "Abba e Pratesi a Pisa." *Italies* 6 (2002), 165–71. http://italies.revues.org/1574

Cheever, Susan. *Louisa May Alcott: A Personal Biography*. New York: Simon and Schuster, 2010.

Ciampini, Raffaele. *Vita di Niccolo Tommaseo*. Florence: Sansoni, 1945.

Croce, Benedetto. "Mario Pratesi." *La Critica* (20 May 1937). Republished in *La letteratura della nuova Italia*, vol. 5. Bari: Laterza, 1950.

De Amicis, Edmondo. *Un salotto fiorentino del secolo scorso*. Florence: Barbèra, 1902.

De Gubernatis, Angelo. *Dizionario biografico degli scrittori contemporanei*. Florence: Le Monnier, 1879.

De Mauro, Tullio. *Storia linguistica dell'Italia unità* Bari: Laterza, 1970.

De Rienzo, Giorgio. *Il poeta fuori gioco: Nostalgia, mitologia e cronaca dell'Ottocento minore*. Rome: Bulzoni, 1981.

Di Tizio, Franco. *Antonietta Treves e D'Annunzio: Carteggio inedito 1909–1938*. Altino, Chieti: Ianieri, 2005.

Falorsi, Guido. *Romanzieri italiani moderni*. Extracts from *La Rassegna nazionale*, 16 Nov. and 1 Dec. 1904. Florence: Ufficio della "Rassegna nazionale," 1904.

Fatini, Giuseppe. "Un romanziere amiatino, Mario Pratesi (Lettere a Giacomo Barzellotti)." *Annuario 1931–32 del Liceo Ginnasio Carducci Ricasoli*. Grosseto: n.p., 1933, 5–46.

Fiorino, Tonia. "Rileggendo Mario Pratesi." *Critica letteraria* 24/4 (1996), 167–203.

Fonnesu, Iolanda, and Leonardo Rombai. *Letteratura e paesaggio in Toscana: Da Pratesi a Cassola*. Florence: Centro Editoriale toscano, 2004.

Fontana Semerano, Sandra, and Paola Gennarelli Pirolo. "Le carte di Emilia Peruzzi nella Biblioteca Nazionale di Firenze," *Rassegna storica toscana* 26 (1980), 187–245, and also in *La Rassegna storica toscana* 30 (1984), 283–305.

Fortunato De Lisle, Lucille Mary. "The Circle of the Pear: Emilia Toscanelli Peruzzi and Her Salon – Political and Cultural Reflections, Issues and Exchange of Ideas in the New Italy, 1860–1880" (1 Jan. 1989). *Boston College Dissertations and Theses*. Paper AAI9015796.

Franchetti, A. "Ruggero Bonghi." *Archivio storico italiano* 17/201 (1896).

Galante Garrone, Alessandro. *La stampa periodica italiana dal 1815 al 1847*. Turin: G. Giappichelli, 1976.

Grillandi, Massimo. *Emilio Treves*. Turin: UTET, 1977.
Guidotti, Mario. *Un'aurora dall'Amiata* Siena: Maia, 1956.
— . *Il romanzo toscano e Mario Pratesi*. Florence: Vallecchi, 1983.
Gunn, Peter. *Vernon Lee: Violet Paget, 1856–1935*. London: Oxford University Press, 1964.
Hay, Louis. "Genetic Criticism: Origins and Perspectives," in Jed Deppman, Daniel Ferrer, and Michael Groden, eds., *Genetic Criticism: Texts and Avant-textes*. Philadelphia: University of Pennsylvania Press, 2004.
Hermet, Augusto. *La ventura delle riviste 1903–1940*. Florence: Vallecchi, 1941.
Hoge, James O. "Introduction," in James O. Hoge, ed., *Literary Reviewing*. Charlottesville: University Press of Virginia, 1987.
Jorio, Marco, ed., and Stiftung Historisches Lexikon der Schweiz. *Historisches Lexikon der Schweiz/Dictionnaire historique de la Suisse/Dizionario storico della Svizzera*. http://www.hls-dhs-dss.ch/textes/i/I30530.php
Lee, Vernon. *The Countess of Albany*. London: W.H. Allen 1884. http://www.gutenberg.ca/ebooks/lee-albany/lee-albany-00-h-dir/lee-albany-00-h.html
— . *Letters*. With a preface by her executor Irene Cooper Willis. London?: Privately printed, 1937.
Libreria Antiquaria Hoepli. *I migliori libri italiani consigliati da cento illustri contemporanei*. Milan: Ulrico Hoepli, 1892.
Lombardo, Mario, and Fabrizio Pignatel. *La stampa periodica in Italia: Mezzo secolo di riviste illustrate*. Rome: Editori Riuniti, 1985.
LoRenzo, Chiarlone. "Giuseppe Cesare Abba protagonista e la Val Bormida." http://www.cairomontenotte.com/biblioteca/vari/150/150ab09.html
Luti, Giorgio. *Narrativa italiana dell'Otto e Novecento*. Florence: Sansoni, 1964.
Macphail, Bruce. "Book Reviews and the Scholarly Publisher," in James O. Hoge, ed., *Literary Reviewing*. Charlottesville: University Press of Virginia, 1987.
Malato, Enrico. Entry in Paolo Orvieto, ed., *Storia della letteratura italiana*, vol. XI, *La Critica letteraria dal Due al Novecento*. Rome: Salerno, 2003.
Mattesini, Franceso. *Letteratura e pubblico: Studi e prospettive di storia letteraria tra Otto e Novecento*. Rome: Bulzoni, 1978.
Mazzoni, Guido. *R. Accademia della Crusca per la Lingua d'Italia: Rapporto accademico per l'anno 1920–21*. Florence: S. Davite, 1922.
McCutcheon, Roger Philip. "The Beginnings of Book-Reviewing in English Periodicals." *PMLA* 37/4 (1922).
Melis, Rossana. "Di paese in paese: Lettere di Mario Pratesi a Emilia Toscanelli Peruzzi," in Chiara Schiavon and Andrea Cecchinato, eds., *Una brigata di voci*. Studi offerti a Ivano Paccagnella per is suoi sessantacinque anni. Padua: CLEUP, 2012.

Morandi, Luigi. *Antologia della nostra critica letteraria moderna*. Edited by Luigi Morandi per le persone colte e per le scuole. Città di Castello: S. Lapi, 1891.

Mutti, Roberto, ed. *Giovanni Verga scrittore fotografo*. With an introduction by Guido Bezzola. Novara: De Agostini, 2004.

Natali, Giulio. "Mario Pratesi (Con sette lettere inedite," in *Ricordi e profili di maestri e amici*. Rome: Edizioni di storia e letteratura, 1965.

"Nel nome del padre, del figliuolo e dello Spirito Santo, Amen." Anonymous commentary in *La Canaglia* (Pavia), undated but end of Jan. 1873.

"Nozze Treves-Pesenti." *L'Illustrazione italiana* (special issue limited to 400 copies, not for public sale) (1 July 1909).

Orteza y Miranda, Evelina. "On Book Reviewing." *Journal of Educational Thought* 30 (Aug. 1996), 191.

Pagliaini, Attilio. *Catalogo generale della libreria italiana: Quarto supplemento dal 1931 al 1940*. 2 vols. Rome: S.A. per Pubblicazioni Bibliografico-Editoriali (S.A.B.E), 1957.

— . *Catalogo generale della libreria italiana dall'anno 1847 a tutto il 1899*. 2 vols. Rome: S.I.A.E, 1964. Print reprint.

— . *Catalogo generale della libreria italiana: Primo supplemento dal 1900 al 1910*. 2 vols. Rome: S.I.A.E, 1964. Print reprint.

— . *Catalogo generale della libreria italiana: Secondo supplemento dal 1901 al 1920*. 2 vols. Rome: S.I.A.E, 1964. Print reprint.

— . *Catalogo generale della libreria italiana: Terzo supplemento dal 1921 al 1930*. 2 vols. Rome: S.I.A.E, 1964. Print reprint.

Peloso, Paolo Francesco, and Tom Dening. "The Abolition of Capital Punishment: Contributions from Two Nineteenth-Century Italian Psychiatrists." *History of Psychiatry* 20/2 (2009), 215–25.

Piccardi, Gian Leopoldo. *Saggio di una storia sommaria della stampa periodica*. Rome: Fratelli Bencini, 1886.

Pratesi, Mario. *Da fanciullo: Memorie del mio amico Tristano; Edizioni 1883 e 1872*, edited by C.A. Madrignani and G. Bertonicini. Pisa: ETS Editrice, 1991.

Pratolini, Vasco. "Introduzione" to Mario Pratesi, *L'Eredità*. Edited by Vasco Pratolini. Milan: Bompiani, 1965 [1942].

Puppo, Mario. *Il romanticismo*. 2nd ed. Rome: Studium, 1973 [1967].

— . *Romanticismo italiano e romanticismo europeo*. Milan: Istituto Propaganda Libraria, 1985.

Ramuzzi, Muzio. "Lettere inedited di Mario Pratesi a Manfredo Vanni." *Ausonia* 16/5 (1961), 33–44.

Ricci, Carolina. *Napoli habillée: Scenari della Napoli aristocratica nelle lettere di Carolina Ricci (1882–1883)*. Edited with comments by Mariella Muscariello. Introduction by Georges Virlogeux, preface by Adele Failla Lemme. Venosa (PZ): Edizioni Osanna Venosa, 1997.

Roper, Derek. *Reviewing before Edinburgh, 1708–1802*. London: Methuen, 1978.
Ross, Silvia. *Tuscan Spaces: Literary Constructions of Place*. Toronto: University of Toronto Press, 2010.
Ruskin, John. *Venezia (Il Riposo di San Marco, La Cappella degli Schiavoni, L'Accademia, Paolo Veronese e gli Inquisitori, Sant'Orsola, Il Tintoretto e Michelangelo)*. Translated with comments by Maria Pezzé Pascolato. Florence: Barbèra, 1901.
Russo, Luigi. "Mario Pratesi," in *I narratori (1850–1950)*. New revised and expanded ed. Milan: Principato, 1951.
Said, Edward. *On Late Style: Music and Literature against the Grain*. New York: Pantheon, 2006.
Santandrea, Luisa. *Io e le cose*. Milan: Treves, 1924.
Sapegno, Natalino. "Pratesi," in *Compendio di storia della letteratura italiana*, vol. 3. Florence: La Nuova Italia, 1956.
— . *Antologia della storia e della critica letteraria*, vol. 3, *Dall'Ottocento ai giorni nostri*. Florence: Giunti-Bemporad Marzocco, 1974.
Savj-Lopez, Paolo. *Dalla vita e dall'arte: Letture moderne di Prosa e Poesia per le scuole secondarie*. Turin: Paravia, 1906.
Soldateschi, Jole. *Il laboratorio della prosa: Pratesi, Palazzeschi, Cicognini*. Florence: Vallecchi, 1986.
Sonnino, Sidney. *Lettere di Sidney Sonnino ad Emilia Peruzzi, 1872–1878*. Edited by Paola Carlucci. Pisa: Scuola Normale Superiore, 1998.
Urbancic, Anne. "The Renaissance Novellas of Mario Pratesi." *Studi rinascimentali* 2 (2004), 135–41.
Werner, Alice. *The Humour of Italy*. London: Walter Scott, 1892.
Woolf, Virginia. *Reviewing*. With a Note by Leonard Woolf. London: Hogarth Press, 1969 [1939], 7.
— . *Diary of Virginia Woolf*. Edited by Anne Oliver Bell and Andrew McNellie, 5 vols. London: Hogarth Press, 1975–80.
Zollino, Antonio. "Letteratura di fine Ottocento nell'officina dannunziana: Verga, Fogazzaro, Pratesi e De Marchi." *Nuova rivista di letteratura italiana* 9/1 (2006), 85–109.

Index

Abba, Giuseppe Cesare 16, 21–5, 26, 28, 29–32, 38, 42, 46, 47, 49–50, 51, 55, 64, 68, 72–3, 78, 82, 85, 89, 90, 93, 97, 101, 103, 110
Academy (journal) 59, 60, 61
Accademia della Crusca 101
"Acque passate" 105
Adorno, Theodor 107
Adriatico Gazzetta di Pesaro (newspaper) 70
Alcott, Louisa May 81–2
Anzoletti, Luisa 77, 99, 101, 102, 105, 133n47
Aramis (reviewer) 69
Arcangeli, Massimo 136n6
Aristodemo B**** (reviewer) 60
"Armonie e dissonanze" 104
Arrigo 23–4, 110
Arte, L' (periodical) 73
avant-texte 6, 7
Avvisatore alessandrino (newspaper) 69

B.A.T (reviewer) 128n87
Baldini e Castoldi (publishing house) 89, 91
"Ballo nel monastero, Un" 55, 57

Bandini, Gino 92, 94, 95, 99, 101, 104, 106, 108
"Barba di Meleagro di Bagnaia, La" 102
Barbèra (publishing house) 46, 56, 57, 61
Barbèra, Piero 57, 58, 65
Barbiera, Raffaello 94, 96
Baretti, Giuseppe 11–12
Barzellotti, Giacomo 4, 16, 18, 31, 33–4, 35–6, 46–50, 52, 54, 56, 58, 62–8, 71, 72, 75, 76, 80, 82, 84–6, 93, 94, 98, 99, 100, 103, 109
Baudelaire, Charles 30, 119n37
"Belisario" 46–51
Bellemin-Noël, Jean 6, 18, 29
Benelli, Sem 146n3
Bertacchini, Renato 78, 79, 80, 138n24
Bertolini Guerrieri-Gonzaga, Sofia 34, 105
Bertoncini, Giancarlo 26
Bianchi, Felicità (Cice) 104
Bloom, Edward A. 9
Bonghi, Ruggero 8, 10–11, 12–15, 20, 60, 61, 71, 77, 88, 113n10
Brunialti, Attilio (pseud. Diogene) 14, 27–8, 34–5

Cacciatore delle Alpi (newspaper) 74
Caffè, Il (periodical) 11
Canaglia, La (newspaper) 36–7, 40, 41, 42, 52
"Canto toscano d'autunno" 102
Capitan cortese, Il (periodical) 74
"Capitano delle corazze, Il" 104
Capuana, Luigi 61, 108
Carcano, Giulio 38–9
Carducci, Giosuè 19, 22, 62, 70, 109, 123n10, 129n93
Cattaneo, Carlo 13
Cellini, Benvenuto 106
Cena, Giovanni 102
Cheever, Susan 82
Chiarini, Giuseppe 73, 91, 92, 101
Colin, Jämes-Ed. 70
Conte, Alfonso 101
Conti, Augusto 56
Cornhill Magazine (periodical) 56
Coronaro, Clotilde Ricci 64, 68, 71
Coronaro, Gaetano 64
Corradini, Enrico 7, 18, 75, 77, 87, 88–9, 100, 101
Corriere della Sera (newspaper) 69, 75, 77
Corriere di Palermo (newspaper) 69
Corsi, Carlo 34
"Corvo fra i selvaggi, Un" 52, 56–7, 127n64
critique génétique 5–7, 23, 29, 109, 111
Croce, Benedetto 112
Cultura, La (periodical) 8, 12–15, 20, 60, 71, 77, 88, 99

D'Annunzio, Gabriele 5, 61, 73, 84, 89, 92, 97
D'Azeglio, Massimo 5, 64, 100
"Dal Monteamiata a Sovana" 53

"Dama del minuetto, La" 102–3, 104
De Amicis, Edmondo 15, 55
De Gubernatis, Angelo 11, 54
De Mauro, Tullio 114n12
de Rienzo, Giorgio 107
Del Lungo, Isidoro 48
Depanis, Giuseppe 128n81
Di Paese in paese 68–71, 89, 98
Dickens, Charles 4, 75
Diodati, John 114n21
Diogene (*see* Brunialti, Attilio)
Diritto, Il (newspaper) 12, 17, 27, 29, 34, 39, 41, 43 49, 68, 69, 87, 109
"Don Angelo e la sua nipote" 105
"Dopo una lettura del Cantico dei Cantici" 55
"Dote di Marcellina, La" 102
"Dottor Febo, Il" 54–5, 60, 102
Dottor Pangloss (reviewer) 74
"Due figliuole dell'ostessa, Le" 103

Eredità, L' 65–8, 81, 95

Fanciulli, Giuseppe 101, 102
Fanfulla della domenica (newspaper) 61, 75, 76
Farulli, Augusta 104
Ferraris, Maggiorino 84
Ferrero Lombroso, Gina 111, 146n3
Figure e paesi d'Italia 98, 101
Flaubert, Gustave 30, 61, 119n37
Fogazzaro, Antonio 67, 73, 76
"Follia del Marchese Roberto, La" 103
Fortuna (Fano) (newspaper) 70
Foscolo, Ugo 9
Franchetti, Leopoldo 52, 53
Frusta letteraria (di Aristarco Scannabue) 11–12
Fucini, Renato 81

Garibaldi, Giuseppe 22
Garlanda, Federico 78
Gazzetta d'Italia, La (newspaper) 38
Gazzetta del Popolo (newspaper) 38
Gazzetta Letteraria (periodical) 59
Gherardi, Alessandro 16, 28, 41, 52, 57, 59, 62, 64, 84, 85, 88, 93, 101
Giornale de' letterati, Il 10
Giornale d'Italia (newspaper) 94, 95
Gropallo, Laura 99
Guasti, Cesare 28, 59
Guidotti, Mario 25, 65, 67, 78, 81, 84, 89, 91–2, 98,102, 103, 106

Hay, Louis 5, 6, 23, 113n6
Hillebrand, Jessie Taylor Laussot 4, 31, 44, 54, 56, 67, 72, 113n2, 117n17
Hillebrand, Karl 31, 44–5, 50, 53, 54, 55
Hoge, James 12

"Iettatura (Catuzza), Una" 62, 69, 70, 102
Illustrazione italiana (periodical) 60–1, 64, 68, 86–7, 89, 94, 96, 99, 102, 142n82
In Provincia 59–63
inter-reader 7
Italie, L' (periodical) 75

Jacopo e Marianna 12, 28, 29–36, 38, 39, 41, 45, 47, 51, 87
Journal des Sçavans 10

Late Style Writing 6, 18, 106–8
Laussot, Jessie Taylor (*see* Hillebrand, Jessie Taylor Laussot)
Lazzaretti, David 98, 99
Lee, Vernon (*see* Paget, Violet)

Leoncavallo, Ruggero (*La Bohème*) 76, 133n54
Lettere e Arti (periodical) 67
Lipparini, Giuseppe 100
Liston, Sir Robert 12
Literacy in Italy in19th century 114n12
Livi, Carlo 25, 26, 118n20
Lombardia, La (periodical) 96
Luzzatti, Luigi 40, 42-43, 73, 109, 122n71

Madrignani, Carlo 26, 27
Manni, Giuseppe 105
Manzoni, Alessandro 8, 19, 23, 31, 35, 45, 61, 64, 87, 89, 109, 121n62
Maraini, Adelaide Pandiani 40, 51, 52, 59, 64, 72, 85, 88, 99
Maraini, Clemente 14, 47, 39–43, 45, 49, 51, 69, 71, 99, 109, 117n17
Maraini, Giulia 40
Maraini, Mimi 40
Martini, Ferdinando 73
Martinozzi, Giuseppe 57, 73
Marzocco, Il (periodical) 18, 75, 88, 100
Masi, Ernesto 7, 73–4, 81, 86, 87–8, 95
Mazzoni, Guido 106
Mazzoni, Nella 101
McCutcheon, Roger Philip 9
Medusa (periodical) 94
Memorie del mio amico Tristano 8, 12, 17, 25–8, 35, 39, 51, 60, 92, 96, 109, 114n13, 118n21
Minerva: Rassegna internazionale (periodical) 78
Mondo di Dolcetta, Il 18, 71–82, 84, 86, 88, 94, 98, 101–2, 104, 132n33, 134n61

Morandi, Luigi 68
Munch, Edvard 66
Mussini, Luisa 105

Natali, Giulio 90–1, 100
Nazione, La (Florence) 87
Nevio (reviewer) 70
Nicolson, Harold 15
Nietzsche, Friedrich 66
"Noterelle prese a Venezia di M.P." 43, 68
Nuova Antologia (journal) 33, 34, 47, 49, 52, 58, 62, 68, 71, 72, 75, 78, 79, 84, 86, 87 100, 101, 102, 103, 104

Oliva, Domenico 69, 75, 94, 95
Opinione, L' (newspaper) 38
Orteza y Miranda, Evelina, 9

"Padre Anacleto da Caprarola" 58, 103
Paget, Violet (pseud. Vernon Lee) 56, 57, 58, 59–60, 61–2, 64, 66, 109
Pallano, Il (newspaper) 74, 75
Panzacchi, Enrico 59
Panzini, Alfredo 90
Peccato del dottore, Il 91–8, 101, 105, 106, 108
Perfidie del Caso, Le 84–9
Perseveranza, La (newspaper) 28, 34, 35, 37, 101
Peruzzi, Emilia Toscanelli 8, 16, 31, 34, 44, 71, 76, 109, 113n3
Piccardi, Gian Leopoldo 38
Piccolo mondo antico 73, 76
Pirandello, Luigi 130n8
Ponti Pasolini, Maria 91
Positivism 4, 47, 76
"Povero militare, Un" 105

Pratesi, Dante 22, 99, 104
Pratesi, Igino 24–5, 52, 117n12
Pro-Caltanissetta e Provincia (periodical) 99
Provincia, La (Teramo) (newspaper) 74
Pseudonyms of reviewers 115n38, 131n15
Puccini, Giacomo *(La Bohème)* 76, 133n54

Rassegna nazionale (journal) 67, 78, 101, 105
Rassegna settimanale universale (periodical) 85, 88, 136n10
Rassegna settimanale, La (periodical) 53, 54, 55, 57, 126n58
Revue Britannique (periodical) 55
Ricchetti, A. (reviewer) 70
Ricci, Matteo 64
Ricordi veneziani 68, 89, 100
Rivista bibliografica di scienze e lettere (periodical) 74
Rivista d'Italia (periodical) 91, 100
Rosso, Gustavo 102
Roux & Viarengo (publishing house) 91, 98
Rovetta, Gerolamo 64, 69, 103
Ruskin, John 90

"Saffo" 64
Said, Edward 107–8
Sandron (publishing house) 89, 102–3, 104
Santandrea, Firenze 104, 111, 146n3
Santandrea, Luisa 105, 111–12
Savj-Lopez, Paolo 99
Scapigliatura 20, 73, 84, 135n6
Sclavo, Francesco 99

Scott, Sir Walter 35
Sentinella bresciana, La (newspaper) 70
Serao, Matilde 61
Shelley, Percy Bysshe 99
Siciliani, Cesira 59
"Signor Diego, Il" 57, 60
Silvius (reviewer) 74
"Sogno del vecchio Benvenuto, Il" 105–6
Söhns, Franz (reviewer) 70
Solimbergo, Giuseppe 3, 38, 39
Sonnino, Sidney 34, 53, 55, 57, 82, 94, 109
Spackman, Barbara 136n6
Spectator 11
Spencer Kennard, Joseph 77
St James Gazette (periodical) 56
Stella di Mondovì (newspaper) 74
Stendhal (Marie-Henri Beyle) 62, 69

"Tarantella sul lido, La" 28
Tenca, Carlo 13
The Humour of Italy 60
Tolstoy, Leo 105
Tommaseo, Caterina 25, 32, 46, 104, 119n41

Tommaseo, Niccolò 24–5, 32–3, 46, 104, 109, 117n11, 119n38
Treves, Emilio 84, 89, 99
Trigona, Lina 47, 112, 146n3
"Troppa grazia Sant'Antonio" 105

Ussi, Stefano 127n68

"Vagabondo, Un" 51, 52
Van Winkle (reviewer) 88
Vannucci, Atto 37, 52, 54
Verdi, Giuseppe 99
Verga, Giovanni 61, 65, 67, 108
"Villa di Massimo D'Azeglio, La'" 68, 70
Vita internazionale (periodical) 90
Vita moderna (periodical) 69
Vita Nuova (periodical) 38
Vitagliano (publishing house) 91

Werner, Alice 60, 130n8, 133n48
Woolf, Leonard 16
Woolf, Virginia 9, 14–16

Zola, Émile 30, 65, 67, 87, 119n37

www.ingramcontent.com/pod-product-compliance
Lightning Source LLC
Chambersburg PA
CBHW020415080526
44584CB00014B/1342